Reading the East India Company, 1720–1840

WOMEN IN CULTURE AND SOCIETY

A Series Edited by Catharine R. Stimpson

READING THE EAST INDIA COMPANY, 1720–1840

Colonial Currencies of Gender

Betty Joseph

The University of Chicago Press
Chicago and London

Betty Joseph is associate professor of English at Rice University.

The University of Chicago Press, Chicago 60637
The University of Chicago Press, Ltd., London

Printed in the United States of America

13 12 11 10 09 08 07 06 05 04 1 2 3 4 5

ISBN: 0-226-41202-4 (cloth)
ISBN: 0-226-41203-2 (paper)

Library of Congress Cataloging-in-Publication Data

Joseph, Betty, 1963–
Reading the East India Company, 1720–1840 : colonial currencies of gender / Betty Joseph.
p. cm. — (Women in culture and society)
Includes bibliographical refrences and index.
ISBN 0-226-41202-4 (cloth : alk. paper) — ISBN 0-226-41203-2 (pbk. : alk. paper)
1. Anglo-Indian literature—History and criticism. 2. India—History—British occupation, 1765–1947—Historiography. 3. Literature and society—India—History—18th century. 4. English literature—18th century—History and criticism. 5. English literature—19th century—History and criticism. 6. English language—India—Rhetoric. 7. East India Company—Historiography. 8. Women and literature—India. 9. Sex role in literature. 10. India—In literature. 11. Women in literature. I. Title II. Series.
PR9489.4 .J67 2004
820.9'358—dc21

2003010412

∞The paper used in this publication meets the minimum requirements of the American National Standard for Information Sciences—Permanence of Paper for Printed Library Materials, ANSI Z39.48-1992.

To the memory of my father
K. J. Joseph
1933–2000

CONTENTS

Reading the East India Company, 1720–1840 is about empire, that colossal system in which one nation—or ruler—controls an array of countries, territories, and peoples. Betty Joseph enters into a crucial period in the history of the British Empire when she takes up the study of India, known as "the jewel in the crown" until it won its independence in 1947. Joseph's fascinating work speaks to us in the first part of the twenty-first century, as we contend with a worldwide struggle about meanings of globalization and another ascendant empire, that of the United States.

As Joseph knows, empires appear neither magically nor miraculously—although their proponents often talk as if they do. Empires evolve in complicated ways because of what people in specific historical circumstances do and because of the institutions these people build, maintain, or resist. *Reading the East India Company* takes place in the middle of the conflict-riddled development of the British Empire. In 1600, Queen Elizabeth I granted the East India Company a charter, which the crown was to renew periodically, to carry on trade with Asia. Thus began a partnership between state and commercial interests. The Company assumed more and more economic, political, and military power in India. In the mid-eighteenth century, widespread violence erupted as the East India Company fought both French and, in Bengal, Indian forces. The soldier joined the merchant in the project of colonization. In 1784, Parliament replaced the crown as the regulator of the Company's charter. Although the Company and the state continued their exploitation of and drastic social engineering in India, in 1813 Parliament amended the charter to allow British citizens greater access to India, be their ambitions economic, social, or religious. In 1858 the Company was disbanded, and direct control of India was assumed by the British crown, specifically Queen Victoria, who gloried in the title "Empress of India."

The story of any empire is of epic dimensions, broad as well as deep, dissolving easy distinctions between tragic and comic, replete with suffering, greed, and grand ambitions that later generations will either scorn or mourn. If we want to avoid error and chauvinism, we need to know about our storytellers and their motives. One of Joseph's strengths is the care and openness with which she establishes herself as a reliable storyteller. She is a literary critic who realizes that we must understand the *culture* as well as the politics and economics of empire. For the builders of empire write about it, draw pictures of it, speak about it, investigate it, justify and rationalize it—in brief, they represent, imagine, and legitimate it. In turn, those who are being colonized, if they can speak, also represent their experience, in different ways. Joseph argues persuasively that history and literary criticism are interdependent. Only together can they show the "cross-relay," the interactions, of the materials of history and their representations. More specifically, "changes in signification or discursive displacements are intimately connected to historical ruptures and crises . . . signs of new forces that have gained entry" (p. 123).

Joseph explores this culture by examining the colonial archive. Readers should discard any notion of archives as dry, dusty, and stupefying. The physical paper in them may be decaying, but under patient and informed scrutiny, the archives reveal vital stories and their meanings. The archives Joseph studies are those of the East India Company itself, which were not made generally public in Britain and India until after 1947. London, the metropolitan center, and India were far away from each other. No colonial official could travel to Southeast Asia by Airbus or 747 and then helicopter to an interior location for an on-site meeting. Nor could he organize a conference call. Governing depended on writing and archiving. Joseph now has at hand parliamentary inquiries; the records of Bengal baptisms, marriages, and burials; pleas to Company officials; and much more. Immense, even potentially unfathomable, as these materials are, Joseph has yet another archive to interrogate: the unofficial writings about India and colonialism, the novels (often read as journalism), the travel guides, and the memoirs. Together, these two archives form an "enunciative field" (p. 15).

A feminist literary critic, Joseph reads archives with her eye on the figure of woman, a practice which inevitably entails the investigation of gender and sexuality. This figure is as complex, multilayered, and heterogeneous as colonial discourse itself. The places where women appear in the official archives, she argues, are "sites of emergence" (a term she takes from the great critic Raymond Williams) that show new forms, values, and meanings being born. Aware of the great differences among women, Joseph makes several crucial distinctions: between the women who speak for themselves and the women who are spoken for; between Englishwomen and Indian women; between elite and non-elite Indian women; and between Indian women and Eurasians, the biracial people who were, by 1830, disenfranchised as a class. Joseph begins with a dramatic comparison between Roxana, the eponymous heroine of Daniel Defoe's 1724 novel, and a native woman raped by an East India Company employee in South India. Roxana is the name of both central character and novel, but the Indian woman is never given her own name. She is "the Bashwar woman." Both novel and trial transcript may show "the transformative power of commerce" (p. 34), but the Indian woman owns neither her identity nor her body. She is a cipher to be exchanged.

As British colonization evolved, so did the figure of woman. To oversimplify Joseph's subtle narrative, between the 1770s and 1830s, the colonizers began to think of India as home. This new domestic sphere, presided over by Englishwomen, was to be a site of European values, "gendered, racially pure, and free of native influence" (p. 92), one part of a binary opposition between the public and the private. (Reading this section of Joseph's book, I thought of the enclosed communities abroad in which contemporary American military and commercial families live.) The opposition was difficult to fix and stabilize, in part because of the presence of the Eurasians, the offspring of unions between Englishmen and Indian women, who had once been taken for granted.

As the figure of the civilizing Englishwoman was gradually being built up, the figure of the Indian woman had simultaneously to be negotiated. For the English, "Hindu women" were often figured as double victims. On the one hand, they might be threatened by loutish lower-class Englishmen, who needed to be controlled in the class dynamics of the colonizers. On the other hand, they were threatened by putatively uncivilized native customs such as despotic enclosure and sati (the immolation of widows). In the dynamics of colonizer and colonized, these local customs, too, needed correction. Indeed, sati was abolished in 1829, an act that is still debated today. Not only the colonizers spoke for the native women. Joseph also traces the rise of "native informants," allied to the colonial elite, who crafted the trope of women as the embodiment of community and tradition. Consistently conscious of the consequences of her historical and literary work for contemporary culture, Joseph points out that a postcolonial elite has burnished this trope, roping the more elite Indian women into the past but freeing Hindu men to be figures of modernity.

Reading the East India Company is a contribution to several fields: literary criticism, through its ideas about archives and archiving; feminist scholarship, through its comparative analysis of the figures of colonizing and colonized women and its detective work about gender in the official records; postcolonial studies and subaltern studies, through its work on the now-broken relations between an empire and the greatest of its colonies. Joseph acknowledges her debts—to Edward Said, Gayatri Chakravorty Spivak, Homi Bhabha, and the feminist scholars of English literature, especially the novel, during the colonial period. In turn, we are in her debt. For she enables us to think about the serious play between history and literature, about a significant period of modern history, and about our roles in the creation of the burgeoning archives of contemporary global history with its neocolonial powers, potentates, and activities. Our archives are being laid down from E-mail, Web sites, CNN and Al Jazeera, embedded journalists, feminist debates, pronouncements from pulpits and mosques, official records (many still secret), corporate reports, and a multitude of other sources. It is impossible, I believe, to read Joseph's fine book and not reflect, in full conscience, about our own archival offerings.

Catharine R. Stimpson

ACKNOWLEDGMENTS

A first book often incurs debts longer in duration and more in number than subsequent projects. Every chapter conjures up past teachers—their seminars, discussions, questions, and cautions. While their lessons are not always calculable in precise ways, their influence on my work has been profound and undeniable: at Jawaharlal Nehru University, Meenakashi Mukherjee and G. J. V. Prasad; at Syracuse University, Jean Howard, Felicity Nussbaum, Bill Readings, and Robyn Wiegman; at the University of Minnesota, John Archer, Nancy Armstrong, Christy Brown, Rey Chow, Abdul R. Jan Mohamed, Prabhakara Jha, John Mowitt, Paula Rabinowitz, Charlie Sugnet, Asha Varadharajan, and Jack Zipes. I owe John Mowitt a special thanks for the generous gift of time and the invaluable feedback that helped this project in the initial stages.

At Rice University, many friends read versions of the book at short notice and gave helpful suggestions at various stages. This book could not have taken its final shape without the help of Lynne Huffer, Susan Lurie, and Helena Michie. Gudrun Klein helped the project along in difficult times with a wonderful blend of criticism and optimism. I am also grateful to Srinivas Aravamudan, Carl Caldwell, Felicity Nussbaum, and Dan Sherman for valuable support at crucial points.

The students in my graduate seminars will recognize their insights and contributions throughout the book. Their interest during the book's trial runs in various courses and lectures has helped in important ways.

For the many years of transatlantic ministering that have sustained me in more ways than they realize, my thanks to Suma Athreye and Sarah Herman. And for the wonderful years of comradeship when thought was most exciting, Chris Chiappari, Susanne Dietzel, Barbara Engh, Jenny Horne, Susan Kollin, Michelle Lekas, Silvia Lopez, Carol Mason, and Monika Mehta.

My aunts, Agnes Idicula, Rose Cloud, and Elsamma Matthew, provided homes away from home in the long years of graduate school and after. The last fifteen years would have happened without them but would have been far less memorable and happy.

I am grateful to the Office of the Dean of Humanities and the Jon and Paula Mosle Fund at Rice University for their generous support of summer travel and research.

For sparing materials at short notice and for his friendship, I am grateful to Donald Johnson at the University of Minnesota's Ames Library. The staff of several libraries provided valuable assistance: the British Library, Cambridge University Library, and Fondren Library at Rice University.

At the University of Chicago Press, Susan Bielstein's commitment to this project gave me the final burst of energy I needed to complete it. For her steadfastness, critical clarity, and efficiency, especially when time was not on our side, I will always be grateful. Anthony Burton was of invaluable assistance in the skillful relay of documents and drafts at various stages. I wish to thank the anonymous readers at the University of Chicago Press whose careful review of the manuscript provided the criticisms and suggestions that helped bring the book together. At Rice, Theresa Munisteri's indispensable proofreading skills have made this a much better product.

Portions of this book have appeared elsewhere. An early version of chapter 1 was first published as "Mutations of the Imperial Contract" in *Genders* 24 (1996), the issue titled *On Your Left: Historical Materialism in the 1990s.* Abridged versions of chapters 4 and 5 appear in *Nineteenth-Century Geographies: The Transformation of Space from the Victorian Age to the American Century,* edited by Helena Michie and Ron Thomas (New Brunswick, N.J.: Rutgers University Press, 2002), and in *The Global Eighteenth Century,* edited by Felicity Nussbaum (Baltimore: Johns Hopkins University Press, 2003).

The Archive without Walls

Can it be, that in your country a woman is permitted to touch the Shaster [Shastra]? Or, are women taught to write?" the astonished Indian narrator asks of his English guest in Elizabeth Hamilton's *Translations of the Letters of a Hindoo Rajah* (1796). The "Hindoo Rajah," however, does not wait for an answer but conjectures commonsensically: "It cannot be. Such things are not proper for women."[1] Like much eighteenth-century writing that used the imagined medium of the foreigner to debate current issues, Hamilton's novel engages contemporary Orientalist scholarship on India (which she had studied), and British gender formations (which she negotiated as a writer), through the perspective of the outsider. While many outsiders offered their perspectives from the vantage point of presumed cultural supremacy over the English, the rajah, a member of the vanquished elite of a conquered colony, has a slightly different function. His astonishment at the cultural differences in the treatment of women means not that equality is the real condition of women in England but only that he thinks it to be the case. Hamilton's rhetorical ploy is to shame English readers into acknowledging that the Indian has obviously misread the superiority of English culture, conflated here with Christianity, and its so-called equal treatment of women. The shaming works precisely because readers are made to sense that behind the misreading there is little to differentiate English women from the women of the supposedly degenerate Hindu culture.

In this fictional confession, an Indian native informant and an English army officer in India debate religious and cultural values through the figure of woman. While this situation may seem a logical choice for Hamilton, who as a woman writer enters the masculine domain of Oriental scholarship in the novel and may need male approbation to shore up her right to do so, there is another principle of cultural comparison operating here. In the eighteenth century, the figure of woman often operated as the general equivalent by which respective cultures were evaluated and assigned their place in the order of civilizations, thus hitching the role and status of women to the level of progress a culture and people had reached.[2] By the nineteenth century, even progressive and radical advocates of European women's advancement (the rights of women) often resorted to cultural comparisons with non-European women. Feminism as a generally conceived set of cultural and political arguments often found itself within the field of the social mission of imperialism. In this discursive nexus, the axioms of feminism and imperialism mirrored each other as the condition of women in non-European cultures was taken to be the measure of their respective civilizations; European women occupied, in this rhetoric, the place of both symbols and agents of European civilizing missions.[3]

Reading the East India Company, 1720–1840: Colonial Currencies of Gender is a genealogical investigation into the political implications of this gendered rhetoric as it emerged in the context of British India. The figure of woman has been used in important ways not only within various representations of imperialism but also within anticolonialism and nationalism, and it continues to inflect a variety of political debates surrounding globalization and development today.[4] Thus a genealogy of the use of this figure in early colonial discourses could advance our understanding of these contemporary deployments. Because of the intimate relationship between nineteenth-century feminist self-representations and imperialism, much postcolonial feminist attention has focused on reading the sparring match between European women and the brown or black women who were summoned and foreclosed in order to consolidate the selfhood and citizenship of the former.[5] This book, by drawing on historical and literary documents that predate this historical moment, tries to avoid the pitfalls of a postcolonial feminist analysis that critiques gendered cultural supremacist rhetoric only to replace it with a nationalist-nativist one. One of the premises of the book is that a globalized reading of the transnational archive of British rule can enable us to locate intersections and shared histories rather than the separation of national traditions. Reading the shared historical links as an inescapable legacy of a long colonial encounter, as well as measuring the effects of these conjunctures today, is crucial to the imagining of any political and cultural practice in the wake of globalization. That is not all. The very use of the figure of woman as the point of reference for a historiographic investigation can transform the premises and blind spots of the dominant history that has marginalized women as actors and agents on the one hand, and the domains of social production and reproduction on the other.

The lacuna of mainstream history—its separation of private and public—

makes it unable to pose woman as a structural issue. As Elizabeth Fox-Genovese points out, modern institutions, including the purportedly neutral market, have "systematically extended gender difference as a fundamental part of the social order," but there is little recognition of gender as a primary category of historical analysis—as "deeply ingrained in social and economic formations and the political institutions to which they give rise as class relations."[6] One way to establish woman as a "structural" rather than a "marginal issue" is to read the importance of sexual difference and sexuality in the very deployment of colonial power.[7] For this we must turn especially to the official records of colonial rule, through which it is possible to access those areas that are normally at the center of conventional colonial history—trade, commerce, modernization, and institution building. The presence of this archive, which includes not only the records of governance but also the unofficial, secondary literature produced by various writers with colonial interests, continues to be felt acutely in contemporary postcolonial cultural studies; it is the very thing that allows us historical knowledge of Britain's general attempt to rule its colonies. However, we cannot see this archive as offering us the singular truth of that encounter, for such a stance would ignore the various ruses through which subjects and objects of knowledge were mutually constituted. Hence, postcolonial criticism's task lies not in excavating the past but in revealing the arenas, agendas, and subjects that are hidden when history is told one way rather than another. Insofar as contemporary interests ultimately mark all histories as histories of the present, *Reading the East India Company* asks what happens if the critical stance of postcolonialism is shot through with a feminist perspective. What happens if the story of colonization is renarrated by placing woman rather than representative man at the center of the telling? Could such realignment do the double work of challenging both the Eurocentric and the gendered designs of colonial historiography?

Contrary to common perception, women are everywhere in the colonial archive, albeit in a fragmented and dispersed way. Yet their fragmentation and dispersal in and across various documents and discursive domains does not necessarily leave us with the problem of a partial and incomplete narrative. Rather, the partial and fragmented appearance of women can provide the occasion for a new telling that ushers in a new subject of history. If feminism is to provide what Gayatri Spivak has termed "a persistent critique of history," then it must not replace the "authoritative male subject," who creates history as "the single, triumphant consciousness," with a female clone.[8] In her classic manifesto on women's writing, Hélène Cixous shows us what it might take to imagine this new subject for history: "As subject for history, woman always occurs simultaneously in several places. Woman un-thinks the unifying, regulating history that homogenizes and channels forces, herding contradictions into a single battlefield. In woman, personal history blends together with the history of all women, as well as national and world history."[9] Here, Cixous is imagining for a new narrativizing of history a subject that is more plural than the individualist bourgeois subject. The historical appearance of women in the historical record simultaneously, in many places at once, is thus not an impasse but a multiplicity of pressure points that reveal the female subject's multiple inscriptions—how she is overdetermined by various discursive networks, such as the sexual, legal, literary, economic, political, and religious.[10]

Feminist critique of mainstream historiography has revealed that when the subject of history is normatively male, sexual difference appears as an agent of historical causation. This appearance, if taken to be a function of social organization, can be a dead end because it does not allow us to open up the historicity of sexual differentiation itself. It is not enough to restore the past appearances of women in history as wives, daughters, mothers, sisters, prostitutes, rape victims, property owners, rulers, or slaves. We must show why the domain of women's agency has been excluded from mainstream accounts and demonstrate, at the same time, how women are put together as subjects and objects of various discourses for the ruses and deployments of colonial power. When the figure of woman makes a fragmented and dispersed appearance in various sites of the colonial archive, it therefore not only provides historical articulations of the discursive networks and their relationship to each other, but also makes woman, in her role as constitutive exclusion, a deconstructive lever for revealing how various sites and arenas of history are repressed at various moments. In this partial and dispersed way, the female as historical subject is pluralized beyond the reach of single-minded attempts to read feminist consciousness in the manner of the bourgeois male historical subject.

Forms of the Archive

The Archive as Colonial Apparatus

Etymologically, *archive* comes from the Greek *arkheia,* a "public office" or "repository for documents." Relatedly, *arkhe,* or "government," also refers to the Greek *archon,* the chief magistrate or ruler, who as the maker and representative of the law used his domicile to store official documents.[11] Thus, the background of the term *archive* reveals its proximity to law, power, and rule—a connection that is obscured by the more recent idea of the archive as a place for public use and scholarly activity. Since I focus mainly on the records of British colonial rule in India, a note here on the East India Company's development of archival methods can serve as a useful reminder that the power/knowledge nexus is unavoidable in any scholarly undertaking.

In an 1819 letter to a friend that describes his job at London's India Office, James Mill's brevity reveals the self-assuredness of a bureaucrat, as well as the consciousness that British "rule" depends on imaginative constructions of the subcontinent. "The Government of India," says Mill, "is carried on by correspondence . . . and . . . I am the only man whose business it is, or who has the time to make himself the master of the facts scattered in a most voluminous correspondence, on which a just decision must rest."[12] Even as the master of correspondence asserts his complete attention to his tasks, the admission that "facts" go unread by higher-ups in London suggests that "just decisions" can also result from misreading or partial knowledge. Today, scholars of the British Empire cannot fail to be struck by this marked disjunction between information production and territoriality, between decision making and the place of implementation in the eighteenth and nineteenth centuries. As imperial governance came to depend on a massive archive of cultural, literary, political, economic, and historical texts, the distance between the subjects and objects of knowledge was more than a geographical issue. On the one hand, the rulers, in making the alien territory and its people into objects of knowledge, initiated a process that gradually denied the colonized any role in this knowledge production. On the other hand, governance was carried out through a practice of archiving, a systematic circulation, preservation, and recall of written texts that allowed rule by remote control from London.

The connection between British territorial expansion and the Company's formal methods of archiving was many centuries in the making. In the seventeenth century, when the Company was still a commercial enterprise trading in the East Indies, copies of letters sent to and received from agents abroad were kept erratically and often assigned to a single employee for safekeeping.[13] In other words, there is little indication of any system of filing or even a permanent dwelling for such documents. As the East India Company's territorial power increased on the subcontinent after 1757 and the output of writing increased exponentially, a formal archive was integrated into the functioning of the Company. In 1776, the first "Keeper of Records" was appointed to overlook the Indian consultations, account books, and other records that were then kept in the "book office." In 1787, the name of this position was changed to "Register of Indian Records," and in 1793, Robert Orme was added to the payroll of the India Office as "historiographer" on a semipermanent basis.[14] By the end of the eighteenth century, the basic record-keeping structure was in place, and it continued till the end of the Company rule in 1858. Permanent archiving of official correspondence was also made compulsory by law as the British Parliament tried to circumscribe the Company's growing power in India in the eighteenth century.

After passage of the 1784 Pitt's India Act, which established the Parliamentary Board of Control to oversee the affairs of the Company, the bifurcation in administrative functions between the two bodies required copies of all incoming letters and outgoing dispatches to be sent to the board from the Company's office. Official dependence on the notion of precedent ("previous communication") and the need for full disclosure guaranteed that the board and Company recorded even the most trivial matters in their meetings for each other's perusal.[15] Yet it is important to remember that such initiatives on the part of the Company were relatively autonomous from the more popular interest in historiography in the eighteenth century, a century often described today as "the historical age."

The period I am describing here did see a growing appetite for history based on primary rather than secondary commentaries.[16] This was also a time of great acceleration in the creation of "national collective memories."[17] But the Company's archive was driven by a different logic. The official record was never deemed to be a repository for public scrutiny; it remained throughout this period an instrument of governance. It was only long after England's first Public Record Office was established in 1838 that Company employees began to propose historiographical and scholarly uses for the Company's records.[18] The fact that Company records in their entirety were made available to the general public only after 1947, the year of Indian independence, tells us that this was a secret archive sheltered from most scholars and historians. Even after the disbanding of the Company in 1858, when India came under the crown, the records simply passed over into the secret archives of the new imperial state.

Without doubt, the gradual opening up of the archives in the twentieth century, both in the United Kingdom and in India, has made possible their ongoing dissemination through printed series, microfiche collections, and scholarly monographs. However, the importance of these records has been recognized primarily by economic and political historians rather than by cultural critics, literary critics, or feminist scholars. Academics in these fields continue to depend more on literary documents for their critique of colonialism. It is my hope that this book will help advance a shift toward using the official documents of colonialism for cultural, literary, and feminist studies. I suspect that the overriding reason feminist scholars have not approached this body of texts to understand the relationship between gender and colonialism is that these documents—factory records, board dispatches, revenue records, district records, and parliamentary committee minutes—do not easily surrender female subjects. The texts for the most part chronicle the busy official routines and misdeeds of male bureaucrats in the economic, political, and military realms of the empire. But there is little question that the assumption that women's subject-status is to be understood mostly in the cultural documents of the empire (novels, memoirs, letters, and travelogues, for instance) has diverted attention from any systematic inquiry into how the official archive itself is constituted through gendered logics.

The Archive as a Tool for Male Legal Subjectivity and the Preservation of Property

The records generated by the East India Company—in published formats or in manuscript records stored at the British Library's India Office Collections and at the National Archives of India—remain the primary source for historians interested in reconstructing the story of the British conquest of India. Here, amid documents chronicling the great economic, political, and military maneuvers that punctuated the Company's progress from a commercial enterprise in 1600 to a colonial formation by 1757, we can also find textual traces of more "mundane" activities. In the lists found in Bengal Baptisms, Marriages, and Burials, for instance, a series whose public audience today is confined to those looking for an ancestral presence in India, we can read the roll call of human reproduction in British India.[19] I will use some bits from this register to set into play the main themes of this book.

These lists, kept in the church at the fortified factory of Fort William in Calcutta till the 1760s, were sent to the Company's court of directors in London every year.[20] This was in keeping with the Company's desire for a complete record of its activities and personnel: all British subjects proceeding to India—in the Company's employ or with any legal connection to it—were listed in various registers depending on their occupations: stockholders lists, cadets lists, ship logs, and so on. The Bengal lists, on the other hand, unconnected with the occupational logics of enumeration, provide us instead with curious instances of human subjects whose very appearance in them seems to disrupt the Company's plans of record keeping.

In the list for 1755, of the thirteen records of marriages seven give us only the name of the English groom; the bride is simply noted as being a "countrywoman."[21] This is an unusual category because it operates as a sort of blank space, denoting the impossibility of assigning identity rather than pointing to a specific referent. By the end of the eighteenth century, the term referred primarily to any Englishwoman born in India, as popular theories of climatic variation distinguished the "country-born" from those freshly arrived from England. These climatic discourses inscribed the "countrywoman" with imagined markers like swarthy skin, a masculine appearance, and sexual promiscuity, thus separating her from the "real" Englishwoman—the more proper (and eligible) woman born in England.[22]

Yet here in the 1755 register, the usage of the term seems to be different, for where brides *are* European, both parties' proper names are given. Thus in the register *countrywoman* signifies a bride who, though unquestionably Christian (she is marrying in church), is not verifiably European in national or racial origin. In the lists, she is a liminal subject—though not "native" she is also not "European," and the records signal her impropriety in colonial space by refusing her any place of origin except India. In a sense, she is already exiled and homeless even though she is marrying an Englishman whose belonging is corroborated by the entering of his proper name in the lists.

Similarly, under the listing of baptisms for 1757, all babies and their English or European parents are named, but Indian names do not appear at all in the list. Yet these baptismal lists are replete with the presence of Indian women; though they are never named as mothers, their existence is marked prominently every time the phrase "natural son of" or "natural daughter of" appears between the infant's name and its father's. In contrast, even the mothers of illegitimate children are listed if they are English or European.

The list does give us, however, one paradoxical way in which a native woman could enter the baptismal records by name—as a Christian convert. Thus, the baptism list for 1769 gives us this entry: "Richard, natural son of John Harper in the pilot's service by a slave called Fanny."[23] Though held in economic and perhaps sexual bondage to her master, "Fanny," as a Christian convert, is momentarily allowed a textual subject position on a par with that of European women.

My reading of these register lists is not meant to merely unearth the religious bias of the church; that is without doubt the primary logic operating here. Rather, I want to draw attention to how the document, faithful to the task of recording and to the logic that shapes it, can also unwittingly give us evidence of the very subject it tries to exclude. That is not all. When the woman in all her variations—countrywoman, slave, English, European, Christian, and non-Christian—appears in the record of a factory settlement, she exposes the operation of a gendered logic in the system of documentation: its requirement that the name of the European, Christian male be the place of primary legal propriety. Moreover, her appearance in these records also reveals ways in which gender is constitutive of colonial relations, indeed of the very ability of colonialism to reproduce itself in a literal sense. In the simple act of separating the European woman from the non-Christian Indian woman, we are also able to read through these lists the failure of discourses that try to discipline sexual relations in the colony. Sexual cohabitation between Christians and "heathens" continues to produce "natural" children.

The lists also give us administrative functions that are specific to the historical role at that time of the East India Company—a trading enterprise that was only beginning to sense its colonial-military function. The use of church records instead of an official census is a sure sign that military consolidation had not yet happened, while the absence of an explicit discourse of race in the lists' organizational logic suggests that hierarchies that were integral to the general attempt to rule India in the nineteenth century were of a different order and politics. The Fort William records show that subjects were refused recognition not because they were nonwhite or promiscuous but because they were not Christian or had no clear nationality. Similarly, the Company at this stage was not particularly interested in questions of sexual or moral propriety. It received these lists without comment year after year in London, simply to keep an account of the growth of its employee base and to confirm the legitimacy of contracted subjects as established by parentage or marriage. These rituals, we may surmise, affected the Company's future obligations—its reimbursements and pensions to family claimants.

Finally, these lists provide an important lesson about the archives: that any one document is just that—a single path to a subject—and it can never exhaustively map the female subject's fate in the social domain. We see this when the religious bias operating at this scene of recording to keep non-Christian Indian women out of the records is contradicted by the logic of recording in another domain: the India Office's collection of wills deposited by East India Company employees in India.[24] Since unclaimed wealth of employees dying in India reverted to the Company, this list was part of the Company's attempt to keep track of potential claims and obligations.

What do we see here? For one thing, we see a sudden plethora of non-Christian Indian women's names, as the rules ensuring their invisibility elsewhere are nullified by the Englishman's legal right to own property and his patriarchal prerogative to bequeath it to his descendants and dependents. Since a will is a document that must ensure the representation of an individual's free will, the Company or the church cannot be the author here. Interracial heterosexual desire and filial love become the primary logic behind the document. Persons with names like Zeenub, Beebun, and Ellisan, none of whom would ordinarily have any claim to English property, are nevertheless installed as legal subjects in the Company records by virtue of being objects of Englishmen's affections. I do not want to make this moment one of radical reversal, for it is difficult to ignore how many of these wills also show the Indian woman's diminished status as she is described variously as "my housekeeper," "my present girl," or "my girl" rather than as "my wife." It is also difficult to say how many of these wills were actually honored by the executors or the Company after the death of these men. However, the very presence of these women in the London archives is proof that domains of affect and sexuality were caught up in the everyday governance of the empire and that the historical effects of these domains could never be determined in advance. If they could, the Company would not find itself in the position of recognizing a woman as a legal subject—as sexual companion of the Englishman and mother of his children—in one set of records while systematically erasing her from another.[25]

This unevenness in the colonial archival record suggests an unevenness in colonial forces, where colonial understanding is limited and the activity of control through recording information is thwarted by the very object that has to be pinned down on paper—the woman. Because the woman appears as a series of displacements and distributions, we can establish her historical place only by a differential reading across a variety of texts and discourses. The official record is thus not a quarry for strict facts and self-evident categories, but rather a window into the processes through which colonial rulers produced their categories of self-understanding and knowledge of the other—whether gendered subjects or natives. For this reason, this book takes as a fundamental premise the belief that although official documents are often closest to the mechanisms of colonial power, it is a mistake to assume that official discourses dependent on and guaranteed by the East India Company's archiving apparatus had sole monopoly over knowledge production about India in the eighteenth century. It seems especially important to contextualize the official record, to remove its continuing documentary power, by reading it within the larger discursive formation in which it emerged—a formation in which multiple cultural sites, texts, and contexts were active in representing British India.

The Archive as a Trope of Women's Textual Appropriation

Most histories of the English novel today acknowledge that the eighteenth-century public was especially drawn to the new fictional form's practiced ambivalence about its relationship to "fact"—its constant insistence that it was history and journalism rather than fiction.[26] This public perception is important to remember today because historians versed in colonial discourse analysis are voicing disgruntlement about the privileging of the literary in postcolonial studies.[27] In the period I focus on, 1720–1840, the novel was for the most part not seen as antithetical to the contents of the historical colonial archive I have described. As my discussion in chapter 2 will show, much of the boundary policing between "literature" and "history" about British India is a more recent undertaking. At this point I will move across the literature/history continuum by tracking the gendered subject from its place in the official record to its place in the domain of the novel.

Consider, for instance, the novel titled *The Lady's Drawing Room,* whose appearance coincides with the very period during which the East India Company was going about making its lists, with their untidy and unmanageable categories. The novel first appeared in 1744 and went on to be reprinted two more times—in 1746 and 1748. After that, the two main stories embedded in the novel—one about the marriage of a Frenchwoman, Henrietta, to an Indian banyan (a native businessman in the service of the East India Company), and the other about the marriage of their daughter Zoa to Rodomond, an English factor—went on to have afterlives in chapbooks and pamphlets till the 1820s.[28]

This novel is useful for my discussion because it plays with the very themes and categories invoked by the Bengal lists, even as it rearranges them in ways that seem to challenge the official discourse. A group of Englishmen and Englishwomen are gathered in Lady Ethelinda's drawing room to partake in "elegant conversation" under her supervision. Two stories from India find their way into this London home, and the assembled group discusses them as a mirroring exercise in manners acquisition; the stories allow them, through their public "reading" and discussion, to sharpen their sensibilities.[29] One of the stories is received as reported speech (Zoa's), and the other arrives as a translated manuscript (Henrietta's). In Henrietta's story we get this startling example of an alternative colonial archive. The unhappy woman, held in religious and cultural tyranny by the banyan she married and prevented from exercising her faith or imparting it to her daughter, had put together a memoir for Zoa to read after her mother's death:

> I cannot die, and leave you with no other Knowledge of yourself, than that you are the daughter of an *Indian Banyan,* and an *Heathen.* O then, if it pleases Heaven, that these Papers fall into your Hands, be careful of them. I conjure you by all that Duty, that Love, and that Respect, which even the Worship you are train'd up in enjoins from Children to their Parents, read them not lightly over, but examine every Article, weigh every Precept; engrave them in your Mind, that, if by any Accident you lose the Original, your Memory may supply you with a faithful Copy.—I command you also, to keep whatever you find here an inviolable Secret, unless Providence, whose Ways are all mysterious, should happily conduct you to some Place, where it may be your advantage to reveal it.[30]

Though the idea of preserving contemporary ideas and lives through the modality of print was firmly entrenched by the latter half of the eighteenth century, the novel stages the preservation of memory in a psychic archive ("engrave them in your mind") as a more secure and permanent act.[31] The undertaking of autobiography by a female subject removed from her community and values is seen as a significant act of self-preservation for the future. Not only that, it is seen as a sort of triumph of the woman's personal, secret archive over the public tyranny of patriarchal power. As the mother successfully bequeaths her memory to her daughter without the father's interception, the memoir becomes an insurgent act that works precisely because it is an activity carried out in seclusion and privacy.

Lennard Davis has made a convincing case that the rise of printed histories and biographies and even unprinted autobiographies from the latter half of the seventeenth century onward performed the cultural work of "embodiment"—of memorializing the lives of ordinary people who could not be found in official or public archives.[32] *Drawing Room* clearly shows this to be the case, and it also makes this alternative modality of transmission from a woman to a woman into a feminist act. Through this alternative channel, the novel creates a subjectivity for one who in normal circumstances would have been an unlisted European woman, shipwrecked, penniless, and orphaned in India, who would never have had a signature or proper name in any official archive.

But Henrietta's story also challenges the idea of self-presence in print, the dominant archival ideology, as it comes through the novel to its readers through a series of mediations—a combination of oral transmission, writing, and memorizing, as well as translation. Henrietta's story is written and preserved for future use by her daughter only because she could not communicate it to her orally. Thus writing—and, by implication, print—is prestructured in the novel as a secondary choice. In the passage I have quoted above, Henrietta warns about the danger of losing the external archive of paper and ink. It is clear that where women have only a tenuous ownership of their own writing, the idea that an external archive guarantees embodiment is questionable. The archive as the cultural stockpile of various individual informants is perceived to be a gendered one whose guarantees of voice and identity can be enjoyed only by the free, male, propertied individual. This alienation from the written text is also foregrounded as Henrietta, the culturally marginal subject, transmits her narrative to her daughter in a foreign language. It is written in Malay rather than in French, as her unhappy marriage has prevented the transmission of her mother tongue. Further, the manuscript reaches its final audience in Ethelinda's drawing room only after Rodomond translates it once again into English.

By bringing together notions of self-preservation, autobiography, and the archive, the novel does the cultural work of demonstrating the archive's various modalities. Archiving is not restricted to official acts undertaken by the East India Company. Though the novel stages through Henrietta a wariness about whether writing or print can actually preserve a marginal woman's memory, *Drawing Room* works against this prestructuring by preserving successfully Henrietta's endangered manuscript. It does this in a couple of ways. The novel itself is an archiving institution—it is a collection of stories. Both stories, Zoa's as well as Henrietta's, are preserved as autonomous units within the novel—they exist as typographically separate pieces with their own headings, rather than as reported speech incorporated within quotation marks or framed within another story. Again, by bringing Henrietta's previously hidden, handwritten, untranslated manuscript into the midst of the novel, the author preserves and protects it at the same time. By releasing it from its house arrest in a box, the novel moves it from a personal, secret archive to the public, cultural one; it now becomes part of the "stock of public knowledge."[33] This textual staging of the colonial archive is also visible in the so-called annotated novels, such as Hamilton's *Translations* and *The Missionary* (1811), by Lady Morgan (Sydney Owenson), both Anglo-Indian novels in which the writers use footnotes to cite historical and ethnographic sources that frame the fictional narrative with "real" facts.[34]

As the drawing room's occupants, mainly Englishwomen, debate the moral implications of a European Christian woman becoming the "Wife of a Man of Complection, Religion and Manners so different from those of her own country," the novel becomes a historical event in itself. It shows us how women were writing themselves into the colonial theater of British

India.[35] The novel, in a sense, archives for us how a historical subject (the anonymous author) imagined the processing of the very information held in the Bengal lists. We also see the novel reversing the historical record by filling in gaps in the official archive. For instance, the official Bengal lists do not give us a single instance of a continental European or English woman marrying an Indian man. When the novel stages for the public an imagined scenario where the Englishwoman is the site of desire, it reveals how the official archive places only the Englishman at the center of desire, marriage, and sexual reproduction. The question here is not whether such incidents involving sexual encounters with native men actually took place during this time, though the strict controls placed by the Company on single women traveling to India made it very unlikely.[36] What the novel does preserve for us is a singular cultural and historical event of "reading": revealing how a set of anxieties that are only faintly visible in the official logic of the lists—racial intermixture, loss of national identity, the equating of Christianity and heathenism, and so on—are actually being processed in a more public setting. The novel responds to these anxieties by fleshing out the empty signifier of the official "countrywoman," forming her into Henrietta, and, through the novel's ideological effect of mirroring, allowing a roomful of Englishwomen (as well as English women readers of the time) to assert themselves as triumphantly Christian when all else—virtue, race, culture, language, and nationality—is lost.

Finally, it is possible for us to read this novel as acting not only as an alternate zone of understanding but as a zone of interference. It does this by translating the story of the mercantilist struggle between the Company and the trading classes in India in the first half of the eighteenth century (before colonial conquest had begun) into a sexual contest. In a powerful recoding act reminiscent of the work of domestic fiction during this time, the novel foreshadows a historical event that will first appear in the official archives during the 1770s—when the governor-general of India, Warren Hastings, commissioned Orientalist scholars like Nathaniel Halhed and William Jones to systematically weed out native agents like banyans, replacing them with English civil servants trained in native languages and law.[37] By reducing these native agents' intermediary control over local trade networks, British mercantilism reworked itself into British colonialism. In *Drawing Room,* the Company employee Rodomond represents already this new generation of Englishmen. Well versed in native languages, he soon replaces the native translator and challenges the hold of the banyan over local trade. Is it possible that colonial logic emerges first in the unofficial record?

If it can be established that the various categories of archival taxonomy are not simply logical, self-evident ways of ordering reality but are themselves mediated, contextualized, and subjective practices, then to what extent are the archival practices of colonial power also part of a general ideological system? One way to understand such a system is to look at the relationships between texts to see when one discourse allows certain utterances whereas another will not. In my discussion so far, I have tried to articulate the novel and the archive, the unofficial and official record, in ways that would allow us to do such an analysis. I have also used *archive* in two senses of the term. First, an archive, as the intended repository of the official historical record of British colonialism in India; this use of the term *archive* will appear in texts such as factory records, consultation books, parliamentary subcommittee reports, and board proceedings. Second, in the Foucauldian sense an archive is the "enunciative field" through which British India emerges, exists, and disappears, the sum of all that can be said and thought about British India at a particular time.[38] The second kind of archive always challenges the first one's monopoly over colonial truth, but it is impossible to get at fully.

In *Reading the East India Company,* I attempt to chart only a partial grammar of the power that determined the emergence and availability of diverse texts and genres in the British India context. I ask, for example, What information was preserved and for what purposes? Who gets left out, and why, when the historical record is put together in a particular way? Why do some subjects rather than others get to be the authors of certain forms of colonial writing? This book frames these questions by using the female subject as a test case for charting the inclusions, exclusions, and deployments of the archive, and it foregrounds the production of the archive as a gendered process. I take as a primary assumption the belief that one must know the rules that determine the constitution or usage of knowledge and the historical conditions that allow various utterances to emerge textually before any meaningful and engaged feminist critique of colonialism can be carried out. Because the records of colonialism for the most part teem with men, all attempts to narrate the gender/colonialism nexus will have to embark on a radical reorganizing of the colonial archive, where the scattered and fragmentary appearance of women must be replotted into a new story. This is the book's ultimate aim, and at a later stage in the introduction I will explore the methodological problems surrounding such an endeavor. Before I spell out how the book engages the role of gender and sexuality in the colonial contest, I will outline the archive's place in recent discussions of colonial historiography and colonial discourse studies. I do this so the reader can have a better sense of how my own use of historical records draws on and departs from the theories and practices of other scholars.

THE ARCHIVE AND CONTEMPORARY POSTCOLONIAL THEORY AND HISTORIOGRAPHY

The Archive and the Critique of Colonialism

Though commonly recognized today as a designated place for storing official and unofficial documents and as a site for public and private use, in colonial studies the archive has always exceeded this definition. Consider, for instance, the notion of *archive* operating in one of the master texts of colonial discourse analysis—Edward Said's *Orientalism:*

> In a sense Orientalism was a library or archive of information commonly and, on some of its aspects, unanimously held. What bound the archive together were a family of ideas and a unifying set of values proven in various ways to be effective. These ideas explained the behavior of Orientals; they supplied Orientals with a mentality, a genealogy, an atmosphere; most important, they allowed Europeans to deal with and even to see Orientals as a phenomenon possessing regular characteristics.[39]

Said is making two important arguments here. The first is that the archive of Orientalism is not a designated space or a known depository but a discursive formation that in its totality created a representation of the object of knowledge (the Orient, the Oriental), enabled its constitution, and defined its limits. By *archive* he means here a unity of knowledge constituted by consensus—of scholars, bureaucrats, travelers, ethnographers, historians, novelists, and reading publics. It is an archive held in common and formed by textual practices of intertextuality, citation, quotation, and referencing.

This Foucauldian notion of the archive takes us beyond its function as a colonial machine and even beyond the priority of the official document. It stretches its operations into the various domains of intelligibility through which people understood the Orient (or for that matter British India). Indeed, since the public had limited access to the official documents of the empire till recently and, as Said shows, the strictly historical "fact" was often suspended as reports on the colonial Other stretched into the fabulous, this extended notion of the archive is perhaps a more accurate depiction of how knowledge production actually took place.[40] Further, as Said's use of the term *mentality* suggests, this body of knowledge was by no means scientifically or historically derived, though it made claims in the name of science and history. Rather, knowledge of the colonial Other was all too often driven by essentialist categories; that is, it was based on unchanging notions of ethnicity, religion, race, and psychology.

The second point Said makes above relates closely to the function of the archive as a tool of governance. He says that this archive, however problematic as a body of knowledge, was actually effective. That is, it allowed the Europeans to govern and "deal with" their colonial subjects. This double use of the archive as a set of both essentialist fictions and effective policy directives for the successful operation of colonial institutions, has been received skeptically by many critics. Robert Young, for instance, has called this a "major theoretical problem."[41] "How can Said argue that the 'Orient' is just representation," Young asks, "if he also wants to claim that 'Orientalism' provided the necessary knowledge for colonial conquest?"[42] If the textual representations of the Orient can create not only knowledge but also the very reality they appear to describe, then what makes it possible for Said to assert that the Orientals did not actually "possess regular characteristics"?—that colonial power only fantasized they did?[43]

This theoretical problem of the relationship of historical representation to historical reality is at the heart of my own project. A response to Young's critique of Said may clarify the issue for my own discussion. Young's question suggests that a double bind of desire grabs postcolonial critics like Said as he confronts the colonial archive. On the one hand, there is the desire to get the story straight and rewrite the story of mastery—to retell it in such a way that the "facts" of colonial history that remain dead weights are challenged, unsettled, and pushed back by a revisiting of the historical record. On the other hand, there is the desire to expose this very colonial record as a fabrication so that what the reader is actually seeing are soldiers, writers, and administrators constructing a representation they can work with. We might frame the problem as a question: How can one expose at the same time the history of colonialism and colonialism's disciplining of history, which in turn produced the very categories and ideas that constitute the "facts" of history? Thus, the challenge for colonial discourse studies today is to formulate what Tejaswini Niranjana has called "a narrativizing strategy in addition to a deconstructive one."[44] How do we go about this task, especially when the endeavor is also complicated by the need to tell the story in a way that will place the gendered subject of colonialism in the forefront? I will address this question by showcasing the work of recent scholars who have specifically used the official record to write a history of the colonized and while doing so have grappled critically with the very discourses and texts that facilitate their work.

Interrogating Official Knowledge

In her now classic study about the founding of English literary studies in India, Gauri Viswanathan tweaks Said's monolithic notion of the Oriental archive by suggesting that the colonizer is also subject to the tyranny of his own representations. On the one hand, because cultural domination needs the presumption of cultural supremacy on the part of the educator/civilizer and of inferiority on the part of the native, domination is often written as goodwill. Thus "detailed records of self-incrimination" are not unusual in the state archives as colonial functionaries talk about the necessity of making Indians subject to humane rule.[45] On the other hand, because the colonial subject is an invention (a "construction"), all calculations of policies and measures involving the native expend vast reams of paper about possible outcomes. In such scenarios, impending historical "events" are always crossed over by the fictional—what happens is often far removed from what must or must not happen according to colonial "intention." While it may be surmised from this reading that the colonial record is already contaminated with fiction-effects that draw the attention of a literary critic, Viswanathan's conclusion about the epistemological distance between colonizer and colonized forecloses the question of native agency. She says, "How the native actually responds is so removed from the colonizer's representation system" that it is a history that "can, and perhaps must, be told separately."[46] Recent work by Priya Joshi and Gaurav Desai, who grapple with similar issues about colonial documentation, has challenged this suggestion that native agency lies in a separate textual realm. They insist, on the contrary, that it can be read within the colonial archive itself or at least around its "proper" epistemological boundaries.

In her study of the English novel in India, Joshi calls for a reexamination of the colonial archive from a "perspective that reconfigures Viswanathan's focus on a hierarchy of [colonial] elites" to one that gives importance to "Indians and their practices."[47] While it is unclear how Joshi's charting of a literate native response is able to move beyond the "elite" factor, her focus on the nineteenth-century Indian novel, Indian letters, and reading groups (as sites of rearticulations of British literary conventions and practices) does show that the colonial archive is much more than a slumbering pile of colonial intentions. As Indians read and wrote in the nineteenth century, even official records manifested traces of this native response as debates ensued about nationalist novels to be banned, vernacular papers to be censored, and periodicals to be policed because they were beginning to represent native voices. In a similar vein, Gaurav Desai, in a recent book on the "colonial library" that collectively "invented" Africa, asks that the archive be understood as "an important terrain of colonial tension and struggle" for African nationalism. Desai's project resonates with my own when he argues that colonial texts are not "reflections" of colonial relations but are "constitutive" of them, and when he therefore requires us to attend to the "configurations" of the archive itself. Most tantalizing for the question of configuration is his final caveat in the introduction, that the "most obvious instantiation" of the library's limitations "is the marginalization of African women in [it] both by European as well as by African writers." Given that Desai declares his desire to reevaluate the archive from the "perspective of a literary critic," it is curious that although decades of feminist literary theory have advanced the gendered analysis of history, the only woman Desai fleshes out in the African colonial archive appears in the text of an African male informant reestablishing continuity with a lost African past through the nostalgic figuration of the precolonial woman.[48]

Viswanathan, Joshi, and Desai share in common the timeline of their historical investigation—mid- to late nineteenth century and after. Thus it is not difficult for them to outline the emergence of native responses to colonialism as print technology allowed the circulation of texts in the vernacular and in English. However, printed or circulated native responses to colonialism from the eighteenth and early nineteenth centuries are practically unavailable. Thus any reading of everyday native responses to colonial rule before the creation of the native elite must be sought in the official colonial archive itself.

The twin problem of reading the official colonial records and reading for the female historical subject is best discussed in Gayatri Spivak's important essay on the rani of Sirmur. In its outlay of various methodological considerations and cautions, it would be no exaggeration to say that this essay serves as a theoretical threshold for *Reading the East India Company*. Spivak's contribution to the debate about the role of official records stems from her avowed focus on restoring the subject-status of the Indian women who have been silenced in them. Spivak's most important claims in "The Rani of Sirmur" appear in a section called "Methodological Preamble," where she explains her desire to "read" a "handful of archival material" that she calls—in terms borrowed from Hayden White—"unprocessed historical record." It is clear that for Spivak such a retroactive reading is a critical activation of historical documents that might have continued to sleep silently in the archives. Yet because Spivak is aware that she undertakes such a task when influential historians like Hayden White and Dominick LaCapra are already questioning the fetishistic use of the archive as a stand-in for the past, she goes on to clarify the status of the textual evidence at which she is looking: "The records I read show the soldiers and administrators of the East India Company constructing the object of representations that becomes the reality of India. On a somewhat precious register of literary theory, it is possible to say that this was the construction of a fiction whose task it was to produce a whole collection of 'effects of the real' and that the 'misreading' of this 'fiction' produced the proper name 'India.' "[49] It is important to note that Spivak does not force herself into the corner where Said found himself by asserting that there is no real Orient to be found. She argues instead that a fiction misread as the real India operates through a powerful reality effect and that such fictions can operate precisely because of the silencing of the natives and their accounts—historical ones in particular.

Thus, when Spivak goes on to assert that the literary critic cannot get access to early-nineteenth-century India, she is saying two things. The first is that we cannot find great works of native literature because the institutional conditions under which they could have flourished did not exist under colonial rule. The second point is more strategic and methodological: since India does not really exist except as the fiction "India," Spivak suggests that reading the colonial archive is the provenance of the literary critic as much as that of the historian. In other words, because the archive is not evidence of the real India but of the ways in which colonial rule went about the task of writing fictions and governing through them, it is also a place to read strategies of representation—rhetoric rather than real referent.

Such a conclusion is not particularly useful, especially if one wants to narrate the story of the silenced subject of the colonial archive in order to restore her as a historical subject. Because Spivak reads the colonial archive completely as a form of "consolidation," she cannot assert any sort of agency in the historical subject she is tracking—the rani of Sirmur. For her, the archival trace is only the signifier for a person who existed at one time, and the lack of a proper name is a sure sign that she is totally written over by colonial rule. As the wife of the deposed king of Sirmur and the mother of the minor heir, the rani seems a logical choice for managing the palace, but Spivak suggests that it is her status as the "weaker vessel" of the two that satisfies the Company, which is bent on annexing Sirmur. The rajah is banished, and the rani and her son live on in the palace, its management overseen by the English resident appointed by the Company. Caught between "patriarchy and imperialism," the rani abruptly declares her intention to be a sati—to participate in the widow's rite of self-immolation.[50]

The rani's declaration forces a crisis of sorts because the Company needs her in order to maintain the semblance of native leadership and legitimacy. Spivak never finds out if the rani did indeed burn herself but does say that the matter is dropped after a few letters that "merely defer the Rajah's further banishment almost as if not to test the Rani's resolution." Thus, Spivak concludes, the reason for her brief surfacing as an "individual" in the records is that she is to be used as an "instrument" by the Company to further the plan of dismembering the kingdom of Sirmur. Spivak then goes on to declare her own intention to track down the rani and "touch the Rani's picture, some remote substance of her" because the records are a dead end: "Caught in the cracks between the production of the archives and indigenous patriarchy, today distanced by the waves of 'hegemonic feminism,' there is no 'real Rani' to be found."[51]

If there is no real rani to be found, has the colonizer's intention to write the rani out of existence succeeded? What if we render the archival document's intention moot since the principle contradiction of the rani's fate did at least catch the literary critic's attention, in some sense defeating that presumed intention? Is it possible that because of an uncompromising individualistic focus Spivak almost desires the rani to be a sovereign subject or nothing? that because the rani lacks a proper name and there is no evidence of her self-will in the archive, Spivak discounts her actions? As Asha Varadharajan asks trenchantly, "Even if the Rani cannot be presented whole and complete and delectable enough for the appetite for knowledge, is there a value to be accorded the brief glimpses one gets of her in [this] and other imperial texts?"[52]

Varadharajan insists that Spivak not read the rani out of existence (as the colonial rulers planned) but instead accord some status of "resistance" to the rani; for can it not be said that her declaration of intent to commit "widow-sacrifice" when her husband was still alive clearly caused political embarrassment? Thus, even if what we have is a "site of failed resistance," to merely read that moment as one of "imperial production" is to hand back the power of truth production to the colonial record.[53] It should be clear from this discussion that one of the problems we face when trying to work with the discontinuous and erratically plotted documents of colonial rule is the nature of the historical subject itself. When representations often operate as facts and have a force in history, what is the relationship between the figure and the historical referent?

Srinivas Aravamudan provides a provocative discussion of the relationship between figural language and historical agency in his recent study of English and French colonialist texts in the eighteenth century, *Tropicopoli-*

tans. In it, he turns the tables on the historian and the historian's anxiety about fiction-effects in the colonial archive by calling for a "genealogical investigation of eighteenth-century literature as *colonial archive* [that] relies on the method of retroactive reading." Using Freud's notion of "deferred action," Aravamudan argues that literary tropes such as the "blackamoor," the "tropicopolitan," and the slave are "memory-traces" of "inherited traumas of colonialism," where we may see less than "conscious replies" to colonialist ideologies. Indeed, as he shows through his reading of a William Blake engraving of a group of African slaves, even the most abject representation of colonial exploitation may hold within itself "stubborn material traces" of "valor, insolence or rebelliousness." These tropes appear as visible reanimations of the past not only in the self-representations of anticolonial and revolutionary subjects ("tropicopolitans" like Olaudah Equiano and Toussaint-Louverture), but also in the texts of metropolitan writers such as Aphra Behn, Daniel Defoe, and Samuel Johnson. These writers are tropicalized retroactively when their own troublesome tropes—Oroonoko, Friday, Rasselas—provide the later militant tropicopolitans with a "literary lingua franca for political and cultural association." By insisting on reading as a form of historical activation (an event) and the production, reception, and institutionalization of literature as historical discursive deployments, Aravamudan demonstrates how the transnational movement and work of tropes from England to the colonies and vice versa can impact present practices. This mode of reading can reconfigure the very boundaries of eighteenth-century studies today: as the textual transactions of the tropicopolitan fragment "the continental shelf of literature" into "manageable textual archipelagoes," they interrupt, like the trope itself, "the monologue of nationalist literary history."[54]

Although Aravamudan's book argues for the importance of literary transactions *within* the historical agency of the colonized, when it comes to reading the female tropicopolitan, literary figuration stands in for the agency of the historical subject. In the final chapter, as he concludes a discussion of Toussaint-Louverture's "masculine sublime," Aravamudan raises the possibility that the woman is again in the margins even as the male "real-world tropicopolitans" get center stage. As "slave rebellion" becomes "national revolution," Aravamudan surmises, the West African cultural sources of slave revolutionary consciousness can be located in voodoo rites, such as a sacrifice of a wild boar on 14 August 1791 and the maroons "kneeling around a voodoo priestess." This anecdote interjects into the discussion—in a way Aravamudan had not undertaken before in the book's discussion of

Western female writers Behn, Mary Wortley Montagu, and Anna Maria Falconbridge—the problem of self-representation in the colonial archive as a gendered problematic: "If Toussaint-Louverture had been a woman, which passage in *Histoire des deux Indes* might she have chosen as a point of departure?"[55]

In the section inaugurated by this question, Aravamudan's concerns resonate with my own in this book. Can the woman question posed in the above terms, albeit counterfactual and speculative, allow us to "measure the elisions in received histories of colonialism"? Confronted with what he terms "the paucity of material on women outside Europe" in the text he is discussing (Raynal's *Histoire des deux Indes*), Aravamudan is forced to settle for figures like Medea and sentimentalized depictions of abject women of Orinoco, overreading them (as a female Toussaint might) into "pressure points" for insights into "gender, slavery and self-possession." Here is his reading of the relationship between historical agency and the literary figuration of woman: "Virtual metaliteracy provides a different advantage, of mining anticolonial subversions in the literary text even as these subversions are not always empirically recuperable from the historical archive. Literature's anticipatory anticolonialisms are seized upon retroactively by nationalization."[56]

In *Tropicopolitans,* Aravamudan consistently asserts the power of the literal and "real-world tropicopolitans" over the virtual ones because the various metropolitan investments in the latter often direct "critical attention from other causes and effects." And as the quote above suggests, it is the relay between literature and history (anticipation *and* seizure) that attests to the former's transformative power; or as Aravamudan puts it elsewhere, "metaphorical slaves" are important because they augur or incite the possibility of "literal ones." Hence, if it makes sense to insist on both sides of the relay, Aravamudan's reading of Raynal's Medea as Obeah woman is only part of the equation; the author gestures to the other part in the very last pages of the book: "Mythical assimilation is not meant, however, as a substitute for historiographic research on female resistance to slavery."[57] While my own discussion has benefited greatly from Aravamudan's elaboration of the "tactical artifice" of his hypothetical female Toussaint, it seeks to address both ends of the relay so that artificial subjects can be replaced as often as possible by speaking ones.

The Figure of Woman and Its Importance for Postcolonial Feminist Studies

The Female Colonial Subject as Historical Subject

Because British colonialism required its rulers to domesticate an Indian reality into an "India" where the native would occupy the "space of the Other on his home ground,"[58] the registers of the real and the fantastic often intersect in ways that make them indistinguishable. In Jenny Sharpe's important study of Anglo-Indian fiction, we see how the figure of the violated Englishwoman circulated widely in fictional and popular narratives around the time of and after the Great Mutiny of 1857, even though there was little actual evidence that such rapes had taken place. Sharpe's demonstration that such figurations had the force of "truth-effects" and enabled the imperial state to embark on a new regime of repression indicates that the state needed a fiction of native barbarism to justify its methods of counterinsurgency.[59] Such representations also went on to affect the status of Englishwomen in India, who subsequently found themselves the object of a paternalist and racialized discourse of male protection. In a similar vein, Felicity Nussbaum shows how women in eighteenth-century England actively engaged in an exercise of self-constitution using images of women from the "torrid zones." These representations, which surfaced in various texts of culture—novels, travel narratives, medical documents, visual artifacts, legal records—ultimately helped consolidate a "cult of domesticity" that further disenfranchised Englishwomen politically even as they were made into racially superior subjects.[60]

In *Reading the East India Company,* I analyze similar historical moments through the official record, when discourse and figure reveal their material effects. In the final chapter, for instance, I show how in 1813 the official construction of the figure of the Hindu woman as protected object was used to stall free-trade and missionary incursion into India. The "truth-effects" of this figure continued into other discursive domains—of social reform as well as of nationalist sentiment—and helped bring about some of the most significant changes in the legal status of modern Indian women. Here, the figure of woman not only was "instrumental in shifting a colonial system of meaning"[61] —an alibi first for the Company's protection of its trade interests and then for the mobilization of native social reform—but also provided an important signifier for the nationalist movement against colonialism.[62]

Yet, despite this evidence of the material effects of figurations, I am not proposing that we ignore the difference between the historical work of figures and the historical/textual records' rendering of women as historical subjects. Unless such a distinction is made, we will compromise the ability of literary analysis to force open issues of distortion and complicity in the historical record; for even if everything is mediated by the act of representation, it does not mean that there is no world external to thought. We need not deny that events, subjects, and objects exist, but only that "they could constitute themselves as objects outside any discursive conditions of emergence."[63] One of the lessons we learn from the work of scholars in the Subaltern Studies Collective is that however bent the official report is on representing its task of imposing law and order as a successful one, a reading against the grain of the accounts of counterinsurgency will always produce evidence of rebellious subjects.[64] Even where there is no option but to cobble together a historical agent by reading in reverse from the acts of colonial power, a reality that is being worked over still emerges from aporias and interruptions in the text. This reality is asserted as a place in the text or a discursive site that is not fully contained by official discourse. At such sites we may not get a fully available empirical subject with all the trademarks of personhood, but we can get another meaning, the "proper" or "literal" meaning against which the tropological function of the officially deployed figure can be read—for if we can make sense of a trope or figure only by distinguishing it from that which is being twisted, such a distinction allows us to assert that something is being worked over. In this book, I ask that we strategically use such moments of reading where these distinctions can be made into assertions of reality—of actually existing social relations and actually existing historical subjects.

When preparing my chapter on *Roxana* and the "Bashwar woman," I faced a dilemma not dissimilar to one Spivak faced when reading about the rani of Sirmur. An unnamed rape victim appears only by her caste nomination as the Bashwar woman. Yet, because the factory records in which she appears were meant to preserve all administrative discussions in great detail, and because the discussion of the woman rudely interrupts that of the factory's commercial concerns, I had little doubt that there was a real woman to be found. Here the difficulty lay not in asserting that a real Bashwar woman existed, but in separating the way she is represented for the Company's manipulations from other possible representations of her. If I could grasp the representations that have to be pushed to the margins of the text so that a "politically interested figuration" or trope could operate as truth, then historical agency could be outlined, even if unrealized.[65] In my chapter on the rani of Burdwan, I explore this issue through another example. There I argue that it is possible to distinguish between a real historical subject, Rani Bishnukumari, and the figure of the secluded woman that also circulates in official discussions. When a figuration is contested and contradicted by another agent in the text, a resistant reality emerges as the result of a differential reading—as we distinguish one set of actions (those of the agent) from the actions preferred by colonial functionaries (the interested figuration). *Reading the East India Company* thus takes stock of women equally as figurations in various cultural and official texts and as historical subjects whose agency is visible at different levels, albeit mediated by colonial discourses and power. By looking at ways in which the textual production of the empire involves the simultaneous production and assignment of subject positions, we also understand the archive to embody a differential relationship between texts and subjectivities.

That is not all. Because such moments of textual production of subject positions are also arrangements of inclusion and exclusion, when we read the archive with the intent of foregrounding a female subject who is otherwise marginalized and rendered almost invisible in it, we also reconstellate the archive by creating new textual links and discursive networks. As marginal subjects, when women appear in the record, they expose the conditions, rules, and constraints that have operated to keep them out of the action. In other words, the grammar of power that underwrites various kinds of colonial writing can be analyzed and deconstructed by tracking women who appear only infrequently and intermittently in the archive. This book explores various moments of women's appearance in order to ask questions such as the following: What conditions have made it possible for a woman to appear in the colonial record? How does she move from official discussions where she is a secluded subject into missionary tracts or novels where she is the object of religious conversion? From Universalist Enlightenment histories where she is sexual slave to parliamentary discussions where she is degenerate mother? All in all, I hope to demonstrate that instances of the faintest presence of women in official and unofficial texts (as figures or historical subjects) can be read as metonyms of significant historical changes. The sites of such emergences of women are potential points on networks that can provide us with various pathways to connect the discursive changes on the textual surface of the colonial archive to the historical shifts in the empire.

Critical Genealogies of Woman: The Gendered Critique of Colonialist Knowledge

One of the problems we face as critical interpreters and interlocutors in the relay between the past and the present is gauging the agency of our own reading. When reading texts that have come out of a dominant social formation like colonialism, how do we ensure that our analysis breaks the hold of colonial power over knowledge? If I were to take the various texts in this study—official ones such as the records of the India Office and the minutes of parliamentary committee proceedings, as well as cultural texts such as novels, memoirs, portraits, and guidebooks—as symptomatic expressions of colonialism, how would my interpretation and analysis prevent a replication of the dominant? This question is also relevant when I am looking at texts that are eccentric or singular instances rather than at those that are close to power or at the cusp of policy making. What is the value of a text even if it is not part of a large-scale cultural trend? Similarly, what is the cultural work performed by a novel, for instance, if it has not single-handedly changed the course of the empire? Such questions, it seems to me, can be addressed satisfactorily if we think about them through the concept of emergence.

The idea of emergence receives its fullest articulation as a term for historical and cultural analysis in the work of the Marxist critic Raymond Williams. Williams takes the fundamental role of cultural or historical analysis to be the recognition of "complex interactions between movements and tendencies," because it is the very notion of movement that enables analysis to "connect with the future as well as with the past." Thus, within the culture of colonialism or imperialism there may be stages or "internal dynamic relations" where we can observe the emergent: "new meanings and values, new practices, new relationships [that] are continually being created." While some of these new meanings and values are only mutations of the dominant culture, others, Williams points out, are substantively alternative or oppositional to it. Our reading of the past can thus perform the task of sifting and separating the strictly emergent from the residual, or elements of the past that continue to form an "effective element of the present," and the dominant, or hegemonic processes that seek to incorporate both the residual and the emergent.[66]

Such a reenvisioning of colonialism as a process rather than a fixed structure, and the archive as a discursive formation rather than a protected body of texts, shows us that the empire is not an a priori totality: it is a hegemonic process that, though always seeking dominance in various areas of lived experience, is never total or exclusive. This suggests that there is virtue in recording not only the power of the powerful but also instances of failure—elements of power that are muted or preemergent and aspects of the cultural that the dominant have neglected or undervalued. In cases where the preemergent failed to materialize, we learn what the dominant had to control or incorporate; in cases where cultural elements are neglected or undervalued, we know what managed to escape the purview of power.

In *Reading the East India Company,* I am particularly interested in mapping such cultural and political stratifications in colonial formations. Thus, in my discussion of *Hartly House, Calcutta,* I show the discourse of sentiments, exhausted for the most part by the 1770s in the English novel, resurfacing as a residual element in the Anglo-Indian fiction of the 1780s. In *Hartly House,* the novel does the cultural work of representing the female psyche as a storehouse of memory that exposes and reinscribes the violence of colonial conquest even as it is being erased by officially sanctioned memorials and histories of the colonial past. In contrast to this case of residue-as-resistance, my chapter on everyday life shows various forms of incorporation into the official project. This analysis begins with early representations of home as an unsupervised site of sexual interaction between English men and native women, and it moves to the widespread cultural activity of archiving personal and private experience. The gradual work of transforming home and the domestic into permanent settlement, or life in India, begins with the simultaneous deployment of the idea of English life as opposed to native life, and a racialized and gendered discourse of English domesticity emerges to separate one from the other. This incorporation of the domestic is complete, I argue, when the novels and memoirs of English women chronicle and archive memories of their life in India.

It may seem surprising that my analysis in much of the book privileges cultural texts (novels, guidebooks, portraits, autobiographical narratives) as sites of both emergence and consolidation, especially since the official documents seem to be closest to the deployments of colonial power. I do this for a reason. The authority of the official document is still understood today as uncontaminated by the subjectivity of the cultural and imaginative text. Part of the undoing of such a claim to authority and power lies in exploring the mutual contamination of the center and margins by examining the relationships between various kinds of texts and the rules and constraints that are put in place to separate them. Thus, as my reading of Daniel Defoe's *Roxana* shows, the novel and the factory record may actually resonate with each other in uncanny ways. In a related manner, the novel *Hartly House, Calcutta* can be read as a zone of interference that ultimately threatens the role of the official archive as a repository of fact.

Because the production of a literary text is ultimately a symbolic act, the text is not useful for documentary evidence about real referents; however, it is unmistakable evidence of a different kind of historical event—that of cultural imagining. We know by reading a novel from a certain historical moment that it was possible to think this way, that the conditions for certain kinds of utterances had already emerged. Furthermore, because the novel was the preferred genre for chronicling the unofficial and marginal sites of eighteenth- and nineteenth-century culture—the private sphere, women's domains, sexuality, and so forth—it is also a useful gauge for measuring the extent to which official processes and ideologies worked their way into various aspects of cultural expression.

By reading emergence as the place where women appear in various texts, I bring together the methodological premises of gendered analysis with those of reading the past critically. It is not surprising that many of the sites Raymond Williams lists for cultural analysis of emergence in modern hegemonic processes are those seen as the normal habitats of women in the period we are studying: autobiography, the novel, structures of feeling, the private, and so on. This helps advance my claim that we can read the various appearances of women as sites of emergence. Women's realms were for the most part tangential sites in dominant formations like colonialism and imperialism, where the political, military, and economic activities accompanying colonization were undertaken mostly by men and in the public sphere. Thus, colonialist histories as well as postcolonial accounts of that encounter did not include till very recently women as historical subjects or accounts of their domains as part of the totality of colonial social relations. But if women exist in the shadow regions of that history and knowledge, then they are likely candidates for the deconstructive power provided not only by Williams's analysis but also by Michel Foucault's historical work in which he employs the twin approaches of archaeology and genealogy. When women appear in the colonial archive as low-ranking and unqualified subjects, they not only bring forth historical contents that have been buried or disguised, but also expose the order imposed by systematizing thought.[67] In other words, the discursive order and arrangement of the archive and its relationship to the social formation as a whole are rendered visible. This is in keeping with the spirit of archaeological analysis.

Further, if we foreground the place of women and read their emergence as a "moment of arising" or a "place of confrontation" where we read also for the "entry of forces" and their "eruption," we have moved into the next stage of analysis, which Foucault terms genealogy.[68] This can happen on a small scale or a large one.[69] Thus, on the one hand, in my discussion of the Bashwar woman we see how the rape trial of a single unnamed Indian woman became an occasion for a Company's trading post to engage in a dress rehearsal of using native law to manage natives. On the other hand, we see how the arrival of the figure of the Hindu woman as a cultural icon in official debates about the East India Company in the 1820s was a sign not only that the missionary societies had begun the task of civilizing the native but also that major changes were afoot in British rule of India—the transformation from rule by a commercial enterprise to rule by an imperial state.

The book gives parallel plottings of various sites of emergence for both the English woman and the Indian woman. These parallel tracks do not provide a continuous or exhaustive history, for that is an impossible task. Instead, I attempt at various points to make woman into a subject of history as Hélène Cixous has imagined her—as someone who "occurs simultaneously in several places." The fragmentary and intermittent nature of her appearances does not make the account incomplete; rather, it forces us to rethink the very premises of historiography that require individuals, empirical persons, or members of a class for legitimacy. A critical genealogy of women as historical subjects can thus "un-think the unifying, regulating history that homogenizes and channels forces, herding contradictions into a single battlefield."[70]

Overview of Chapters

In chapter 1, I approach the figure of the female-as-individualist through Daniel Defoe's *Roxana* (1724) and read it alongside the rape trial of an unnamed woman recorded in the East India's Company's 1721 factory records from a settlement in south India. In creating this temporal conjuncture, I aim to extend the discussion of European women's self-constitution as bearers of rights into a globally dispersed setting. When we thus extend the discussion, we see that the character Roxana does not simply approach the colonial margins in order to make herself into a bourgeois individual; her fate in the novel is similar to that of the subaltern woman in south India. On one side of the world, an Englishman (Defoe) constitutes the English woman's self at the scene of colonial trade. On the other side, an Indian woman's self is negated by English traders who decide she is the property of Indian men. By showing how the novel resonates with the representational strategies of the rape trial in the colonial archive, I expose the novel's use of female individualism as a ruse to further financial interests. In both cases, a male author and male colonial functionaries stage the woman as a counter to gauge the place of patriarchal power in existing economic relations.

In chapter 2, I explore how colonial violence in India, which is only preemergent in chapter 1, becomes a major point of discussion in mid- and late-eighteenth-century literature. Through a reading of three texts—John Z. Holwell's *A Genuine Narrative of the Deplorable Deaths* (1758), Robert Bage's *Mount Henneth* (1782), and Phebe Gibbes's *Hartly House, Calcutta* (1789)—I show how this violence is both contained and utilized for various political gains. All three texts, a primary historical document and two novels, are inscribed within a discourse of sentiments and sensibility. Such a discourse allows male writers to stage themselves as feminized victims of native violence. However, with the publication of *Hartly House* we see that a woman writer exploring female themes of empire can establish forms of female solidarity with native women as well as expose the forms of colonial violence that masculinist histories try to hide. The chapter concludes by showing how the arrival of the woman writer on the scene of writing about India creates a zone of interference for the "truths" of the official archive.

In chapter 3, I continue my discussion of historical shifts that install new subject positions for the Englishwoman in India by tracing the changing notions between 1770 and 1830 of the domestic, home, and life. I use Mrs. Monkland's *Life in India* (1828), a domestic novel, to establish when accounts of everyday life are complicit with colonialism. When the domestic is seen no longer as a description of English foibles but as a mnemonic device for inscribing memories of Anglo-Indian life, then the novel becomes an important archiving tool and can be incorporated into a politics of settlement. Unlike chapters 1 and 2, chapter 3 surveys a wide array of texts—portraiture, parliamentary debates, a guidebook, and a novel—to show the ideological dispersal of the notion of archiving memory as an act of reinscribing India and possessing it more securely.

While the earlier chapters focus mainly on the Englishwoman and show the native woman emerging as a marginal subject at the scene of the former's self-constitution, the last two chapters of the book reverse this trend. Since the Indian woman cannot be accessed as a producer of cultural texts in the period I am discussing, in chapters 4 and 5, I attempt a genealogy of the Indian woman mainly through official records. In chapter 4, I show how a historical subject, the rani of Burdwan, combats a Company-deployed figuration of her as the secluded woman. By reading the psychobiography of this female landholder from 1770s Bengal, I demonstrate that it is possible to read her agency by tracking the ripple effects of her actions through various documents in the official archive—primary reports, letters, dispatches, parliamentary minutes, and so on. In a reverse reading, I also show how the European woman, though absent at the scene of the rani's original actions, arrives years later as the main frame within which the rani's role is understood in the nineteenth century. The rani becomes a footnote in J. S. Mills's famous essay on the subjection of women.[71]

In chapter 5, the final chapter of the book, I show how the earlier discourse that disciplined the rani of Burdwan in the 1780s—an Orientalist discourse of the secluded woman—is replaced by a nativist discourse of the

Hindu woman as cultural emblem by the 1820s. I follow the movement of official and unofficial discussions toward this emergence by reading three textual sources: parliamentary discussions leading to the renewal of the Company charter in 1813, which first gave official sanction to missionary work in India; selected works of Raja Rammohun Roy, one of the most prominent Indian social reformers of this time; and parliamentary debates of 1832, when Roy was invited to England as the first native expert witness before a select committee. By intertwining the official exercises in constructing the figure of the Hindu woman in 1813 with the subsequent activism of Rammohun Roy, I trace the genealogy of the male Hindu "native informant." I argue that he gains visibility and authority through his activism on the behalf of Indian women and that he is the forerunner of the residual power of tradition in gendered politics in contemporary India. I track these early historical moments into the present—into the nationalist use of women as objects of protection from "westernization" and the metaphorizing of female subjects for religious rather than class critiques of globalization. Both exercises, I contend, serve to keep the power base of the nationalist elites secure in postcolonial India.

Each of the chapters in this book identifies moments of emergence and charts the social forces that accompany such textual and historical acts. The Englishwoman appears as female individualist, she-merchant, author, domestic subject, civilizer, and moral thermometer, while the Indian woman appears as rape victim, mistress, secluded landholder, and cultural emblem. The chapters do not move in a strict chronological order; instead, they convey in their succession a series of uncoverings of representations of women and by women as they move across the surface of the textual record: from fictional narratives to official discussions and vice versa, and from the eighteenth to the nineteenth century.

CHAPTER ONE

Globalizing Defoe

> The Latter Part of her History lay Abroad, and cou'd not so well be vouch'd as the First; yet, as she has told it herself, we have the less Reason to question the Truth of that Part also.
>
> —Daniel Defoe, preface to *Roxana* (1724)

> In perusing your Consultations We find great Carelessness, partly in the Writing, but more in the Mistakes for the want of careful Examination afterwards. In some places there is no entry of the Persons Names who Sign'd them . . . whereas in other Our Settlements the President and Council each sign the Consultations they send Us, and as it used to be at Fort St. George We expect it shall be in all time coming.
>
> —Court of Directors to Council at Fort St. George, 1724

When working with literary texts from the eighteenth century it is often difficult to extend the story of Europe into its colonial margins in a way that would allow a simultaneous articulation of both the center and the periphery. Daniel Defoe's *Roxana* (1724) stages the self-constitution of its female protagonist against the background of British commercial expansion. The novel's representation of the rising empire, albeit short-circuited in the novel's preface when the unverifiable aspects of Roxana's tale are made to line up with the unknown geography of overseas trade, uses the "East Indies" in crucial, constitutive ways. The Indies provide a convenient ruse for Roxana to acquire respectability. Her wealth, amassed through various sexual exchanges, is laundered into legitimacy by her claims that it was accumulated in the Indies. The colonial margins operate also as places of real economic gain when they provide employment for Roxana's young sons. Thus the far-flung spaces of colonial trade represent both places beyond epistemological limits, where truth cannot be verified, and places of enrichment that wait for characters dispatched from the main scene of the action. How do we read this narrative ambivalence of the colony? How do we understand its simultaneous presence as constitutive of Roxana's autobiography and exclusion as unrepresentable space? To what extent does the novel's narrative blind spot also remain a scholarly one in the reassessments of eighteenth-century literature today? What will it take to transform that space of the heroine's dissimulation into a reading position—a textual space from which one can write back in the wake of European expansion?

To revise *Roxana*'s story of colonialism, told as the unidirectional, and often pretended, movement of entrepreneurs into non-European spaces, one might start by filling in the shadowy regions that lie around the main plot. Ideally, for the critic, such an undertaking would involve rereading a cultural archive with what Edward Said has called "a simultaneous awareness" both of the metropolitan history that is narrated and of those "other histories against which (and together with which) the dominating discourse acts."[1] This is a difficult task, given that the English literary tradition has been representing non-Western spaces since the sixteenth century, but printed texts that responded to the phenomenon of European worlding did not emerge in many of the eastern colonies till the nineteenth century.[2] In light of this unequal textual production, is it possible for the literary critic to put together an alternative story of interplay and contestation between European and non-European elements in the earlier stages of colonialism in India?

Roxana provides a very apt metropolitan strand in this anticipated story because it not only incorporates within its plot the commercial sites where the East India Company was active in the early eighteenth century, but also generates a form of expression that resembles the ebbs and flows of mercantilism. Defoe's economic and fictional writing reveals an obsessive charting of the transformative power of commerce, its logic of exchange and its ability to transform the identity of people and things through various determinations of economic value. In that a novel like *Roxana* chooses to explore this symbolic economy through a female figure who uses her sex as labor-in-exchange, prostitution rather than commerce proper is the chosen entry point into a vast discursive field where various concepts are being rapidly redefined—individualism, private property, subjectivity, rights, and so on. There is a strategic reason for such narrative transvestism on Defoe's part, a point I will come back to later. But first, why does this novel of female individualism advance the problematic of reading Europe as Self and as Other?

The eighteenth-century novel develops female individualism by evaluating the status of English women against various forms of non-English subject positions. In *Roxana,* the most common tropes are those of slave and Turkish woman.[3] However, Orientalist tropes were not the primary way of depicting the relationship between female agency and the structures of colonialism. Feminist postcolonial scholarship over the last two decades has established that representations of British female individualism were used for cultural comparisons with an inchoate mass of "other women" of the colonies well into the nineteenth century.[4] Thus, a retroactive reading that turns narratively emptied colonial space into a site where a British and a native woman can be read together in their proximity and difference may help forestall similar tendencies in globalist feminist criticism today. A case in point: the renewed efforts under contemporary globalization to install "women's rights" for people within different cultural inscriptions seems to take the "goodwill" of feminism as a "guarantee,"[5] but historical attention to textual and cultural sources that show good-willed men representing women, figuratively and legally, to further various economic agendas in the name of these female subjects may provide useful lessons about "woman" as a ruse for financial control.

In this chapter, I will read Daniel Defoe's *Roxana* alongside some excerpts from the East India Company's factory records from 1721 to 1723.[6] By coupling the novel with coeval material from the Company archives I mean to do three things. First, I attempt a global reading of the historical construction and distribution of the figure of the female individualist and its deployment within colonialist discourses. The archival records of the East India Company allow us to translate this figure historically into the arenas the novel only outlines as the "East Indies." In this case we will focus on a fortified factory in South India where Company employees carry out trade and plan the slow steps from trade to conquest. The factory records reveal the various agendas that are dissimulated around the discussions of the trial of a Company employee for the rape/seduction of a native woman.

Second, with this textual juxtaposition I provide a way of reading the female figure's deployment as a textual resolution of existing social contradictions. Both the novel and the factory records reveal an instrumental use of the female figure where the social haunts her body's sexuality. We see how sex-related differences between bodies are continually summoned as testimony to social relations and other phenomena that have little to do with sexuality as such—not only as testimony *to* these phenomena, but also as testimony *for* them, or as "legitimation."[7] Joan Scott, from whose discussion I have gleaned this point, asserts that such displacements occur also because "hierarchical structures rely on generalized understandings of the so-called natural relationships between male and female."[8] In such narrativizations, both novels and official records become spaces of trial where we can read the figure of woman as "instrumental in shifting a colonial system of meaning."[9]

Finally, I identify the uncanny narrative resemblances between Defoe's novel and the record keeping of the trading company, which show the growing imbrication of commerce in the cultural practices surrounding text—its production, preservation, circulation, and reading by various communities within and outside Britain. *Roxana*'s narrative format closely approximates the ebbs and flows of the mercantilist world system as Defoe, like the bookkeepers and writers of the East India Company, charts the transformative power of commerce and its ability to change anything and everything into a commodity. While the Company imagines continued accumulation through the careful archiving of all information that can translate into future economic gain, the novel scripts the phenomenon by plotting the relentless onward movement of its heroine—the accumulative drive of a female picara as prostitute. The debate ensuing about the fate of Roxana in England and that of the rape victim in India generates more writing and reading as novel readers, on the one hand, and Company officials, on the other, create new networks of social relations. The power struggles between various communities of readers are negotiated and established through their common participation in the moral, economic, political, and legal discussions about the status of the two women.

By reading the transformations of these women's status as partial requirements of colonialist processes and capital accumulation at a historical moment, I ask what the relationship between imperialism and feminism is today. The textual juxtaposition argues for the need to read for historical conjunctures—rather than for separate histories—as a way of measuring the legacy of colonialism and its role in securing a position not only for the advocate of feminism in the West but also for the feminist in decolonized space who might see her struggle as incommensurable with the presuppositions of Western liberal rights.[10]

The Moral Geography of the Individualist

Choosing a female speaking subject is not an unusual novelistic maneuver for eighteenth-century male writers. The works of critics such as Nancy Armstrong and Madeleine Kahn have shown convincingly that the "narrative transvestism" of writers like Samuel Richardson and Defoe enables rhetorical reversals that transform all social conflicts, whether of class or rank, into sexual conflicts between men and women.[11] Armstrong in particular argues that Richardson's heroines, because they are women, can be considered apart from polity and economy and thus prove apt vehicles for representing an interiority shorn of public interests. Though presupposing such interiority for a subject of rights is clearly a political project, the domesticated woman provides liberal bourgeois ideology with the fantasy of a nonpolitical space. The woman's "natural" predilection for the private and the psychological therefore provides the textual opportunity to establish the mental states of the modern individual as such.[12] Kahn, on the other hand, shows that when Defoe plays woman in *Roxana* he uses his access to female subjectivity through the heroine's mental states to consolidate masculinity rather than to diminish it.[13] In the works of Richardson and Defoe, the common element is the use of marginalized female figures—the sexually violable servant (Pamela), the raped lover estranged from her family (Clarissa), and the abandoned wife turned prostitute (Roxana)—as rhetorical tools to define the role of women as well as the legal subjecthood and political identity of men through and in terms of women.

In Defoe's *Roxana* we see how the author's use of a female heroine is symptomatic of a wider social crisis of legitimation. Commerce, or mercantile capitalism, enlarged existing social networks through trade in the eighteenth century, and global trade was a web in which all markers of identity and subjectivity (whether of gender, nationality, or race), previously held to be "natural," were rendered ambivalent and unstable.[14] Even as the novel provided a powerful instrument for the imagined resolution of these social contradictions, the figure of woman allowed this debate to be staged in a multilayered way. Just as the raped or about-to-be-raped woman problematized the relationship between the body and the mind, as well as accompanying notions of intention—mental states and consent, for instance—the prostitute focused attention on the problematic relationship between the body and economic value-in-exchange. Because both women are subjects of physical, moral, or legal violation, these feminine representations allow male authors to stage the limits of violation for all individuals. What becomes at least possible for a woman—inviolable self, will, instincts, love—becomes inalienable for a man in a cultural scenario where economic exchange threatened the very meaning of selfhood, property in the person, and identity.

Defoe establishes Roxana as a female individualist through a narrative strategy that resembles his conjurings with Robinson Crusoe on the island. Because individualism posits an autonomous producer of value—one who simultaneously owns both self and property—such autonomy must be established by sleight of hand.[15] Crusoe, for instance, can be posited as *Homo economicus* and as the origin of value only because he is cast off on a deserted island, shorn of sociality, and unhindered by competing claims for his habitat. In *Roxana,* Defoe tries a similar magical formula to posit the female individualist embarking on the creation of value. The protagonist-narrator is stripped of the security of her household and her means of support by a foolish, squandering husband. Like Crusoe, she is cast into the world with nothing but her labor power as a means of improving herself, but Roxana does not manifest the work ethic that has become the hallmark of the solitary exile Crusoe because she is "not bred to Work" (*Roxana*, 48).

Having denied Roxana's ability to work, or her capacity to support herself as members of the lower-class female workforce of that time did, Defoe can now posit that she is ready to embark on becoming an individualist through the use of sexuality as labor power.[16] At the same time, in order to establish Roxana as the subject of contractual relations (the primary discourse that produces the individualist), Defoe must present sexual relations as contractual. Roxana reaches this point when, in her penury, she is forced to imagine the possibility of having to lie with her landlord for bread. Her indigent circumstances are momentarily suspended as she and the landlord debate the possibility of another contract: "My Dear, *says he,* I have taken such Measures as shall make an Equality still; and with that, he shew'd me a Contract in Writing, wherein he engag'd himself to me; to cohabit constantly with me; to provide for me in all Respects as a Wife; and repeating in the Preamble, a long Account of the Nature and Reason of our living together, and an Obligation in the Penalty of 7000 *l.* never to abandon me" (*Roxana*, 76, emphasis in original).

In tune with the powerful emerging ideology that determined discussions of polity, economy, and sexuality at that time, the framework of the social contract is mapped onto marriage (a thesis now well established by the work of Nancy Armstrong and Carole Pateman, among others), and accordingly the narrative now paves the way for an evaluation of the heroine's attempts to better herself through the use of her sexuality.[17] However, once the social contract has become the sexual contract for the female as individualist, the narrative is transformed into a moral fable that is to be judged by the criteria of nature, decency, and politeness, rather than by questions of women's unequal status as signatories to such contracts. To understand the implications of what it means to make Roxana a signatory to a sexual rather than a social contract, we have to look at the important role this displacement played in the changing social relations within Britain at that time.

Contractual ideology, coming as it did when individual rights had become the rallying cry for popular movements leading up to the two revolutions in the late eighteenth century, produced the sexual contract not only as a paradigm for a discussion of women's rights, but also as a rhetorical strategy to displace the ideology of possessive individualism from the marketplace to the domain of the family. In all activities relating to the production, reproduction, and consumption of wealth, the white bourgeois male remained the property-bearing subject.[18] To the woman went a "new form of political power"—authority over the household and the various activities organized around leisure, courtship, family, and child rearing. Under her "jurisdiction," Nancy Armstrong argues, "the most basic qualities of human identity were supposed to develop."[19]

In *Roxana,* the expected domestic resolution in which female individualism is displaced and is in retreat from the public to the private does not take place for the heroine. Instead, the narrative locates the production of economic value precisely at the site of the female body. The "home" becomes the marketplace instead of a space alternative to it as Roxana moves through a spectrum of sexual contracts: wife, common-law wife, mistress, and kept woman. At the end of each of these liaisons she takes stock of the multiple forms of wealth she has accumulated: portions, pin money, jointures, gifts, pensions, and even dowers. The novel goes one step further by making Roxana, now the subject of a sexual contract, into the freelance signatory of the social contract. This happens when Roxana refuses an offer of marriage from a Dutch merchant and her refusal is couched in the language of individual autonomy. Roxana asserts that "the very Nature of the Marriage-Contract was, in short, nothing but giving up Liberty, Estate, Authority, and every-thing, to the Man, and the Woman was indeed a meer Woman ever after, that is to say, a Slave" (*Roxana,* 187). At this point in Defoe's narrative, it is possible to say that Roxana is not just a prostitute, driven by necessity to sell her services. Using her sexuality, she has become a woman of means, the dreaded *femme seule* and the figure of real contractual relations.

However, this moment of refusal that establishes a female contractual subject who is not domesticated is also an occasion for the narrative to signal a warning. When Roxana does not freely choose the Dutchman, he tells her, "Dear Madam, you argue for Liberty at the same time that you restrain yourself from that Liberty, which God and Nature has directed you to take." The novel now replaces Roxana's language of necessity and need, employed earlier to justify the use of her sexuality, with the foreboding language of unnatural vice or "vicious Liberty, which is neither honourable or religious" (*Roxana,* 197). A "liberty" that is "directed" by "God and Nature" is now offered as guaranteeing true female autonomy, while the specter of natural female instincts begins to haunt Roxana's attempt to appropriate the subject position of possessive individualism. Dire consequences are also foretold when Roxana informs the reader of the contents of the letter the disappointed Dutchman wrote before leaving her: He "forgave me every-thing, *he said*, but the Cruelty of refusing him, which he own'd he cou'd not forgive me . . . because he was satisfied it was an Injury to myself; would be an Introduction to my Ruin; and that I wou'd seriously repent of it; he foretold some fatal things, which, *he said*, he was well assur'd I shou'd fall into; and that, at least I wou'd be ruin'd by a bad Husband" (*Roxana*, 200, emphasis in original). The letter sufficiently mortifies Roxana to leave her "melancholy" and crying. Her admission of hubris follows soon after this when she enjoins her audience to read her as a "Monument of the Madness" that women run into when they "follow the Dictates of an ambitious Mind" (*Roxana*, 201).

Various critical accounts of the eighteenth-century novel have noted how the bourgeois cultural revolution in the eighteenth century debated its new human subject through the literature of the time. Pamela, Clarissa, Charles Grandison—and Roxana, for that matter—are not only "fictional characters: they are also public mythologies, coordinates of a mighty moral debate, symbolic spaces within which dialogues may be conducted, pacts concluded and ideological battles waged."[20] These spatializations of narrative forms transform the novel into the space of a trial. It is not hard to see that *Roxana* performs a similar ideological function: it stages not a space of prohibitive law, but what Derrida calls a "fictive institution," which in principle allows anything to be said.[21] This freedom of expression is crucial for instituting new forms of subjectivity because it mystifies the operation of law at other levels. For instance, the novel's judgment about the economic and sexual transgressions of the female subject must seem to originate from Roxana herself, just as juridical discourse must seem to have no other basis to exist but the protection of law itself. On the other hand, as Peter Fitzpatrick explains, "Disorder on law's part cannot . . . be located in law itself. The sources of disorder must exist outside the law—in the eruptions and disruptions of untamed nature or barely contained human passion against which an orderly law is intrinsically set."[22] In *Roxana* we see the operation of this discourse when bourgeois morality arrives as a Lacanian law or name-of-the-father, a censuring and castrating agency that limits the very desire it has brought into being.[23] When law has been internalized as morality and a subject desires to be made over and reformed, what we see is the successful consolidation of hegemonic power that uses not the mechanisms of prohibition but the mechanisms of consent.

Through Roxana's confession and descent into despair, Defoe sets the stage for the victory of domesticity. Her growing self-introspection (and the comfortable income she has amassed) allows her to lead a retired life in London with her maid, Amy. But her constant regret at not having married the Dutchman indicates to the readers that she is finally ready for rehabilitation.

The Dutchman soon reappears in England, they are married, and he assumes paternal responsibility for the son he had earlier abandoned to Roxana's care. The novel suggests through Roxana's great approbation of this parental gesture that she is to do the same, albeit secretly, with the children she has also abandoned at various points in her sexual career (*Roxana,* 308).

The Dutchman's moral authority is signified by the kind of wealth he owns. In a symbolic reenactment of a Lockean voluntary compact of marriage, the newlyweds disclose their wealth to each other and discover it to be equal, but with a difference. His is the new wealth: "Account-Courants," maritime contracts, shares in ships, stocks in the East India Company, and shares in cargo lying at foreign docks. Her wealth, on the other hand, symbolizes more traditional attempts at social mobility—mortgages upon land and buildings, securities of fee-farm rents, and money deposits. At this point Roxana muses, "*Unhappy Wretch . . . shall my ill-got Wealth, the Product of* prosperous Lust, *and of a vile and vicious Life* of Whoredom and Adultery *be intermingled with the honest well-gotten Estate of this innocent Gentleman to be a Moth and Catterpiller among it!*" (*Roxana,* 304, emphasis in original). In that the profits of colonial trade are established as moral and proper compared to the rewards of prostitution, the narrative transforms the exemplary merchant into a paterfamilias and provides a paternalistic and ethical basis for such trade.[24]

This nexus between colonial wealth and the bourgeois patriarchal family is made more evident in a later version of *Roxana.* In the 1745 version, which I have discussed elsewhere, the Dutchman becomes the preferred agent of Roxana's punishment. He takes over her property and her children.[25] Unlike Roxana, for whom maternity and commercial activity are irreconcilable, the Dutchman manifests no contradiction between paternity and the profit instinct. In fact, his success at trade serves to polish his abilities as a parent. What creates base instincts in Roxana effects paternity par excellence. The Dutchman takes care of not only his own children but Roxana's too. In this version of the novel, he marries off Roxana's daughter with a sizable dowry to a factor in the Dutch East India Company on the Malabar coast and gives her son Thomas a large plantation in Virginia. The Dutchman's children from his previous marriage are also given shares in Roxana's assets, which the Dutchman appropriates by virtue of existing law that makes all property in marriage that of the husband. Before his death, these children are given five thousand pounds each in East India stock. Roxana's capital accumulated through prostitution and avarice is thus morally transformed into inheritance through its insertion into the political economy of colonialism.[26]

In Defoe's *Roxana* of 1724, by contrast, moral disciplining is effected by the heroine's self-recrimination rather than by an external agent. We sense this plot shift when the reformed prostitute's entry into matrimony does not provide closure for the marriage plot. For moral closure, it seems, the narrative must persist till Roxana has internalized a "human" law. We read on to find that Roxana, despite a new life filled with "humane Felicity," looks back on her former life with "detestation" and "utmost affliction" (*Roxana,* 310). The guilt increases till Roxana, ridden with nightmares, grows "sad, heavy, pensive and melancholly." She languishes in this condition for two years, and would have done so for longer, the novel implies, if "Providence had not reliev'd" her (*Roxana,* 311). Roxana's later repentance and renewed religious faith do not seem adequate, for Defoe does not stop here either but persists at the risk of self-contradiction. It is not enough that Roxana relinquish her quest for profit, repent bitterly, and replace female individualism with conjugal love. She must be punished for forgetting her so-called natural instinct as mother.

The children Roxana abandoned in the past are now given center stage; they reappear on the scene and threaten to expose their mother's past behavior. Roxana even goes so far as to sanction the murder of her eldest daughter, Susan, who stalks her in the hope being reunited with her. Bad mothering—now "the most secret [of] Crimes," which is, by the "most unforeseen Accidents, brought to light and discover'd"—proves decisive for Roxana's fate (*Roxana,* 345). Abruptly the novel provides its third and final moment of closure: "After some few Years of flourishing, and outwardly happy Circumstances, I fell into the dreadful Course of Calamities, and *Amy* also; the very Reverse of our former Good Days; the Blast of Heaven seem'd to follow the Injury done the poor Girl, by us both; and I was brought so low again, that my Repentance seem'd to be only the Consequence of my Misery, as my Misery was of my Crime" (*Roxana,* 379).

This confessional ending clinches the paradoxical positioning of the female as individualist. Roxana is punished by moral law, which acts as the restraint on her capitalist aspirations, and her repentance reinforces the juridical power of a masculist bourgeois morality. She confesses to the educative role of law, she admits that the little value she placed on her children is the reason why she placed too much value on "vice," and she accepts poverty and misfortune as just due for her unnatural instincts. Roxana's movement through Defoe's narrative as a figuration of possessive individualism is short-circuited when she is simultaneously mapped onto the fields of affective relations and gendered natural instincts. When Roxana, as female entrepreneur, fails at domestic life, love, and motherhood, "natural law" is invoked to produce a disciplined and responsible female subject.

When Defoe brings forward biological laws and natural instincts as a check to sexual and gender transgressions in an unquestioning way, it is easy to see that he can also use this logic in other discursive domains. What we know today as economic theory and economic laws were still in the making at this time. What Defoe calls "evil influence" or "secret overruling decree" in *Robinson Crusoe* is not yet Adam Smith's invisible hand but is its discursive precursor. That sexual difference has explanatory power in uncertain epistemological terrain is clear in Defoe's writing, and its capacity for allegorical or generalizing power is demonstrated when the Roxana figure appears in other discursive domains: the mighty debates about class and national identity in the eighteenth century, for instance.

Defoe's readers outlived his authorial intentions about *Roxana* and went on to take over the task of deciding an appropriate fate for the heroine. In subsequent printings, some editors responded to the public's dissatisfaction with several aspects of the novel—its abrupt ending, Roxana's half-hearted confession, and the unresolved question of the missing children—by adding sizable numbers of new narrative twists and turns. In one of these continuations, the novel is recast in the style of French popular romances and acquires a happy ending when Roxana is reunited with her children. In a 1775 version, she becomes the middle-class wife happy in her companionate marriage.[27] In the well-known continuation published in 1745 (often attributed to Defoe himself), the ending is bleak and deals out an extended, harsh sentence to Roxana.[28] She loses all her assets playing she-merchant, and the Dutchman abandons her and assumes parental rights over her children as Roxana ends up in a debtor's prison and dies before her release. Her autobiography is "finished" by a former maid who adds only that her mistress died a repentant woman. When readers of all these versions became arbiters, it is clear that Roxana ceased to be a fictional character and became a textual cipher with allegorical power. Through a discussion of her fate, various social-interest groups debated in the literature of the time the role of emergent middle-class subject positions associated with domesticity and privacy. Similarly, *Roxana*'s use of sexual difference as a coding for economic debates can be perceived in a new historicist anecdote from some of Defoe's writing that predates the novel.

In 1717 the consumption of calico rose sharply in Britain and threatened the livelihood of local woolen and linen manufacturers, because although Indian-printed calicoes had been banned in Britain since 1696, those sold by the East India Company in Holland and France were being smuggled into domestic markets.[29] In 1719, Defoe threw in his lot with domestic weavers and issued a series of papers, titled *The Manufacturer*, that defended home industry against foreign trade. The brunt of his attack was borne not by the East India Company or the cloth smugglers, however, but by the English women who bought banned imports:

> Those especially such as are Mothers of Children, and are yet Wearers of Callicoes; I say, let them consider how many families of Mothers and Children they help to starve, by gratifying their Callico-Fancy, at the Expence of the Poor, and encouraging that Trade which takes the Milk from the Breasts of the Mothers, and the Bread from the Mouths of their Children. Let them consider, how a just and Christian Compassion would move them to detest and abhor the Dress, which merely because 'tis a Mode or Fashion, and that too of their own making, engages them in a Cruelty against nature and makes them little less than Murtherers and Destroyers. Let them look on their Children and represent to their Imaginations the torment of a mother, when she sees her Off-Spring starving and calling upon her for Bread when she has none to give them.[30]

The English mother who murders and destroys children for a dress is the later fictional Roxana. In the novel, Roxana's ubiquitous Turkish dress made of banned imported fabric—"Persian or Indian Damask" (*Roxana*, 215)—comes back in several afterlives as a sign of her fetishism of the foreign and exotic, and it also functions as the ultimate instrument of her ruin. Even in Defoe's subsequent papers on the subject of foreign imports, there is little doubt that the Englishwoman is not only a metonymic representation of unwarranted consumption but also the national cultural boundary that is in danger of being breached: "Every Woman whether rich or poor, that is seen in a Gown or Dress of printed Callico or Linnen shall be reputed an enemy to her Country. . . . We should soon see the ladies leave the Callicoes, and the callicoes, by Consequence, leave the Nation."[31]

Defoe's anxieties about England's unfavorable balance of payments are dominant in his economic writings. In order for Europe to maintain economic supremacy over those he terms "Pagans and Indians, mahometans, and Chineses [*sic*]," who gain employment at the expense of "Christians and Britains,"[32] Defoe calls for a Dutch-English coalition against foreign imports from the colonies. The allegorical power of the desired outcome of the Roxana-Dutchman marriage in the novel is clear in this wording: "It is our Undisputed Interest to maintain a constant, steady Union with the Dutch and the Civil Interests of the two nations, are, as Europe is now stated, Inseparable."[33]

The above examples from Defoe's economic prose show that the ideology of free trade, then as now, needs to interpellate all participants as equal inheritors under a future shared heaven while it places, at the same time, various constraints or limits to ensure that some—Europeans—will benefit more than others. The economic insecurity of England in the age of mercantile trade is thus staged and resolved by the seeming natural order of sexual difference, when the woman's body is used to draw the limits of free trade and a national community. On the one hand, for Defoe, the crossing of national, racial, and ethnic boundaries creates anxiety about losing economic control. On the other hand, the redrawing of affective and proprietary domains in the age of commerce drives the desire to naturalize gender at the site of the female body. Roxana resolves the first by becoming a good student and the reformed wife of the Dutchman; she resolves the other by admitting that the existence of a "man-woman" is self-destructive and against natural instincts.

In this discussion, I have tried to establish an entry point for the consideration of "women's rights" within the rubric of colonialism and have argued for a critical reading of the complicity of representations of female individualism with the history of conquest and domination. A contrapuntal reading that places the female subject of the social contract and property relations in eighteenth-century Britain within the framework of Britain as an empire may help us understand the historical connections and parameters that govern the alleged dissonance between "feminism" and "rights of woman" today. This dissonance establishes another important point: that colonialism manifested a contradiction central to the political institutions and ideologies of the time—the collusion of British liberal discourse with despotism. In the metropolitan context, we see this in the contradictions that lie at the heart of the discourse of individual rights, where affective relations and possessive relations short-circuit each other to disallow women a central place in the narrative. Within discourses of colonialism this collusion is revealed as we explore the uneven application of legal concepts within economic, legal, and political discourse when they travel to an alien context. Peter Fitzpatrick explains this procedural export of the law in the following way:

> The amnesiac quality of modern law's origins avoids a momentous paradox. An advanced Occidental law, wedded in its apotheosis to freedom and a certain equality becomes thoroughly despotic when shipped to the rest of the world in the formal colonizations from the late eighteenth to the early twentieth centuries. . . . This law was a prime justification and instrument of imperialism, one which, in the

> assessments of [a] great practitioner-theorist of imperialism [was] a gift which should "deserve the gratitude of the silent and ignorant millions."[34]

Reading in the colony the caricature of the theories of liberal rights and the premises on which they were founded can expose the limits of what is still today a very powerful discourse. It is to that end that I read the record of the colonizer as he unpacks the gift on Indian soil. At the very instant that the discourse of possessive individualism rears up as despotism in its unguarded, illegitimate existence as alien rule, the tracks of ideology are revealed. Here in some archival fragments of the East India Company, we can perhaps clarify better what the literary text of Defoe relinquishes reluctantly in its untidy ending. Although Defoe's fictional work ceases, it can be taken up in the East India Company's acts of inscription. As in Defoe's narrative, which leaves us with a female figure who is reduced to being a transmitter of wealth from one generation to another, in South India caricatured British law is summoned to render a woman not the owner of her self or body, but an exchangeable cipher for colonial reciprocity and the property of native men.

THE EAST INDIA COMPANY AS JUDGE

First the setting. A group of English traders and their native employees conducted their activities from a fortified factory in South India, the first one erected in India after a special dispensation of land from local rulers in 1640. The factory was in the middle of a "black town" (Madras) where a large number of natives had settled to participate in the trade network surrounding the settlement. The English depended on native translators and agents to negotiate the still unknowable web of class, caste, linguistic, religious, gender, and racial differences. The fortified factory faced a military threat at this point not from the Indians around the fort but from the French and the isolated groups of pirates who operated along the coast. Trade was maintained through a delicate balance of appeasement of local rulers, coaxing of local traders, and public displays of English ceremony.

In the entry for 23 February 1721, the Diary and Consultation Book of the factory at Fort St. George (cited parenthetically as Diary) records the arrival of a petition to the president, Francis Hastings, and the council from Vinketrauze, "an Inhabitant of this place of the Rashboot Cast":

> The Import of the said Petition being a complaint against Devaroy the Warehouse Conicoply [*sic*] for seducing his sister from her

> Lawfull Husband, debauching her and forcibly detaining her when she was demanded by himself and her said husband . . . the Complainant being very pressing and Importunate for Justice and being so much exasperated at the Shame and disgrace which their family was like to Suffer on ye occasion that they could scarcely be restrain'd from murdering themselves as well as the Woman, the Cast or tribe to which they belong being so nicely strict in their rules with reguard [*sic*] to matters that Concern their honour that they chuse much rather to suffer death than Ignominy or reproach. (Diary, 31)[35]

Normal entries about the arrival and departure of ships, outstanding bills, and receipt of revenues, consignments of goods, and dispatches are interrupted by this petition for justice. The case was a native affair: a local employee of the company, the warehouse "conicoply" (clerk) named Devaroy, was accused of "seducing" and "forcibly detaining" the wife of an upper-caste (Rajput) man. The factory council had ordered a preliminary roundup of the four people named in the suit, and their testimonies are summarized in the records. The defendant, Devaroy, stated that he had only provided shelter to the woman. She had run away from home and appeared at his door with a local washerwoman asking for protection from her relatives, who would "use her ill whenever she returned to them" (Diary, 31).

Vinketrauze (the brother-in-law of the woman) now told the council that he had sent his brother's wife away to her relatives because she had kept frequent company with a lower-caste washerwoman of "no very reputable Character" (Diary, 31). Later, when he was informed that she had escaped from her relatives' home and had been seen at Devaroy's compound, Vinketrauze had gone there and demanded that Devaroy hand her over. Devaroy had denied that she was at his house.

In her testimony, the washerwoman stated that Vinketrauze had solicited her help to locate his missing sister-in-law. She had done accordingly and had found her "amongst the Cooley Washerwomen." The two women then stopped at Devaroy's for shelter because it was too late in the day to travel. The next day, the washerwoman told Devaroy that the "Girl" had no place to go and her relatives would "murther her" if she returned to them. Devaroy gave them permission to stay three days, "two of which she . . . remain'd with the Girl but confesses that the third day she was absent" (Diary, 31). And finally there is the "testimony" of the "Girl," also called the Bashwar woman: "The sister to the Plaintiff Vinketrauze being brot before the board was ask'd if Deveroy [*sic*] was guilty of the several perticulars [*sic*] wherewith, he now Stood Charg'd in answer whereto the Woman declar'd in the affirmative and offer'd her Oath to the same" (Diary, 32).

This is not a case without potential for skepticism. Although the Bashwar woman had spent three nights at Devaroy's house, at least one of which was unchaperoned, the charge against the conicopoly of seduction, debauchery, and forcible detention rests wholly on the woman's oath that sex was nonconsensual. But it is also clear from all four accounts that the woman had come to Devaroy's house of her own accord and was not lured there by him.

As crimes go, says Frances Ferguson, rape is "remarkable for focusing attention on the mental states and their apprehension." Thus, discussions of rape invariably find themselves on the ground of subjectivity: "who or what counts as a person who can consent, whose consent is significant." Historically, Ferguson points out, because legal notions such as body-as-property, consent, will, and intention refer to the psychological states of individuals, they make rape into a complex act that requires narratives or storytelling to back up the often limited physical evidence. On the one hand, the "story of rape" is often contradicted by the model of statutory rape that "establishes consent and intention as potentially self-evacuating terms." On the other hand, in the more complicated cases, where "intention and consent are required to manifest themselves" without the statutory mechanism of age, for instance, there is always much skepticism: "It quickly collapses into itself with a competition between the story and the narrator."

Ferguson's insight that the tendency for the subject's self-contradiction was not only part and parcel of eighteenth-century legal debates about rape but also part of the dramatic treatment of female individualism in the eighteenth-century novel provides an important intersection for our discussion here. It allows us to see the relationship between fictional narratives and the "fictitious certainty" of law, as well as the way in which female legal subjectivity is always caught up in a displacement. As the "circumstances" of the rape displace the "act as the subject of the account," the legal effort to deduce "individual intention" begins to move into the social: patterns of behavior, general character, and past history arrive to establish or deny credibility. The rape victim, most often a woman, finds that her mental state is never adequate evidence and must be replaced by extraneous factors that negate the very kind of subject the law was to protect: the bourgeois individual who is able to represent her own mental state.[36]

In what follows I will take the cue about the individualist subject's potential for self-contradiction to follow the movement of the Bashwar woman from her appearance as a subject before English law through her transformation into a textual referent drained of proper identity. Dispersed and evacuated into a cipher, she becomes little more than a sign to be circulated and exchanged between classes, kin, castes, and institutions. The clash between the various interest groups (caste communities, trading groups, and English merchants) that collectively staged and silenced this woman allows us to read how law, whether "imported" or "native," provides a structure of power sharing, rather than justice for the supposed victim. Indeed law serves as a dissimulation of how patriarchal structures haunt the supposedly gender-neutral world of colonial trade.

In the eighteenth century, as in the present, rape was considered a crime of a secret nature, and English laws governing its prosecution acknowledged that the "party injured is . . . an admissible witness."[37] In the case under discussion here, the woman's oath before the council thus represented the first stage of the application of this legal precedent. But it is soon clear that there was disagreement in the council about Devaroy's guilt, and the matter had to be put to a vote. Six councillors agreed that Devaroy had to be punished, while three voted against the motion. Taken together, the opinions of the three dissenting councillors attempted to discredit the Bashwar woman's oath and prove that her "character," suspicious behavior, and reputation made her accusation that Devaroy was guilty of "forcing or lying with her" the account of a "very light Woman if not a Whore" (Diary, 37). While all three dissenting councillors acknowledged Devaroy's prehistory of "vile behaviour" and "debauchery," they also insisted that the woman was "wicked," "lewd," and of "loose behaviour" and that her false oath was being used by the "indigent husband and brother" to extort money from Devaroy.

It is in the paradox of consensual rape that this unnamed woman comes closest to displaying deliberate will and to being an individualized subject—she was *asking* to be raped. This paradox represents not only general disbelief in the woman's testimony, but also the inherent contradictions of possessive individualism as it constitutes a legal subject; this is borne out by Ferguson's argument that the notion of consent, when extended to women, establishes rape through an evaluation of the mental states of both parties involved. Though consent presupposes a deliberating will and inalienable property in the person (rights), renowned scholars, such as Sir Matthew Hale, included a built-in warning in their definition of rape. While acknowledging that rape violates the woman's will and shows the perpetrator's disregard for his victim's consent, Hale wrote that it is also "an accusation easily to be made and hard to be proved, and harder to be defended by the party accused, tho never so innocent."[38] In one stroke, raped women, though subjects of will, were disallowed credibility in the eyes of the law.

Other aspects of the woman's place in the proceedings belie the tendency to reduce her legal personhood and ability to testify on her own behalf. The discussion about her history and intentions aside, the woman appears in the records not as the appellant but as a referent. It was not from her that the petition for justice originated. Not only was she spoken for by her brother-in-law, Vinketrauze, but she was also left unnamed in the entire proceedings. She appears variously as "the Bashwar woman," "Girl," "wife," and "sister of the plaintiff," and her anonymity precludes her from being read as the willed and individuated speaking subject in the liberal tradition of legal discourse. The erasing of her proper name while all the male players were named had a function that will emerge only as the case unfolds. It is usual for proper names of natives to appear in the Company's factory records when there were financial or legal transactions at stake. Because it refused to grant the woman a similar status—what within liberal jurisprudence would signal "the self-presence of the subject, that truth which the proper name embodies and which the civil code verifies"[39] —the trial was not really about her. Instead, what we see is the powerful pursuance of various financial interests using patriarchal structures so that this woman remains the object of other people's discourse rather than a subject with her own utterances.

This marginality is especially visible in the relative importance given to each of the testimonies. Devaroy's summary is the longest one in the records, followed by Vinketrauze's testimony. (These do not appear as direct speech but as reported speech, because the English writer on the premises was transcribing past events into the Diary.) Not only is the Bashwar woman's "testimony" the last to appear, but it is also the one that merits the least attention in the records, and there is no summary of it. Instead we have to read it simply as affirmation or denial or as a voice reconstructed in the interstices of Vinketrauze's and Devaroy's testimonies and in the scattered references to her version of the story in the councillors' debates.

In addition to this refusal to extend a basic legal standing (even by English standards) to the woman, we also have a further dispersal of her legal status through the staging of collective victimization. In such a scenario we cannot easily read for a Roxana or a Pamela. It is difficult to extricate the Bashwar woman, the victim of alleged rape by Devaroy or violence by her kin, from the records as a person with will and sovereignty—one who claims a violation of her self and her body—when rape is depicted as a violence against a community. In direct contrast to the British legal framework of rape as an act that involves penetration of one body by another, the assault on one will by another, in the case proceedings rape is represented largely as a transgression that affects and throws into disarray a larger social body—the woman's kin and members of her caste. Rape is a caste transgression more than it is an individual assault.[40] And in this legal paradigm, where all sexual intercourse between upper-caste women and lower-caste men is forbidden, the woman's yes will always mean no—thus her consent or nonconsent becomes irrelevant. All sexual transgression, whether adultery or intercaste sexual intercourse, is rape against the caste communities to which the man and woman belong.

In offering this different paradigm for rape, I am not suggesting that the woman's alleged rape is justifiably read as a form of violence against a community, or the caste's honor, for such metaphoric displacements erase the materiality of her body. Rather, my aim is to show how reading one way rather than another exposes through the alternative the constructedness of the bourgeois legal subject's claim that self-presence and originary meaning are strictly located within the body. As readers, we are faced with the possibility that even if the Bashwar woman can barely speak in the records, her presence as a limit to the English legal paradigm does allow us to perform an interruptive reading. That is, we expose both the constructed nature of the modern legal subject as individualist, and this subject's unraveling in the face of various financial interests. The factory records show us that in this trial there is no prior existence of a real legal subject, English or native, but rather a caricatured invention created by the factory officers out of a catachrestical use of "British law" and "native law."

This unholy mixing took place formally when the council decided to consult caste leaders for their opinions. British attempts to codify Indian law began only in the 1770s, after they had amassed vast amounts of land and people to govern in Bengal. But the experiment in recruiting native agents to legitimize the operations of the Company on Indian soil had already begun in 1721. The Company had acquired Fort St. George in 1640 through a grant, and the village around it, Madras, a year earlier in 1639. Ceded colonies like these were the only spaces where the East India Company had the absolute prerogative to govern and subject Indians to the jurisdiction of British law. In the Company's 1726 charter, mayor's courts were established at Madras, Bombay, and Calcutta with prescriptions for the involvement of local *panchayats* and caste councils in intercaste disputes and of inferior courts with Indian merchants and local leaders for other cases involving trade disputes.[41] By the time of the case under discussion here (1721), some complications were beginning to emerge.

The growing alliance between the Company and local trade interests and comprador classes had resulted in disputes between natives and British subjects, as well as between native traders and native agents employed by the Company. The factory records show, for instance, that the petitioner in the

Bashwar woman case, Vinketrauze, was a peon in the employ of tobacco farmers who were suppliers to the Company. The handling of these disputes needed more delicate applications of law. Fort St. George, where the councillors staged the trial, was an area of partial sovereignty. The larger province was not under British territorial authority, thus explaining the need to deal with autonomous caste councils, unlike the incorporated ones in Bombay, and the use of competing systems of law. In the absence of absolute territorial control and under pressure to keep the climate conducive to trade, the Company needed to find ways to respect local customary and criminal law, even when the offender was one of its employees. However, as we shall see, the doctoring of the outcome by pressuring the caste council and the undermining of its decision in form (if not content) also were part of the flexible rearrangements to maintain superiority of British rule over native opinion.

A body of local caste leaders was hastily constituted by the council headed by Hastings and asked to give its opinion. The caste leaders' "verdict" was entered soon after, in the proceedings of the council's next meeting: "That Devroy [*sic*] kept in his house the Wife of a Rajah three or four days together and would not deliver her up tho he was Requir'd to do it several times by ye said Rajah and we believe as she her self like-wise declares and will [have] her Oath that he lay with her by Force for which transgress[ion] We leave to your Honour and company to punish him as ye may think fit" (Diary, 39). In this account, the Bashwar woman's husband had been promoted to rajah (king). It is possible that the English writer transcribing the proceedings made an error and repeated it throughout. Whatever the origin of the title, the emphasis on the husband's caste suggests that there was some agreement that Devaroy's main crime, whether the sex was forced or consensual, had been sexual contact with a social superior.

The caste leaders concluded that Devaroy had committed not just rape ("he lay with her by force"), but a multiple violation, which included infringement on conjugal privileges (refusing to deliver her up), as well as a caste offense (abducting the "Wife of a Rajah"). By accepting the woman's oath that she was forced, the caste leaders strengthened the case against Devaroy and made it difficult for the dissenting councillors to insist on him being let off. One must note, however, that the native legal body prescribed no punishment; the power of sentencing was delegated to Hastings and the factory council. One can read this in one of two ways: either the native authorities had already acknowledged that the Company was not subject to their law, or the cooperation between the two parties in response to a common threat (Devaroy) was seen as more crucial than a unilateral decision by one party.

The Company's recognition that a "correct" outcome of this trial would allow further consolidation of its power and influence in the area is apparent from the trial records. Since the law-merchant presence was not yet alien rule, the Company still trod carefully. It did not have military control in the area, so it had to show willingness to cooperate with local groups, but without capitulation, in order to keep its trade interests safe and still be capable of asserting a strong influence. For this reason, the factory council had to act as judge rather than prosecutor; it had to seek advice from local vested interests but without losing the position of dominance. The records tell us that the factory councillors reached a consensus against holding a formal trial: "The admission of a formal tryal and hearing of the Several partys before the said Castes would have been in a manner forming them [the caste leaders] into a Court of Judicature Superiour to ourselves as they were to Judge of a matter with which they then might reasonably suppose they were better acquainted than our selves" (Diary, 41). So while the Company employed the local juridical institutions (leaders of the castes) to advise them, and everyone in some sense had a say, whether as "opinion" or "testimony," the Company officials had to subordinate in spirit the judgment of the natives.

Here, then, are the salient points of the verdict that was delivered by the president, Francis Hastings, at a hastily arranged meeting of the factory council. It is the closest approximation we have of the intentions of the councillors: The woman's testimony could not be disallowed for lack of evidence because of "common rules of Justice in England where the woman is often times allow'd to be a substan[tive] evidence against the man in such a case" (Diary, 35).[42] Devaroy, we are told, was not being tried for rape but for refusing to return the woman to her husband when demanded by her husband: "We think he ought to suffer because *the Crime is in itself of a very heinous nature and no less than the invading another mans right and property* as well as the possessing and detaining it from him which is in Effect a Robbery and is always punish'd with severity by the Laws of our Country" (Diary, 35, my emphasis).

It is important to note that it is British law that was invoked to justify the acceptance of the woman's testimony and that the caste leaders' acceptance of the same is not mentioned.[43] Furthermore, British law was invoked here to change the nature of the crime from rape to robbery—a change obviously made to accommodate the dissenting council members who agreed that the woman had been restrained but could not concede that she had been raped—and to avoid the harsher sentence prescribed by customary law. The change from rape to robbery is also in concert with the idea of the sexual encounter as a caste transgression; both deny the woman a mental state, will, and consent. Now the question of protecting the woman's rights—her ownership of her own person—was suspended as the councillors came forward as guardians of the "property" of the husband and the other male members of the caste. In a fascinating reversal of Rousseau's fiction about the unsocialized individual submitting to the law to become a social body, here the native male as a social body upholding caste honor submitted to the law to become a property-bearing subject: he now owned women.[44] What might in different circumstances have been collective reparation paid to a community or family was now transformed into a more private economic transaction. It was the native husband who became the beneficiary of possessive individualism. As husband he was transformed into property owner and was to be compensated for that which he had lost—caste and wife.

The factory council was aware that this case also presented an opportunity to consolidate its standing among the upper castes. Hastings rationalized the verdict for the council in these terms: "We think ourselves under an indispensable Obligation to make a very Publick example, . . . that by such an open piece of Justice the Inhabitants may be convinc'd that we will not Suffer such persons to be thereby screen'd and protected from having due punishment inflicted on them when they committ unwarrentable [*sic*] actions" (Diary, 35). Devaroy was given a sentence that reflected the council's feelings that this was a case not about rape but about wrongful possession of another man's property: "He should be dismissed from the honourable Company's Service . . . he should stand in the Pillory and he should pay to the Injur'd Husband such a sum of mon[ey] as should be sufficient for the procuring another Wife in the room of her whom he debauched" (Diary, 35).[45] Devaroy was ordered to pay four hundred pagodas to the husband on the recommendation of the caste leaders. He was also ordered to pay a fine of five hundred pagodas to the Company, upon the receipt of which he was to be released (Diary, 101). The Bashwar woman had become an object of exchange—she was property that was temporarily displaced in ownership, an error to be rectified by actual monetary transactions in the amount of her value. The woman's husband was richer by four hundred pagodas, and the Company's treasury by five hundred pagodas.

The matter did not end there. Eight months later, in November 1721, Francis Hastings was dead, and the case was resurrected in order to settle old accounts between in-fighting councillors. Only one of the original group of councillors who voted to punish Devaroy still remained on the council. We do not know why all the others were dismissed, but a letter written by the newly constituted council to London at this time suggests that the late governor was siphoning money from the Company's coffers for his own private trade. The letter also says, "Mr. Hastings would singly direct all the Madrass shipping [and] sold the Goods at under rates by private Contracts . . . in which all the Councill joyn'd except Messrs Turner, Benyon, and Emmerson."[46] The three dissenting councillors, the thorns in the governor's side, were the same three who had dissented in the verdict against Devaroy. In the letter of 12 November to Company headquarters, a single paragraph is devoted to the case. It states that Hastings "intimidated" the caste leaders into giving a verdict against Devaroy, that Hastings subjected Devaroy to "ill usage." The fate of the fines reveals even cruder forms of appropriation. Though Devaroy paid four hundred pagodas to "buy" the peon a new wife, the peon, we are told, "never had a penny." The letter goes on to add that Devaroy "was fin'd 500 pagodas to the Company which is paid, desire directions about it, Messrs. Turner, Benyon and Emmerson dissented knowing the accusation false."[47]

In this hurried transcription, the shorthand hides little. The official view from the factory is that Hastings's underhanded dealings essentially made the proceedings of 1721 into the mistrial of a loyal Company employee. The only person who gained from this trial was not, as might be expected, the husband, who never got his money, but Hastings, who seems to have pocketed the fine collected to get the man a new wife.

The Company's response arrived a year and two months later, in February 1723: "It appears evident to Us that Mr. Hastings whole Presidentship may be reckon'd as one continued act of Arbitrary Power exemplefy'd in various Instances." The Company, worried that his tenure might have affected trade adversely, advised the factory council to try harder to draw "rich trading people to Madrass." The directors assured the factory council that "cultivating a good Understanding and on all occasions checking the first beginnings of dispute between them [the castes] must make the Place flourish."[48]

In the new arrangements, the conicopoly's fate was decided again. The Company directors in London decided to reverse the previous decision made by the council under Hastings and ask that the fine paid to the Company be refunded to Devaroy. The fine that was to go to the husband, however, was upheld, but it had to be recovered from whoever had intercepted it. There is no mention at all of the woman. She slipped away into oblivion after creating a structure for the giving and taking of money and after her price had been calculated. In 1724, the factory sent the last word on the case to London: "Devaroy shall be repaid the 500 pagodas fine about the Rashwar woman [*sic*], have let the Black inhabitants know how strictly the company forbid oppressions."[49]

The attempt of the Company headquarters to repair the damage done by a corrupt employee (Hastings) thus transformed retroactively the entire text of the legal proceedings recorded in the Diary and Consultation Book into a fiction. If the outcome of the trial was fixed and Devaroy did not have a chance from the start under Hastings, then the proceedings as recorded in the diary are all subsequent readings haunted by actions that are conducted backstage by Hastings and never appear in the transcript. The very act of archiving is now a scene of fabrication, where the semblance of due process—the inclusion of dissent, testimonies, and petitions—disguises the maneuvers that take place outside the margins of the text.

Reading as Arbitration

The factory's policy of summarizing written petitions and privileging them over oral ones is apparent in its records. So how do we counter this textual stifling of the Bashwar woman's testimony? Can we read a trace of her agency in the interstices of the opposing testimonies? It is, after all, *her* spatial, social, and caste transgressions—refusing to go to her brother's house, refusing to forgo the company of a low-caste washerwoman, and entering factory space—that form the subtext of this crisis. There is enough evidence in the brother's petition to indicate that she had left her home of her own accord before running into Devaroy. Her presence in the records attests to the considerable danger this incident posed to the trading interests of the Company and to its relations with the locals around the fort.[50] Though she could conceivably have caused a caste riot given the number of people involved in petitioning for her, the Bashwar woman also functioned as a sign that was exchanged to create a new level of relations between the English and the locals, a function that precludes our reading of her merely as the legal subject of possessive individualism. Because she had entered the Company's legal space, her status was now carefully parceled out into two alternatives: she could be an object of protection (according to Devaroy's claim that he was protecting her from her relatives) or an object of coercion (according to her relatives' claim about her forcible detention). Here a woman had become the catalyst of a political crisis without bearing the deliberate will of the usual social agent—that is, without intention. Yet her fate is unknown. The records do not follow her after the employee crisis is solved. Was she only discarded by her family? Or did they follow up the threat of violence and punish her for running away? It is clear that she was never the recipient of justice but was only a handy instrument for the enrichment of her menfolk and the factory officials.

In such instances of a female subject's violent erasure, the role of the critic as arbiter becomes crucial. Much has been made of the task of the critic in locating historical examples of resistance in Third World studies, whether it is in Gayatri Chakravorty Spivak's reading for the subaltern as textual silence in the official account of the rani of Sirmur, or in Homi Bhabha's formulations of the mimic man.[51] To the question about the strategy by which the critic makes her analysis an intervention—making visible agency that is not easily available even to the sympathetic reader—Spivak proposes the reading for subaltern subject-effect. Here, the account of stifled voices is replaced by a meticulous reading for the predication of another will to which the powers that be are reacting.[52] For instance, we cannot judge the truth of the matter in these summarized transcripts, which leave out the testimony of the victim. But we can (and must) read here the terms under which a native woman who was not yet the juridical subject of rights under British law had her fate decided by the representatives of a pseudolegal institution—an English fortified factory. We can read here how she effected the crisis: it was produced by her transgression of social boundaries determined by status and consanguinity. Thus, not only is an agent displayed but a certain totality of social relations is revealed. We see how gender codings are written into the relations between the alien merchants and the comprador classes, the native upper-caste men who benefited from trade with the English. The confrontation thus becomes symbolic of large-scale transformations that are yet to take place. Just as Roxana's story is an allegory of Dutch-English commercial relations, the case of the Bashwar woman is an allegory of the gradual transformation of mercantilism into colonialism. It is prefigured through the appearance of law as the authority of the alien power and through a grotesque staging of the "rights" of the subaltern female subject.

This excursus into the proceedings of the Bashwar woman's rape trial is not an attempt to make causal links between the novel *Roxana* and the archived material of the Company. I do not think Defoe, the factory councillors, and the court of directors learned lessons from each other. Yet there is little doubt when looking at the parallels between the case of Roxana and that of the Bashwar woman that each articulates in an uncanny way the shared epistemology of Defoe's commercial fictions and the Company's textualized links to its far-flung factories. Staging commercial relations as sexual relations is one way of assigning subject positions without conflict through the consensual, or shared, framework of patriarchy, rather than through the uncharted and uncertain arena of new commercial relations. But there are other parallels: both texts emerged out of a vast eighteenth-century network of writing that provided not only commodities and services but also the very means by which economic activity was carried out (with bills of exchange, correspondence, accounts, dispatches, and so on). The novel and the factory records lend themselves to similar interpretive modes of reading. Indeed, even though one text is a fictional account and the other a historical record, both make sense of the world in similar ways and through similar narrative prestructures.

In the factory Diary and Consultation Book of 1721, we have writing that is intended not only as a self-recording and a legal archive, but also as a message to London so that the head office can keep track of activities at its outposts. Like *Roxana,* in which Defoe as author, Roxana as self-indicted adventuress, and the readers who rewrite the novel to reflect public opinion all cast judgment, the factory correspondence also reveals multiple levels of judgment at each site of reading and writing. The caste council defers judgment to the factory council only to see that council's decision overturned by the Company directors in London, who have the final say through remote control, after they complete their own reading of the various discrepant accounts coming in from the factory.

This deferral of judgment shows the very textuality—indeed, the discursivity—of the historical formation we call mercantilism. Each act of reading is implicitly transformed into an attempt to regain control over this unfamiliar and displaced context. The court of directors, separated from its outpost, reversed the factory council's decisions to let its members know that London, rather than Hastings, was ultimately in charge. There is little chance that the short, badly written trial transcripts the directors received helped their deliberations. It is more plausible that they saw the trial, held on factory premises, as a dangerous overstepping of boundaries. Their decision to reverse the earlier judgment thus cut the factory "judges" down to size and let them know that they were being read carefully in London.

On the other hand, the narrative space of the literary text is not unlike the scenes of trials or fortified factories. When *Roxana* is subjected to various rewritings, the novel enacts through its readers not a space of prohibitive law but a freedom of expression that is crucial for instituting new forms of subjectivity because it mystifies the operation of law at other levels. In the factory books of the East India Company, a similar freedom of expression enjoyed by the Englishmen as traders makes the factory records a perfect place to read the discrepancy between intention and effect. We get to see how colonial power imagined itself into being and when and where a deliberate will can be sensed behind historical events. In the papers relating to the Bashwar woman, we see the gradual development of a desire for more control over native resources and trade networks. But the force that will consolidate these still fictional events into history will not happen for another two decades, when the East India Company adopts a policy of open warfare with local rulers.

If I were to insist that the factory record and the novel are irreducible in their respective places within the true and the fabricated, such a position would resemble the colonizer's project of codifying law; both attempt to arrest textuality. To fictionalize the law, to provide its genealogy, is therefore to challenge its duration: "It seems that the law as such should never give rise to any story. To be invested with its categorical authority, the law must be without history, genesis, or any possible derivation."[53] Not only does a story about the law establish the legal process as an act of reading and interpretation, but it also suggests the importance of the power of the script. The fields of law and history, like the field of the literary, are fraught with countersignatures. Just as the critic appears before a text and contaminates its pastness with her reading, the subject before the law, in applying it to herself, creates something new. The text of legal commentary is in that sense like the text of literary criticism—both display the sociality and production that go on at the scene of the text.[54]

Such an undoing of the distinctions between the literary, the historical, and the legal can help us address other questions about rereading the past, or for that matter questions about rewriting the social text. For instance, there can be no legitimate claim by anticolonialist Indians that women's rights are always available from ancient legal texts (like the Shastras used by the caste council), for that discussion is itself a response to colonial rule. It is in this sense that rights and individualism have been secured by the history of imperialism, and not in the simplistic sense as a legacy or gift of Western social missionaries, whether Orientalists, administrators, or legal historians. This reading of the case of the Bashwar woman and a novel of female individualism makes it clear that at the level of the social text, spatial demarcations like the public and private do not exist prior to the law but are set in place by legal discourse. The politics of domestication that circumscribed Roxana in the private sphere went hand in hand with the large-scale capital accumulation required by mercantilism, which was speeding on its way to colonialism and imperialism. On the other hand, the scrupulous protection of personal law by the British in India was a strategic deployment of similar categories to service colonialist rule. With the separation of personal (or women's) rights from the law of colonial governance (the common criminal and civil procedure for instance), the illusion of cultural noninterference could be maintained. As the ruling in the case of the Bashwar woman indicates, women and the traditions associated with them are promoted as the separate property of the indigenous patriarchy at one historical moment, while at another moment they become objects for Western transformation and liberation (see chapter 5).

The final irony is that it is in the arbitrary divisions created by legal discourse that the agency of the female subaltern realizes its most far-reaching implications. In contrast to Roxana, whose possessive individualism is short-circuited by a definition of the female simultaneously as individualist and as the subject of affective relations (bourgeois love and motherhood), the Bashwar woman presents a different sort of agency. Denied representation through speech or a proper name, she reveals how agency is often an activation of relations that seem to exclude the woman structurally. In this sense the Bashwar woman provoked her community to action without intending to. This crisis with all its ramifications would not have been possible if her subject status were purely private—that is, outside the political. This sort of agency proves, if nothing else, that "woman" was a structural rather than a peripheral issue in the communities forming around British trade in south India.

By paying attention to such slippages and disjunctures when acceding to unavoidable structures also creates something new, one sees how the position of the subaltern performs a politics of interruption. As historical subject she not only interrupts intellectual projects that construct her as totally Other, for she shares the history of colonialism with the woman in the West, but she also destabilizes attempts to diminish her agency: her presence rewrites the law. By exploring this historical link that has simultaneously produced the European woman and the colonized woman, and by acknowledging the differential privilege that history has finally accorded them, feminists in the West may learn from the subaltern in postcolonial space.

CHAPTER TWO

ARCHIVAL FICTIONS: MEMORIES OF VIOLENCE IN THE AGE OF SENSIBILITY

By the 1750s large-scale colonial violence, which was only preemergent in *Roxana* and the factory records of the 1720s, had effected a temporal break in the processes of mercantilism and brought about a change in the sign systems of commerce. One significant such change was from the sign of *merchant* to that of *soldier*. Figures like the Dutchman, who in *Roxana* represented the virtuous, benevolent, and civilizing aspects of commerce, could no longer appear in literature without being followed by the shadowy presence of violence. After the East India Company's wars against French interests in south India (1744–1760) and the war in Bengal against the nawab Sirāj-ud-Dawlah (1756–1757), there was little doubt that English trade in India went hand in hand with military force. However, it was also the case that in the mid-eighteenth century a general perception prevailed that the preeminent function of commerce was "to refine the passions and polish the manners."[1] At this time, a notion of civic humanism held in place by discourses of sentiment and sensibility (which named both a feeling and a guide to moral conduct) espoused the legitimacy of a middle-class rather than an aristocratic vision of society.[2] But as the poster child of commercial success, the East India Company, embarked on controversial military campaigns, the unleashing of colonial violence injected a visible contradiction into the notion of commerce as the middle-class's civilizing process.

In novels written in the 1770s and 1780s, middle-class writers coming to terms with this discursive shift displayed a visible unease with their class's mercantile alliance as its historical function was exposed in the colonial periphery. On the one hand, there was outright condemnation, such as Matthew Bramble's invective in Tobias Smollett's *Humphry Clinker* (1771) against the clerks and factors from the East Indies who appeared at Bath "loaded with the soil of plundered provinces."[3] On the other hand, there was crisis management as colonialism was recoded as a theater of virtue.

Consider, for instance, Helenus Scott's *Adventures of an East-India Rupee* (1782), where an Englishman, Melvil, leaving England to join the East India Company's army, receives these instructions from his father: "Your particular province is to protect the trade of our country, against the insults of European powers, or of the Indian nations, who ignorant of the blessings that commerce diffuses, even to themselves, are often disposed to interrupt its equitable course. The prosperity therefore of trade, is what you are to have in view, not the extension of settlement and much less your private advantage."[4] The soldier going out to India to advance the protection of trade, rather than "extension of settlement" or "private advantage," is a literary figuration of this crisis of legitimation. Scott's novel also reworks the historical narrativizing of conquest. Decisive battles, which had already given the East India Company a trade monopoly in south India and sovereign power over Bengal by this time, are represented as necessary acts for the protection of commerce's "blessings" from rival European powers as well as from Indian rulers who might "interrupt its equitable course."

In this chapter, I will look at similar narratives that equate colonialism with virtue by using a new kind of colonial subject—one who advances an argument for conquest by dissimulating it as the protection of just and equitable principles. Through a close reading of an autobiographical captivity narrative and two novels, I will explore how certain notions of subjectivity perfected in the English novel of the 1760s and 1770s, the man and woman of sentiment especially, were actively reworked for colonial settings. These narratives also introduced into the historical discussion of colonial violence a gendered rhetoric of suffering, victimization, and sensibility that appropriated, in a gynetic move, the figure of woman for the merchant-soldier.

It is well established that sentimental narratives of the eighteenth century assumed and asserted the values of a middle-class culture that was intent, as Robert Markley puts it, "on demonstrating the naturalness and benevolence of its moral authority." Furthermore, this "affective spectacle" was a gendered appropriation. The same "complex of strategies" that was designed to relegate women to subservient roles as perpetual victims, passive sufferers, and docile and emotional beings was mobilized to valorize men and their "masculine sensitivity" as a virtue, "as an indication of a 'natural' sympathy possessed by men of feeling."[5] In the various colonial graftings of sentimentality, we see the arrival of the merchant-soldier as a victim and sufferer whose profound sensibility allows him to recast historical events as individual traumas. Like novels that allowed their readers a vicarious participation in the individualized theatrics of characters with hypersensitized bodies and minds (such as Henry Mackenzie's Harley, Samuel Richardson's Clarissa, or Laurence Sterne's Yorick), these narratives had colonial subjects who also drew in their readers and allowed them to participate in the timeline of the nascent empire by recasting large-scale historical events into various emotions at the level of individual perception; battles and skirmishes in far-flung places could now be experienced or registered as bodily effects on singular individuals.

This newfound proximity between the historical and literary narration of the emerging Indian empire is especially clear when we follow the textual relays from historical document to novel and vice versa. My discussion in this chapter will track the textual relay of historical memory and trauma primarily through the trope of the Black Hole. This textual itinerary will allow us to see not only how dominant colonial myths and stories got instituted in the eighteenth century, but also how they were utilized by and for subjects who did not have a place in the original story—women for instance. Because sentimentality and its subject positions were gendered appropriations by male writers and characters, a consideration of work by a writer like Phebe Gibbes, who also fictionalized British India, can reveal how female writers, after watching from the sidelines, ultimately reappropriated sentimental discourse as their proper object.

My discussion of eighteenth-century negotiations of colonial virtue will unfold in four sections. In the first section, I will look at John Zephaniah Holwell's *A Genuine Narrative of the Deplorable Deaths of the English Gentlemen* (1758), which is now regarded as one of the most authoritative primary documents on Sirāj-ud-Dawlah's attack on the English factory at Fort William in 1756. In this text we see the use of a new language for archiving the East India Company's activities in India. Holwell's text is not simply a positivist document in which the event seems to tell itself without the interruption of a subjective voice or figurative language; rather, it is a text that represents historical trauma through the individualized discourse of sensibility.

In the second section I read Robert Bage's *Mount Henneth* (1782), a novel about mercantile virtue that, though set in rural Wales, is interrupted by a digression that takes it into the midst of the Company's 1756–1757 war in Bengal. The war becomes a moral allegory of class conflict in Britain, but the colonial setting also serves as a training ground for the merchant of sentiment, whose suffering and virtuous behavior in the face of great temptation make him, like Richardson's Pamela, a prime candidate for deferred rewards. As the merchant returns home to the Welsh countryside with uncontaminated wealth ("gifts") from India, the novel advocates a kinder and gentler mercantilism in which colonialism is questioned but held in place at the same time.

In the third and fourth sections, I turn to Phebe Gibbes's *Hartly House, Calcutta* (1789). Ostensibly written by its protagonist, Sophia Goldsborne, *Hartly House* is one of the earliest novels set in India. In it, I read how in the hands of an Englishwoman sojourning in Calcutta the discourse of sentiments and sensibility becomes a critique of colonialism as a masculinist undertaking. When British women writers like Phebe Gibbes entered the arena of Anglo-Indian fiction in the 1780s, male sentimental fiction was on the wane, and sensibility or sentimentality was associated primarily with female writers and characters. Because women presumably embodied sensibility and sentimentality naturally, they could also become the real arbiters of the moral levels among the potentially violent expatriate Englishmen in India. Gibbes's strategic use of this narrative subject position overturns the abject subject positions assigned to women in both Holwell's and Bage's texts.[6]

The Black Hole as Historical Trauma

Holwell's *Genuine Narrative* was published in London in 1758 while he was on a short visit home from India. As one of the key administrators at Fort William in Calcutta (he was a tax collector, a district magistrate, and a member of the governor's council), Holwell is believed to have remained at his post while Fort William was under siege. Thus his account draws much of its authority from his official rank and his role as an eyewitness to and survivor of what transpired. Later in this discussion, I will address the mystifying power of the purportedly eyewitness accounts of the Black Hole incident and the implications of finding that nearly all of them lead back to and are various iterations of Holwell's text.[7] But first I will provide a shorthand version of the incident as it is generally presented in standard English histories.

The Black Hole was a jail cell, approximately eighteen feet square, built at Fort William, Bengal, to house English subjects arrested for misdemeanors. In June 1756, after weeks of rising tensions between Company officials and the nawab of Bengal, the latter attacked the fort and effected an English surrender after only four days of fighting. At this point, Holwell's account alleges, the nawab personally ordered the confinement of 146 prisoners, mostly English, on the night of 20 June. By morning, 123 had suffocated to death and only 23, including Holwell, had survived. We are told that on the nawab's orders the victims were buried in a mass grave on the fort's premises.

This event became one of the most charged topics of discussion in the eighteenth century. Though the story always had its skeptics, the connotative power of the Black Hole and its hold on the popular imagination were unparalleled till the Great Mutiny of 1857 provided a new national trauma. The passions aroused by the Black Hole event did much to justify the subsequent Company-funded "revolution" in Bengal, which replaced the local potentate with a puppet who furthered the interests of the Company. After the Battle of Plassey (1757), which saw the defeat of Sirāj-ud-Dawlah, the Company became a territorial ruler, not just a trading entity. It was now possible to believe that British rule in India was born not out of naked English aggression but out of justifiable actions taken to punish the Indian perpetrators of the Black Hole.

In the *Genuine Narrative,* Holwell depicts in compelling detail the horrific night spent in the Black Hole. We hear the cries and groans of the wounded and the delirious calls for water; we feel the heat and perspiration, the weight of dead bodies, the slow suffocation; we smell the stench of urine and death as the hours crawl by in slow motion. In view of such clarity of description, Holwell's long caveat in the first few pages about the impossibility of representing the incident of the Black Hole warrants some attention. It is here that we see the first relay of historical event as memory-trace into a personal archive that can be accessed only by the merchant-soldier of sentiment:

> Few survived capable of giving any detail of the manner in which it happened; and of these I believe none have attempted it: for my own part, I have often set down with this resolution, and as often relinquished the melancholy talk, not only from the disturbance and affliction it raised a-fresh in my remembrance, but from the consideration of the impossibility of finding language capable of raising an adequate idea of the horrors of the scene I essayed to draw. But as I believe the annals of the world cannot produce an incident like it in any degree or proportion to all the dismal circumstances attending it, and as my own health of body and peace of mind are once again, in a great measure, recovered from the injuries they suffered from that fatal night, I cannot allow it to be buried in oblivion; though still conscious that however high the colouring my retentive memory may supply, it will fall infinitely short of the horrors accompanying this scene.[8]

These, as Holwell presents them, are the conditions of his textual production. Not mentioned in the passage is the setting for the writing itself: "on board the vessel in which the author returned from the East-Indies, when he had the leisure to reflect, and was at liberty to throw upon paper, what was too strongly impressed upon his memory, ever to wear out" (*Narrative,* iii–iv). Though the long excerpt above gives us a Holwell conscious that he is the first to archive this event, the sentence from the introduction suggests that a prior archiving had already taken place internally—in his mind. Here "impressed upon his memory" brings forth the notion of a substrate on which the event itself has left its deposits as a trace.[9] The writing of the *Genuine Narrative* is thus only a secondary moment, and act in which he tries to "throw upon paper," or re-archive, what is already a "private calamity" stored within himself (*Narrative,* iv). By presenting the Black Hole as an event that can only be inadequately archived for a public as writing, Holwell protects the version that is already in his possession—the original event that exists only for him and has not been accessed by anyone else.

Yet when Holwell represents the truth as "buried" in his mind, he is also led to speculate on possible ways to retrieve it. (He would actually rather leave it there, he says, but for the pressure to "gratify public expectation" [*Narrative,* v].) In the excerpt above, Holwell makes writing into a technology of retrieval when he complains about the "impossibility of finding language capable of raising an adequate idea of the horrors of the scene I essayed to draw." But it is not only language that is inadequate. As though sensing that his use of the metaphor of visual representation ("draw," "colouring") could suggest other, more adequate, forms of representation, Holwell withdraws the Black Hole from the act of representation itself. Now even the primary archive of "retentive memory" cannot visualize for him the "horrors" he wants to show. By enacting another moment of deferral for the Black Hole, making it a signified without signifiers, he suggests that neither Holwell the writer nor Holwell the owner of consciousness and memory can represent the event. Holwell, in other words, cannot represent the event even to himself.

I have already suggested in the introduction that the general condition of the archive and of archiving is one in which the historical event is always deferred—that all textual deposits of the past are always moving us away from unmediated access to the events themselves and that we cannot use the archival text as a stand-in or substitute for the past without accounting for the very problem of representation itself and the various interests that collaborate, clash, or are excluded in that process. But Holwell's attempt to plumb his depths is an attempt not to deconstruct the event but to lay a singular claim to it as personal experience and memory and yet protect himself from any future textualizations that may unsettle the primary status of his own text. How does he do that? Consider this bit from the introduction, where he appeals to the nature of trauma as a primary determinant of his text: "If therefore it appears in some places, a little passionate; in others, somewhat diffuse; and through the whole tinctured with the disposition under which it was written; the occasion, and the nature of the performance, will sufficiently excuse what might have been considered as imperfections, if it had been intended for the public view" (*Narrative*, iv). Here Holwell uses a popular eighteenth-century novelistic device, the accidental arrival into publication, to assert the truth of the *Genuine Narrative*. It is important to note that Holwell leaves "imperfections" and "diffuse" unspecified. Does he mean stylistic or factual imperfections and diffuseness? Is this primary document of a foundational event in the conquest of India replacing fact with diffuseness and rationality with passion?

While eighteenth-century writers often used the confused frames of fact and fiction because they could not find a category for a genre that was somewhere in between news and novel, Holwell, it seems to me, was inventing a new species of writing for reporting trauma.[10] He was also inventing for the Company's archive a new species of document that challenges the earlier formats of official writing. Unlike the standard reports on various activities from Company officials, reports that transcribed details of transactions involving Company interests and resources, this account makes the author himself the source of the narrative. Like the authors of the New World captivity narratives popular in the eighteenth century, in which an "abducted body," often female, became a "historically new basis for national identity," Holwell writes from a position usually reserved for women and children.[11] In the importation of this format into the Indian setting, we see the transculturation of a narrative form already familiar to British readers taking on a new role: the sort of originary violence that allowed English identity to congeal in North America is reenacted in Bengal.

It is important also to note that unlike official reports that bore the signatures of Company employees to attest to their facts, the nature of Holwell's account seems to protect him from being accountable for his words. Holwell offers a kind of historical documentation that does not have the objective narrator of historical discourse, one who gives the impression of a discourse that seems to speak for itself. Instead, his *Genuine Narrative* presupposes a subjective and limited narrator who cannot get a handle on what he has to represent. Holwell's appeal for imperfections as part of the natural weave in the fabric of the text is thus part and parcel of an argument about the role of historical trauma and the kind of externalization needed to record it. He installs the event of the Black Hole as a trauma experienced bodily and psychically, but at the same time he puts in place an opposition between the originality of the event, memory, consciousness as self-presence, and the supplementary nature of writing. This separation is enacted by positioning the sensible body as the primary receiving surface for impressions, the surface of writing for historical violence, thus making the preserved event almost impossible to subsequently reach and retrieve for representation:

> With some difficulty, I raised myself, and gained the platform a second time, where I presently lost all sensation: the last trace of sensibility that I have been able to recollect after my laying down, was my sash being uneasy about my waste [*sic*] which I untied and threw from me. . . . Of what passed in this interval to the time of my resurrection from this hole of horrors, I can give you no account; and indeed, the particulars mentioned by some of the gentlemen who survived . . . were so excessively absurd and contradictory, as to convince me, very few of them retained their senses. (*Narrative*, 30–31)

Thus Holwell enacts this separation of word and event by distinguishing his narrative from a standard autobiography, a genre that Lennard Davis has described as the eighteenth century's unofficial archive of individual lives—the preservation of individuals through their embodiment in writing.[12] When Holwell's hysterical, frantic, and then senseless body stops recording, the historical event ceases. The "texts" of other survivors, whose bodies continued to record, can no longer be accessed except as delirium. In this way, Holwell uses the collapse of the sensible body to explain the contradictions among the various accounts that had already surfaced in the two years since the war. Soon Holwell draws a distinction also between the writing of the pen and the writing of the body, with the body as an instrument of writing rather than as a surface to receive it, when he recounts how he came back to his senses: "But oh! Sir, what words shall I adopt to tell you the whole that my soul suffered at reviewing the dreadful destruction round me? I will not attempt it; and indeed tears, (a tribute I believe I shall ever pay to the remembrance of this scene, and to the memory of those brave and valuable men) stop my pen" (*Narrative*, 33).

This is an important moment for the question of archiving, for Holwell is asserting that where the pen fails to produce a document and preserve memory, the body produces another text more representative of the scene, as well as a more adequate memorial to those who have died. Real preservation of the event happens inside the body, but this "archive" disseminates its texts through signs of distress—tears—on the surface.[13] As indicated before, this separation of word from event will serve him well in the future as his account comes under attack for its contradictions.

In Holwell's act of endless deferral, horror becomes the site of origin or self-presence; it is both the original scene and the unrepresentable. The image, or impression, in the psyche becomes a supplement or substitute, a flawed and partial version of the real thing. The deconstructive deferral of the event is manipulated to provide Holwell with a prophylactic for his account. He uses the impossibility of true representation to protect himself from charges of inconsistency and fabrication. Thus, though Holwell's account may be accused of being partial, fragmented, and inconsistent in parts, it is, Holwell seems to suggest, the closest anyone can get to an accurate recounting of the events. What other historians may perceive today as a profound lack of archival evidence about the Black Hole is thus explained away as the result of an extraordinary trauma. None of the other survivors, we must conclude, could perform the externalization of the event as well as Holwell could.

There are no contemporary Indian accounts of the incident. One well-known native historian's version of the events in Bengal does not even mention the Black Hole.[14] Various French communiqués from the same time do not mention the Black Hole, though they sometimes refer to varying numbers of prisoners who were shut up in the fort and perished there. Two Dutch accounts also talk of prisoners being shut up and perishing at the hands of the nawab, but do so only in official letters written in November 1756, almost five months after the alleged incident. It is now generally believed that while many accounts of the Black Hole appeared in subsequent years, all of them ultimately lead back to Holwell.[15] The primacy of Holwell's account is so well established that he can be held single-handedly responsible for publicizing the Black Hole.[16]

Yet it is clear that by 1764, when Holwell published his voluminous *India Tracts*—a collection of several works, including a new edition of the *Genuine Narrative*—his version of the events was already under attack. Alongside the new edition of the *Genuine Narrative*, Holwell included various supporting papers, especially letters, that were meant to corroborate his account of his actions at the time of the siege. One of the letters is particularly interesting because it demonstrates the impossibility of controlling the paper trail of the Black Hole. On 30 November 1756, five months after the incident, Holwell was under considerable pressure because the Company headquarters was being inundated with various explanations of the heavy losses incurred by the Company during its military failure in Bengal. Holwell fired off a letter to the court of directors in which he begins by apologizing—for not having sent along a

> particular narrative of the causes, and various accidents, which brought on the heavy loss you have sustained: this I promised to forward as soon as my health would enable me. The slow recovery of my sight, much impaired by the shock and injury my nerves suffered that fatal night in the Black Hole, and from being exposed to the sun on my passage to Muxadabad, must plead my pardon for your not receiving the narrative I promised. . . . You will receive many different narratives and accounts of the causes of our misfortunes; leaving those to your impartial consideration—I sit down to discharge this part of my duty, humbly intreating you will believe me determined to pay the strictest regard to truth to the best of my knowledge.[17]

It is clear from this letter that although Holwell's *Genuine Narrative* was the first detailed account of the Black Hole incident, it was a long time coming, and this delay grated against the East India Company's policy about immediate and constant reports from its employees in the East. Holwell was thus caught in the double bind of having to get his "true" version in before those of the other survivors even as he had to ask for time to recover in order to be able to recount the event. What is also clear is that instead of corroborating his account by multiplying the evidence, the proliferation of writing about the events in Bengal was actually undermining it. I have mentioned the case of spurious and belated eyewitness accounts that have led several historians to question whether the Black Hole incident actually took place. The role of iteration thus undermines the mystified power of eyewitness accounts as they begin to differ from each other, altering one another in turn by their various appearances.

Archivists and historians have puzzled over that night's events and tried to piece together many aspects: Who was there? How many died? And who was ultimately responsible for the deaths? Indian as well as British historians who have charged Holwell with fabrication have done so under the belief that he probably was attempting to avoid responsibility for the loss of the Company's property and to support a demand that the defeated rulers of Bengal pay reparations to the sufferers. But clearly the more significant role of the account goes beyond local and metropolitan discussions of loss and reparations. The Black Hole captured the public imagination in a way that helped the Company avoid much public and political scrutiny of the crucial shift that had taken place in its role in India. Through this skirmish with the rulers of Bengal and their later defeat at Plassey, the Company moved from being a commercial enterprise trading with the Indies to a territorial power ruling a portion of India. It was the beginning of the conquest of India.

If we look at the function of the Black Hole in this way, the debate can shift from questions about individual blame and loss to the many historical effects. Indeed, as Iris Macfarlane puts it in her extremely skeptical analysis: "The importance it assumed in history books, in the national imagination, was not related in any way to its truth. When it was not necessary to believe it, it was taken or left according to taste."[18] What rises to the foreground then is the critical task of identifying the different versions of the event and the significant substitutions and iterations that signal the uses to which each retelling was put. One such moment of repetition with a difference is visible when Holwell's *Genuine Narrative* of 1758 includes a new inscription, one that had not emerged in any of the previous accounts of the Black Hole, including Holwell's earlier reports to the Company. This is the inscription of a woman—the figure of Mrs. Carey.

None of the official accounts indicates the presence of a woman in the Black Hole. In the *Genuine Narrative,* however, Holwell facilitates this historical subject's arrival in two places. First, she appears parenthetically as the devoted spouse of an English soldier: "Close behind me was an officer of one of the ships, whose name was Carey, and who had behaved with much bravery during the siege, (his wife a fine woman tho' country-born, would not quit him, but accompanied him into the prison and was one who survived)" (*Narrative,* 29). And then there is the ominous single line at the end of the *Genuine Narrative,* where she is announced and foreclosed at the same time: "The rest, who survived the fatal night, gained their liberty, except Mrs. Carey, who was too young and handsome" (*Narrative,* 36). The hint of rape changes the tenor of the Black Hole incident, transforming it at once from a function of economic, political, and military relations to a case of sexual violence. Though the suffering of the prisoners is described as having made little impression "on a breast the most brutal" (that of the nawab), in the sentence about Mrs. Carey, there is no specific referent. Are we to assume that the soldiers carried Mrs. Carey away?

Textual evidence suggests that this slightest of references in Holwell's text was sufficient to invoke the public's nascent phantasmic image of oriental despotism as sexual as well as political vice. Let us catch this figure as it surfaces almost a hundred years later in H. E. Busteed's *Echoes from Old Calcutta* (1888). Here, this well-known chronicler of British India discusses a paragraph found scribbled into the flyleaf of a copy of Holwell's *Tracts.*

The book's owner, Thomas Boileau, was, we are told, an attorney practicing in Calcutta, and he had been so moved by Holwell's account that in 1799 he went in search of the "last survivor" of the Black Hole. Here is Busteed's reproduction of Boileau's account as the latter penned it in coda form onto the leaves of his own personal copy of Holwell's *Genuine Narrative.*

> This lady now 58 years of age as she herself told me, is of a size rather above the common stature and very well proportioned; of a fair mesticia colour, with correct regular features which give evident marks of beauty which must once have attracted admiration. She confirmed all that Mr. Holwell had said on the subject of the Black Hole in the foregoing letters [the *Tracts*] and added that besides her husband, her mother Mrs Eleanor Weston . . . and her sister aged about ten years had also perished there-in and that other women, the wives of soldiers and children had shared a like fate there. Signed, Thomas Boileau.[19]

Boileau's visit to Mrs. Carey suggests that the list of the proper names of survivors and the dead that appears at the end of Holwell's *Genuine Narrative* had a special place in readers' minds. Yet Mrs. Carey's conversation with Boileau does not merely add her signature to Holwell's testimony; it actually undermines it somewhat. Because there was no mention of any other women or children in Holwell's earlier accounts or the other official accounts, we are led to ask whether Mrs. Carey was a strategic inclusion intended to produce a resonating allegory of oriental despotism. The iterative principle is at work again as Mrs. Carey multiplies her own suffering in the Black Hole by adding women and children who were not on any of the official lists. In this scene of testimonial excess, where corroboration gives way to fabrication, we see a sufferer who, grateful for all the attention long after the events and their tellers are gone, gives more than she is asked for. There is a whole story to unearth here, but I cannot follow the strands to their archival conclusions. At this point I will simply straighten out some of the loose ends.

Most English accounts concur that before the siege of the fort was under way, all the English women and children had been sent off to safety on a ship downriver. Now we find that a half-caste woman, Mrs. Carey, was left behind. Although her lineage did not get her a place on the ship, it was sufficient, it seems, to earn her the sole place in an allegorical tale of native violence against Englishwomen. (She gets as close as the native sufferers do to a signature, for the native soldiers who perished alongside the English in the Black Hole are only counted, never named, and they are even erased from Holwell's title, which announces primarily the death of Englishmen.) Boileau confirms that, her color aside, her great beauty warranted the attention. But the real indication of Mrs. Carey's symbolic resonance in the public imagination comes via this observation by Busteed. After running into some direct lineal descendants of Mrs. Carey in India, Busteed concludes his anecdote about Boileau with this observation: "I may however authoritatively say this much, Mrs. Carey was not carried off by the Moors at all." Not only rape, but also forced abductions for the nawab's harem were, it seems, part of the ghost chapters written by an avid public continuing Holwell's *Genuine Narrative* into the next century of the British Empire.[20]

Historian Dominick LaCapra has argued in another context that a violent and destructive historical event can be converted into an "occasion for sublimity" to "transvalue [trauma] into a test of the self or the group and an entry into the extraordinary." Some violent events may even become occasions for "negative sublimity or displaced sacralization." By this LaCapra means that often survivors and others do not want so much to forget the past as to compulsively repeat the scene of prior violence. Such an obsession, LaCapra argues, can give rise to "founding traumas"—traumas that become the "valorized or intensely cathected basis of identity for an individual or a group rather than events that pose the problematic question of identity."[21] In the next section, I will look at how the Black Hole becomes a founding trauma in a narrative by a male writer claiming authority and leadership for the middle classes in Britain's economic transformation. Holwell's account of the Black Hole has shown us that although the discourse of sensibility operates in the official document to undermine the truth content of the historical event, it also adds to the event's ideological power in colonial discourse. After Holwell's initial recording of this event, various novels and historical narratives of the late eighteenth century take it up and disseminate it to a larger reading public, so much so that after a while the Black Hole takes on the task of being the violent origin of the merchant's shift to soldier.

Virtue Rewarded

Toward the end of the eighteenth century, a host of novelists like Robert Bage, Agnes Maria Bennett, and Henry Brooke explored the compatibility between commerce, on the one hand, and sensibility and femininity, on the other. The merchant became a major player in a new fictional trend.[22] In Bage's *Mount Henneth* (1782) and Brooke's *Fool of Quality* (1766–1770), for instance, middle-class protagonists drawn from mercantile professions are pitted against characters of aristocratic excess and vice to expose the latter's moral bankruptcy and economic ineffectiveness. They do this by drawing on benevolence as a just mode of social action and a sort of judgment based on "naïve" responses of "personal feeling."[23]

What is also remarkable is that these novels, especially those by Bage and Bennett, make a concerted effort to discuss the origin of the wealth that came to Britain from the colonies. For instance, in *Mount Henneth,* Mr. Foston receives his fortune as a "gift" from a rich Indian for saving his and his daughter's lives. In Bennett's *Anna; or, Memoirs of a Welch Heiress* (1785), Mr. Mordant's fortune from the West Indies is carefully set apart as superior to and morally cleaner than that of Colonel Gorget, a Company soldier from India. It is as though in the political climate of the 1780s, the merchant must prove that his wealth was accumulated without violence. (Obviously, in the previous example slavery is being read as a nonviolent mode of production.) In the case of *Mount Henneth,* what we see is not colonial wealth acquired without violence but a case of narrative laundering. Wealth acquired abroad is cleaned through a set of narrative transactions at its origin so that the merchant can come home uncontaminated by violence and still be in possession of the virtues of sentimentality and sensibility.

In Bage's novel, Mr. Foston, a wealthy merchant from India, has just purchased Mount Henneth, an estate in rural Wales, from Sir Howell Henneth, an aristocrat who has over the years reduced it to a mismanaged, unproductive, and debt-ridden property. Foston takes over the estate and uses his huge stock of capital, commercial expertise, and civic virtue to transform it into a thriving self-sufficient community. This story of justifiable mercantile takeover is called into question when Tom Sutton, the hardworking young steward of the estate, receives a letter from a friend insinuating that his employer, Mr. Foston, may have a hidden story behind his fortune. There may be, Sutton is told, "some monopoly of betel nut, or some purchase of a whole district of rice; some rajah deposed and his treasures and territories plundered; or some tale of mercantile or military oppression for which our countrymen are at present famous."[24] Sutton defends his employer by narrating in a series of letters Foston's self-reported story of his service in India. Here is the preamble to the story:

> Mr Foston . . . went out a writer in the service of the East India Company, but was a lieutenant under Colonel Clive, when the chapter of accidents, and the exercise of all the virtues of humanity, gave him possession of a fortune, that exceeded his wishes, almost as much as it exceeded his hopes. . . . The *virtues* of humanity, Henry! what word would your proud metropolitan nabobs substitute for

> this, were they to account for *their* acquisitions with a strict regard to truth? Fear not that any action of this man should make thee blush, except at thy own—inanity. (*Mount Henneth,* 120, emphasis in original)

When virtue appears as the framework within which colonial violence is unpacked, the novel is busily folding one discourse into another. A gendered discourse of virtue that dispensed judgment on eighteenth-century heroines who were either coerced subjects of marriage (Clarissa) or wanton subjects of sexual exchanges (Roxana) or celebrated subjects of social mobility (Pamela), is generalized as "virtues of humanity." When the possession of a fortune in India is read as a tale of virtue rewarded, it transforms Foston's colonial adventure into a story with a different plot, one that makes its protagonist closer to a Pamela than a Crusoe. The novel operates a series of substitutions and displacements in order to transform Foston from the figure of the plundering nabob to a feminized figure who resists the temptation of the colonial vices of greed and rapacity, stands up to threats against his body and property, and is finally rewarded with the very social mobility he had refused to trade for virtue. In India, native violence becomes the occasion for Foston's transformation from merchant to soldier, and the Black Hole is already a trope for English suffering that summons horror instantaneously without the need for historical specifics: "When I was preparing to return to Bengal, news arrived of the war begun by Surajah Dowlaw [*sic*], of his having taken Calcutta, and of the well-known horrible catastrophe of the black hole there. All this was confirmed by a letter from Lewis, who informed me farther, that our friend Sorrell was amongst the number of the unfortunate wretches who perished there, and that himself escaped by lingering a few days with his Arady longer than his business at her village required" (*Mount Henneth,* 157).

In Bage's novel, the fictional characters Sorrell and Lewis are added to the burgeoning list of victims and survivors of the Black Hole. Like Holwell, whose account speaks of the fevers brought on by the trauma, Foston is kept inactive for several months by a debilitating fever brought on by news of the war and the ensuing destruction of his property in Bengal. When he recovers and leaves to join his friend Lewis in Calcutta, he is transformed from merchant to soldier.

On his way to Calcutta, Foston is subjected to a series of assaults, including one in which he is substituted for a victim of feigned rape: "We heard a cry of lamentation; it proceeded from the right of the road; my black servant advised me to ride on without regarding it; but a piercing shriek, which seemed to be from a woman, carried me towards the sound, in spite of fear or prudence." Despite being held back by his native servant, Foston goes to assist this woman and her companions, who have been "stripped half naked and tied to separate trees" (*Mount Henneth*, 158). The woman, we soon learn, is only feigning assault and rape; in fact, she is with a band of thieves who use her as bait to rob travelers. Now Foston and his friend lose their horses and money. Foston's emasculation is completed when he is tied to the very tree that was occupied by the native woman. In effect, they trade places—the woman was the fake victim and the man is the real victim.

When Foston arrives in Calcutta, his mental transformation from merchant to soldier is complete. It is effected, paradoxically, by the discourse of sentiments operating hand in hand with a discourse of military force:

> I had been accustomed to . . . cast a transient glance at misery; . . . but now I had seen a thousand wants, and my own feelings had communicated the soft sensation of sympathy to my bosom. May I never lose it! My vanity too had suffered in the conflict; . . . and this disposed me to accept the lieutenancy under Colonel Clive; for, in the present state of things, soldiers were more wanted than clerks. The grand object was the humiliation of the Nabob of Bengal, upon whom all vowed revenge for the black catastrophe of Calcutta. Chandernagore was taken and many gallant things performed before we arrived at the finishing of the contest. (*Mount Henneth*, 158)

However, for Foston the subject position of a virtuous soldier is only a rest stop on the journey. One more scene of rape transforms the soldier back into a merchant. The novelist seems bent on presenting violence as the means of protecting virtue and not as the means of getting wealth. After the British retake Fort William, Foston is sent on a mission to find the defeated nawab Sirāj-ud-Dawlah. While on this tour he spies deserting soldiers from the nawab's army pillaging a house. Inside the house, Foston finds an old man tied up in bed; in another room two native soldiers are assaulting the man's daughter, Caralia, and her maid. Enraged, Foston kills the soldiers and rescues the two women. The old man, Duverda, a local merchant who has made his money trading with the British, takes Foston to a safe room filled with money and bills and offers him everything (*Mount Henneth*, 160).

The prevailing public discourse about the ongoing rape of India and the accusations of plunder leveled by the British press against Robert Clive and (later) Hastings and their armies is reversed by Foston's solitary act of rescuing a native merchant and his daughter from this scene of assault and rape by native men. The Englishman is now offered a fortune as the reward for his attempts to protect native property and virtue. When Foston refuses to put a price on his "human virtue," the old man offers his daughter in marriage, saying, "Never will my Cara find [her] mate amongst the sons of slavery or rapine" (*Mount Henneth*, 162).

When Foston and Cara are married, we see a simultaneous transfer of capital from the native merchant to the British merchant: "We were united according to the English rites; and, with his daughter Duverda gave me possession of all his effects in all the formalities of the Hindostan law. Circular letters were sent to notify this to all foreign correspondents; no difficulties arose from any of these" (*Mount Henneth*, 166). Cara's function seems to be merely to convey £160,000 to Foston. Two paragraphs later in the novel she is dead, and the fortune reappears as the capital invested in Mount Henneth.

How do we account for this fracture within the novel of Bage condemning British colonialist policies on the one hand, while granting moral power to characters who get and spend wealth accumulated in the colonies on the other? The no-no-yes moral reversal that finally allows Pamela to accept a reformed rake also operates here. Colonial wealth is the gift given to the reformed adventurer as a reward for his virtuous conduct. This novelistic resolution is one attempt to write out the violence of capital accumulation in the late eighteenth century. Mary Pratt has described this phenomenon succinctly:

> Euroimperialism faced a legitimation crisis. The histories of broken treaties, genocides, mass displacements and enslavements became less and less acceptable as rationalist and humanitarian ideologies took hold. . . . Yet the demands of capital remained. Competition among Euroimperial nations would only intensify as capital expanded. And as always, it was their own competition with each other that bound European powers together in finding new forms for Euroimperial interventions, and new legitimating ideologies: the civilizing missions, scientific racism, and technology-based paradigms of progress and development.[25]

In Bage's novel, which was written before the language of the civilizing mission was fully operational, the discourse of sentiments is the ideological lever for displacing the aristocracy's power with middle-class values. But the demands of capital existed then as well: colonial wealth was an inescapable part of the political change in Britain, where the growing power of the middle classes undermined the hold of the aristocracy. The feminizing power of sentimental discourse allowed the woman to be placed as a figure within the paternal fiction of capital accumulation so the transfer of resources could be staged as a gift. In *Mount Henneth,* the woman's anchoring role further dissimulates the violence of large-scale British primitive accumulation by displacing it onto the violence of singular native male bodies against singular female ones—onto rape.[26]

It is significant that when Karl Marx describes so-called primitive accumulation by the British colonial state, one of the historical examples he uses to illustrate the use of force and violence is that of Warren Hastings's maneuvers in Bengal. We cannot miss Marx's sarcasm when he refers to trade as the "inexhaustible mines of wealth" through which "the officials themselves fixed the price and plundered the Hindus at will" and the governor-general's favorites "received contracts under conditions whereby they, cleverer than the alchemists, made gold out of nothing." We also have Marx's reading of the tale of adventure as it leaves the venue of fiction and arrives in the public eye of the court during the Warren Hastings trial: "Great fortunes sprang up like mushrooms in a day; primitive accumulation proceeded without the advance of even a shilling. The trial of Warren Hastings swarms with such cases."[27]

Shuddering to Name It: The Reiteration of Violence

At the end of the eighteenth century, the trial of Warren Hastings brought sensational stories of colonial violence home to Britain, and the empire found some of its severest critics.[28] In this climate, the man of sentiment could no longer operate as a virtuous subject in the colony; however, into the space vacated by this subject in a rapidly evaporating discourse entered the woman of sentiment.

Rape, as Jenny Sharpe's analysis of Anglo-Indian fiction has shown, is "not a consistent and stable signifier but one that surfaces at significant moments."[29] Sharpe's reading of the allegory of rape as it emerges at the moment of native rebellion suggests that the insinuation of potential or past native (male) violence can be a legitimizing or justifying force for greater mechanisms of repression in the name of protecting the British (female). While her reading privileges the large-scale insurrection of the 1857 mutiny, which provided the first real threat to the permanence of the Indian empire, mine pauses at a point between the mutiny and the earlier moments of violence in 1756–1757 that inaugurated the empire. In 1789, Britain was in the midst of another legitimation crisis as reports of plunder and pillage in India by Company officials reignited the tensions between Parliament and the East India Company and between aristocratic interests and the rapidly growing power base of the expatriate merchants. The trial of Warren Hastings at this time gave all these interests a venue in which to stage their discordant agendas. Various forms of sexualized and gendered representations of colonial violence began to surface in cultural and popular texts as singular events took on allegorical import.

In Sara Suleri's nuanced reading of materials from the highly spectacular parliamentary trial of Governor-General Warren Hastings from 1788 to 1795, she marks the place of the legitimation crisis in the "difficulty of finding the appropriate idioms to describe the colonization of India or Hastings's possible violation of the law."[30] Suleri tells us that in the trial's opening speeches, which were made by the most vocal member of the prosecuting force, Edmund Burke, the figure of woman provided one of the "most powerful weapons" against Hastings. Accounts of women being dragged from the "innermost recesses of their houses," exposed naked to public view, raped, and subjected to physical mutilation soon provided a gendered idiom of colonialist excess where the female body was "ushered in only to be transmuted into a figure for the damage Burke wishe[d] on Hastings's political credibility."[31] This discourse was also visible in other realms of public culture. Consider, for instance, contemporary political caricaturist James Gillray's 1788 print titled *Blood on Thunder Fording the Red Sea* (fig. 1), which shows Chancellor Thurlow, who presided over but was opposed to the impeachment of Hastings, wading through a sea of blood from Indian victims with a comfortably placed—and dry—Warren Hastings on his shoulders.[32] Weighing Thurlow down further are the huge moneybags he holds in each arm, signifying payoffs from Indian interests. Unnoticed in most commentaries on this print but clearly visible in the foreground is a figure floating in the water, bobbing in the path of the wading pair. It is the corpse of a woman with torn nipples—a figure borrowed directly from Burke's speeches, which list such mutilations among the atrocities committed on women by Hastings's hoodlums, who were hired to exact payments from native debtors in Bengal.

When colonial relations are metaphorically represented in this way, as the violation of female bodies, Suleri cautions, it is "less an event than a deflection from a contemplation of male embattlement." For the British public, mourning violence against a female body using "sentimentality's greatest excess" forecloses the reading of the struggle over the boundaries of colonial power as a struggle among themselves, the diverse class interests in Britain, displacing it instead into other arenas.[33] However, such forms of mourning

Figure 1. James Gillray, *Blood on Thunder Fording the Red Sea,* 1788 (shelfmark BM 7278; © The British Museum)

can also clear subject positions for those who are not implicated in colonial violence per se, but are drawn to it by its gendered rhetoric. Consider, for instance, Phebe Gibbes's *Hartly House, Calcutta,* which appeared in print the year after the opening of the Warren Hastings trial. The female writer of the novel uses the historic occasion to rework sentimentality's excess to her advantage—to represent a woman's ability to be the "moral barometer" in this great debate among men.[34]

Hartly House is written as a series of letters from the fictional author and protagonist Sophia Goldsborne to her friend Arabella in England after the former embarks on a voyage to India. In the first letter from Sophia to Arabella, we see that the protagonist's position—that of a single English-woman going to India—is not a ready-made position of authority. Unlike men, to whom various subject positions have always been made available since the seventeenth century—as soldiers, civil servants, adventurers, and so on—the female subject has to embark first on a scrupulous clearing of space. Male and female travelers to India did not enjoy the same status. The East India Company's strict controls over women proceeding to India contributed to this discrepancy. Wives were often allowed to join husbands in India, but single women were always viewed with suspicion because they had nothing to exchange but themselves.

Thus it is not surprising that from the 1760s onward literature makes the woman traveling to the colonies either an object of pity or an object of suspicion and ridicule. In Sarah Scott's *The History of Sir George Ellison* (1766), Ms. Almon is offered a position in the colonies to escape a forced marriage in Britain. She accepts it on the condition that it is made clear to everyone that she is not doing it for "personal advantages" or with the intention of seeking a husband, for she had always looked upon such "proceeding" to the colonies as "prostitution." Ms. Almon insists that "virtue and pride" forbid "making a traffic of her person."[35] In 1780, Henry Fred Thompson's *The Intrigues of a Nabob; or, Bengal the Fittest Soil for the Growth of Lust, Injustice, and Dishonesty,* appeared in print and confirmed what may already have been apparent to many—that in the new racialized order of colonial rule (see chapter 3) Englishwomen were valuable commodities.[36] *Intrigues* is the scandalous disclosure of adulterous letters written by Richard Barwell, a powerful civil servant and close friend of Warren Hastings, to Thompson's wife while the couple resided in Bengal. Included in this book of intercepted correspondence is an agreement signed between Thompson and Barwell in which the former agreed to concede his rights over his wife to Barwell in exchange for an annuity to be paid to him upon his return to London.

Even in theatrical circles, debates about sojourning women were not uncommon. In Mariana Starke's comedy *The Sword of Peace; or, A Voyage of Love,* "female adventuresses" are the objects of satire. Two young women who have gone to India to fulfill a personal obligation (to retrieve a sword) use their short sojourn to attack Mrs. Tartar, the "First Woman" of the settlement in Calcutta, for her role in forcing Englishwomen to marry in India. In a confrontation with her, the young women express their hope "that the traffic will be abolished, as still more disgraceful to our sex than that of the poor slaves to a nation."[37] Even as late as 1804, we have Mrs. H. Lefanu's novel *The India Voyage,* the happy ending of which is produced by the revelation that the heroine will not have to undertake the voyage after all because she managed to find a husband in Britain before the ship was to sail.[38] It is clear that at a time when the ideology of the domestic woman had enabled middle-class women to imagine themselves as being valued more for their "essential qualities of mind" than for their class and economic status,[39] the colony displayed contradictory and threatening versions of the very notions that had been banished from metropolitan circles.

In order to avoid this discourse of the traffic of females in the colonies, *Hartly House* begins with the setting up of the heroine's good intentions: "I love you too well," Sophia writes Arabella in her first letter, "to suffer you to suppose caprice, or the wild curiosity of seeing foreign sights had any share in my instantaneous resolution to visit the eastern continent."[40] The "particulars of" Sophia's "motives and consequential conduct" follow this declaration and justify her travel to India:

> I was retiring, and the final farewell appeared to tremble on my father's lips; again I approached, and again, to embrace him. My manner unspeakably affected him. It was nature's work; and when did nature ever work in vain. He held me for a short space, with silent anguish, in his arms, and I could alone articulate, "My father!—my dearest father!" . . . "Oh Sir!" cried I, "revoke, I conjure you, your own decree; nor be so cruel to yourself, when it is my anxious wish to accompany you, as to leave me behind." (*Hartly House*, 5)

Sensibility is the manifestation of "nature's work," and because the father's state is one of "silent anguish," it is Sophia alone who can "articulate" the agony of parting for both of them. The common masculinist understanding of adventure is of flight from domesticity as a result of wanderlust or greed, but here the conventions of the sentimental novel that celebrate filial ties are used to allow Sophia to accompany her father to India. Thus Sophia is released from the scriptural economy of the colonial adventurer, the administrator, the soldier, or the merchant. Instead, *sensibility* is made into another name for a moral and virtuous (dis)interest in India. Sophia then performs a speech act in her letter, making a vow that positions both Arabella and the novel's readers as witnesses: "This letter shall therefore be constituted the repository of a private vow I have entered into with myself, never to marry in Indostan, lest it should become difficult, at some future period to ascertain my genuine impulse for quitting the country of my birth; a vow, take notice Arabella, I will not violate to be a nabobess" (*Hartly House*, 6).

Several things are being staged here. By mimicking the covenant that writers sign with the Company before proceeding to India, Sophia displaces that official, and often secret, document with a more democratic, public one signed with Arabella and the reading public. By refusing to marry in India, Sophia also thwarts a conventional novelistic ending and suggests that marrying in the colony only facilitates female complicity with colonial power. Her refusal to participate in the growing marriage market in the colonies and her eschewing of the feminized appellation of *nabob* suggest that Sophia is aware that women can gain entry into the networks of colonial wealth, that they are not always innocent bystanders in such social relations. Through the use of a discourse of sentiments, Sophia Goldsborne creates a transcendental position for herself. She can circulate in India without being implicated in British violence or rapacity.

In her important work on sensibility, Janet Todd locates a radical shift in the users of this discourse. By the 1780s, she argues, "the man of feeling ha[s] died" and a host of professional women have adopted the conventions of sentimentality to depict a fictional subject yet unimagined: powerful virgins who use female friendships and familial fellowships to make their way in the world. Rather than being objects of weakness, the female body and female beauty are summoned to denote "moral worth."[41] In *Hartly House*, sensibility is conjured with greater power than that given to female sensibility in the metropolitan context because the colonial setting exiles the female subject from the constraining structures of family and society in the metropole. In her excellent reading of *Hartly House*, Felicity Nussbaum makes the point that the colonial arena, though a place for temporary "rebellion," is ultimately a training site for the Englishwoman's "proper domesticity" after the divesting of these energies.[42] This is certainly one of the ideological ends of the novel, for Sophia does marry in the end despite her initial protests. But at another level, the text is also doing an important cultural work: it is engaged in the production of authority—a female-centered moral authority, tied to the female body, that can evaluate the moral condition of the British in Calcutta. From the outset, sentimentalism had "opposed the individualistic and thrusting values that were transforming Britain into an industrial and imperial power."[43] When the novel *Hartly House* extends this critique into the colony by celebrating virtue and natural morality while the climate is saturated with news of colonial excesses in India, the discourse of sentiments takes on an explicitly political function.

The novel gives us a grand tour as Sophia moves among various institutional and cultural spheres of Anglo-Indian life, passing through the Writers' Building, the fort, the hospital, the playhouse, the governor's mansion, the children's nurseries, and the native bazaars. As Sophia moves through these venues, the narrative is suffused with terms that mark her approval: *grace, genteel, dignity, affectionate, delightful, softest, handsomest, elegant, fine, picturesque, pleasing, striking, desirable, splendor, dazzling, delicate,* and so on. These descriptions leave readers with little doubt that, contrary to popular imagination, the Calcutta of the 1780s was not a frightening outpost, but a civilized place. But these initial descriptions soon give way to darker overtones. Because the novel first casts the colonial landscape of Calcutta as a pleasurable sight for the woman of sentiment, when colonial violence does enter the scene, it suggests a contradictory impulse to the novelist's seeming desire to demonstrate through a sensible agent the civility of the British in India.

The catalyst for this memory of violence is a familiar one. In one of her letters, Sophia takes Arabella on an architectural tour of English Calcutta. After describing in detail the Company's offices, the governor's mansion, and various pleasure spots, Sophia pauses before the old Fort William and stages this uncanny unearthing of past violence:

> At the Old Fort, which is situated at the extremity of those streets terminated by the Esplanade (I shudder to name it) are the ruins of the Black Hole, where the no less memorable than tragical event took place in 1756: for out of one hundred and forty-five British subjects, only twenty-three survived the horrors of one night's imprisonment. . . . The Soubah, a capricious and unfeeling tyrant . . . forced his prisoners into a secure hold, only about eighteen feet square, and shut them in from almost all communication of free air. But I draw a shade over miseries I am unequal to paint. (*Hartly House*, 61)

The use of literary allusion usually implies the existence of a collective fund, a sort of list sufficiently memorized so that the reader, already familiar with the literary or historical reference, can fill in its gaps in the act of reading. Yet here the novel's allusion to the Black Hole is not an invitation to the reader to fill in the blanks. Rather, Gibbes, through Sophia's act of remembrance, re-creates the event for a reading public already separated from the events by several decades. Sophia's shudder creates a fresh knowledge of the event even as she pretends to recollect only what is already known in the public memory. Though Sophia presumes the event of the Black Hole to be "no less memorable than tragical," she repeats the details of who, when, and how many. The Black Hole, it seems, is not really archived in popular memory; the details have been forgotten and only the affect remains. We also notice that the historical description of the event is forestalled by the plea that it is impossible to represent or "paint" its horrors. But the truth of the event's effect on Sophia's body is unmistakable. The recollection "affected [Sophia's] spirits" so severely that she begs to return home. The reader is left with this textual blank: "Having committed my morning's excursion to paper, [I] shall endeavour to remember the concluding part of it no more" (*Hartly House*, 62). Sophia's sensibility recalls the Black Hole and registers it as historical memory, while her body draws it to the surface. The shudder is the mark left on the body's writing surface to be read by others.

Sophia's shudder is also a staging of the structure of the historical event as it enters the lived time of human subjectivity. We have a double gesture of remembering and resolving to forget as Sophia withdraws from the fort. The novel, strangely enough, works against this resolve by forcing Sophia to recollect again. Almost 150 pages later, we have an unexpected trigger for the memory: "I was startled, within this half hour, by the discharge of guns; for, though the affair of the Black Hole is but little remembered at this distant period in Calcutta, I myself am unable to forget it" (*Hartly House,* 219). Is Sophia unable to forget it? Or is Gibbes reminding the audience about this violence, as a result of which the English became "just" rulers and protectors, in order to make another point?

This representation of an active present-past recalls Ernest Renan's articulation of national will in his essay "What Is a Nation?" Here, Renan argues that national communities are constituted through the collective act of forgetting the violence that engendered the nation in the first place, the originary violence through which unity was forged in order to begin the nation. Renan's examples for France are the Saint Bartholomew's Night Massacre and the thirteenth-century massacres in the Midi. These, he says, every French citizen is obliged to forget.[44] Sophia's expression of the desire to forget is a belated gesture, for she has already reactivated the memory for her readers. The question is whether this particular allusion to the Black Hole as a site of willed remembrance (rather than of forgetting) uses the memory of native violence to erase the subsequent and continuing violence of the English in India in the 1780s.[45]

The effect of this repeated memory in the novel does not lie in the use of trauma as a site for identity consolidation for the British (Sophia, after all, does suggest that no one else but her remembers the Black Hole at this point). Rather, it interjects violence right into the middle of a narrative that has painstakingly described the moral sentiments and civility of the English at Calcutta. Having established her sensitivity to violence, and thus her ability to function as a barometer, Sophia begins to rework unexpected characters and players into a new plotting of colonial violence. The apparent randomness of her itinerary in Calcutta gives way to deliberate choices, and we realize that a strand of violence has always paralleled the narrative strand of civility in the novel. Sophia's criticism of the popularity of English dueling, for instance, can now be linked to her refusal to go fishing—an amusement for which she was "disqualified by a painful degree of sensibility." What is ironic, of course, is that Sophia insists that her sensibility to violence has been sharpened to acuteness since her acquaintance with the Hindus, whose "hearts are softened into a tender concern for the kind treatment of every creature living" (*Hartly House,* 132).

Next Sophia goes one step further and transforms the nabob, the English figuration of sexual and political tyranny, into a potential suitor. In a replay of Lady Wortley Montagu's account of being noticed by the grand seignior of Turkey in *The Turkish Embassy Letters,* Sophia tells Arabella that she caught the nabob's eye while he was on a visit to the fort. Sophia neutralizes the trope of oriental despotism as sexual power by inserting it within a lover's discourse. "The Nabob," she says, "has *carried off the heart* of our unfortunate friend" (*Hartly House,* 269, my emphasis). Later Sophia seems to let this moment of reversal slide as she jokes to Arabella about her uncertainty about going to the fort, lest "the Nabob should form plans for carrying me off" (*Hartly House,* 269). But Sophia is not interested in a retroactive reading that would place her in the Black Hole (i.e., in Mrs. Carey's position). Rather, she undercuts the fear of rape by observing that "an Englishwoman was not born to fear giant knights or enchanted castles; and the more especially, where an army would stand forth in her protection and defence" (*Hartly House,* 274). This passage is typical of the way in which the writer of *Hartly House* continually undermines the novel's own propositions by the use of irony. When Sophia implies that fears of rape are not unlike the stuff of childhood myths, she points to their irrationality and poses the implicit questions: Is such fear justified in a settlement where the Company has visible military might? Is it possible that native elite men like the nawab could abduct Englishwomen when the former have no political power?

These moments of ambiguity make the novel into an effective tool of critique even as it pretends to work its way through colonial reality using the map of feelings, without transgressing the narrative conventions of sentimental fiction. In other words, overt discussions of Company politics are kept to a minimum and are often prefaced with long apologies for such "diversions." Then, in a surprise move, the final letter enacts a complete reversal of the novel's celebration of English sentiments in Calcutta. The rape of a young native woman by a soldier in the East India Company's service interrupts Sophia's heady life in the high society of Calcutta. This incident functions as the turning point for Sophia's own impressions: "There are monsters, Arabella, in human shapes and the eastern world is (what I should have returned without conceiving it to be, but for the incident of this morning) the scene of tragedies that dishonour mankind" (*Hartly House,* 277–78). Sophia spells out the details:

> [A]n officer in the army . . . discovered an old man's daughter to be lovely beyond whatever this country has produced, basely resolved to rob him of her. To her father's house he went, on this diabolical design and was received by its innocent and unsuspecting inhabitants with the utmost kindness; in consequence of which reception, he changed his plan of outrage—and instead of bearing her off, as he intended, he settled it to violate the laws of hospitality—of God and of man—and accomplished his work of darkness under the paternal roof. (*Hartly House*, 278)

The myths of native violence are replaced with the reality of British violence as a reversed scenario of rape interrupts the scene of British civility in Calcutta. By stating that her opinion of colonial society would have remained unchanged if she had not heard about this incident, Sophia implies that this incident has canceled her entire approval of English society in India. In this scene of violence against the female body, which also operates as a continued allegory for the plunder of India, the novel paradigmatically substitutes the body of the violated native woman for the body of the English sufferer of the Black Hole. In its iterative role, this violence also expels Sophia from the scene into which she had arrived with such excitement: "I now rejoice, more than ever that I am about to leave a country where fiend-like acts are I fear, much oftener perpetrated than detected; for the grave complains not and gold can unnerve the arm of justice" (*Hartly House*, 270). The language of sentiments no longer suffices, it seems, to describe Sophia's state. Her prose breaks up as she says in the final letter: "I am all agitation, terror, compassion and agitation:—the young woman survives, however, to appall the guilty wretch by her mellow testimony" (*Hartly House*, 279).

The word *testimony* is significant because it hands over the act of truth production to the native woman whose mellow tale is now the eyewitness account of colonial violence. *Hartly House* is not a novel that enacts its closure neatly, but it does display, in its awkward and abrupt narrative turns, the almost parallel movement of historical violence in the timeline of the empire. It is in this sense that the novel's use of the female body to register the shock of history or indeed the use of the body as an inscriptive surface, or archive, is particularly interesting. By bringing the female subject, otherwise constrained by the gendered conventions of writing, into a mode of truth production through her body, the novelist enables us to displace history from its textual existence to a form of scripting done in everyday lives. This use of sensibility resembles that of Holwell and Bage, but also departs from their usage in significant ways.

In Holwell's *Narrative,* male sensibility provides him with an effective protection against accusations of fabrication and against being held responsible for loss of property. (Later, he was also to benefit from reparations from the defeated nawab's treasury for his suffering and would receive a top Company appointment in Calcutta.) In Bage's *Mount Henneth,* the image of the merchant-soldier caught in an agonistic struggle or appearing as a figure of virtue in distress provided a new way to justify the acquisition of colonial wealth after the Bengal war, when the levels of expropriation from the local population were impossible to hide. In the case of *Hartly House,* the subject position that opens up in the novel enables the voicing of a more thorough critique of colonialism as the gendering of sensibility allows a woman writer to gain access to self-representation in the colony.

It has been established by the work of recent critics, such as G. J. Barker-Benfield, that the "culture of sensibility" provided end-of-century feminists like Mary Wollstonecraft with the means to express "felt oppression" or mistreatment by men. In *Hartly House,* we see that this politics had gone one step further—to forms of identification with other victims, victims who shared with English women their common oppression by English men. The novel thus provides at least a single case to show that female sensibility did not always represent an "antiworld view" or a retreat into privacy.[46]

I could stop here—at what seems to be a place to end a satisfying but discontinuous story of female appropriation. But *Hartly House* had an afterlife in the twentieth century that few early novels written about India did. The novel caught the attention of three prominent archivists, and through their conjurings it provides us today with a parable about the arbiters of what is truth in the colonial archive. The final section in this chapter is therefore a coda to the larger discussion. It follows the ripples created in the colonial archive by the novel's arrival into uncharted territory. As we shall see, even a novel can upset the machinery of colonial truth production.

HACKING INDIA

In his introduction to the 1908 reprint of *Hartly House, Calcutta,* G. F. Barwick, the superintendent of the British Museum Reading Room, voices his regret that "the ordinary sources from which the author of an anonymous work is often discovered, such as private correspondence, presentation copies duly signed, or in a known handwriting, have all, so far, refused to give up the secret."[47] This failure to discover the proper name of the author is compounded when we notice that Barwick's introduction also serves as an epitaph for another archivist, the late John MacFarlane, librarian of the Imperial

Library, Calcutta, whose years of research into the real person behind Sophia Goldsborne also failed to yield positive identification: "My late colleague and friend did not live to edit this book, and to give, with abler pen, the results of his researches in his own words."[48]

The last player in this literary relay, Sir William Foster, entered the debate a decade later and participated from a venue more official than the public museum or library. Foster speaks as the master archon, the man in charge of the official archive of the British Empire: the Registry and Record Department of the India Office in London.[49] In 1919, while serving his term as the superintendent of records, Foster published an essay titled "Who Wrote *Hartly House*?" in which he describes the novel as a work composed of "fictitious" letters. But it is not the fictionality of the novel that motivates Foster's essay as much as the possibility that the author might be a fiction operating a fabricated India without the credentials of "actual experience of life in" the colony.[50] Admittedly, any eighteenth-century text claiming to be a woman's collection of letters written from India should be enough to rouse the historian's interest. The only close contenders are Mrs. Kindersley's highly acclaimed *Letters from the Island of Teneriffe, Brazil, the Cape of Good Hope, and the East Indies,* published in 1777, and Eliza Fay's *Original Letters from India,* written in the 1770s but published in 1817.

Foster's essay is an exercise in separating the fake from the authentic, the woman from the man, and the hack from the real writer. It is less about privileging real ethnographic and autobiographical materials about India than it is Foster's demonstration that as an archivist he can tell the difference. With the arrival of the three archivists into the domain of literary criticism in the early part of the twentieth century, the official colonial archive had already unhinged itself from its function as record keeper for the imperial state and was undertaking the more public function of helping readers separate fact from fiction. Monica Clough has pointed out that even the eminent social historian of colonial India H. E. Busteed, in his *Echoes from Old Calcutta,* quotes verbatim from *Hartly House,* thinking it to be a genuine autobiographical and journalistic account.[51]

It is not surprising then that as a custodian of a patriarchive, Foster was bent on proving that the person behind Sophia Goldsborne was a male hack. Foster lists misused words, inaccurate details, and incorrect dates to conclude that the author had never lived in the colony, though "he" had an "obvious acquaintance with life in India." Once Foster concedes the novelist's "obvious acquaintance," his next step is to imagine the archive that had presumably allowed this "London literary hack" to substitute a fake India for the real one. Foster speculates that "he" must have had "access to a collection of private letters written in Calcutta [and] conceived the idea of working up some of their details into a novel, adopting for that purpose the then fashionable framework of a correspondence between one gushing young woman and another."[52] Foster never seriously considers the possibility that the hack might be a woman, for he has already determined that the writing is that of a man. Only a man, Foster insists, would use "Latin quotations," write "dissertations" upon Indian history and Indian religion, and give particulars concerning the Company's stock; for these are "all topics unlikely to occur to a woman writer."[53]

It was not difficult for Foster and the other two archivists to establish that the name on *Hartly House*'s title page was a fiction. The East India Company's meticulous record keeping was a form of both mastery and strict control. Till 1833, anyone proceeding to India had to apply for a license from the Board of Control, and a Sophia Goldsborne residing at Calcutta from 1775 to 1777 or later would have shown up in one or more overlapping records: marine and ship's logs that kept passenger lists; personal records of employees; bonds, agreements, and warrants signed by people standing sureties for civil servants, dependents, visitors, or residents; or even the most comprehensive enumerative effort, the "Europeans in India Records," which list every European inhabitant in Bengal since 1793.[54]

The gender and epistemological confusion created by *Hartly House* shows that the official archive is a patriarchive not because its formats of writing are inherently male, but because the conditions of truth production, the assignment of expertise, and the bias of the disseminators of knowledge, such as Foster, determine access to subject positions of authority in colonial knowledge. But although "India" as a new discursive domain was unavailable to women as historians, it was clearly available to women as novelists. We now know for sure that *Hartly House* was indeed written by a woman and that her name was not Sophia Goldsborne but Phebe Gibbes. She had never been to India, but she used the letters her son had sent her from there before his death to write the novel. Isobel Grundy, whose research unearthed this proper name, tells us that the proof of the author's identity lies in another archive, that of the Royal Literary Fund, which has a statement by a Phebe Gibbes giving information about the circumstances surrounding the writing of the novel. The publisher, Robert Dodsley, recorded in his own correspondence that he paid Phebe Gibbes twenty pounds for the manuscript in 1789.[55]

The three texts I have examined in this chapter represent the history of colonial violence in alternative ways, using narrative strategies that are in the domain of literary rather than historical discourse. By so doing, they disseminate the historical event of the Black Hole by compulsively repeating it on affective registers, yet each repetition exposes the original story's fabricated nature. Holwell's desire to multiply the accounts of his experience in the Black Hole only creates more doubt about his veracity. Bage's *Mount Henneth* could add undeniably fictional characters to the Black Hole because the truth of that experience was still up for grabs. Finally, *Hartly House* goes beyond the historical representation of the two earlier texts as it threatens the machinery of truth production. It brings out the archivists in force to install a boundary to separate an archive of the real from an archive of fiction. Whereas the official colonial archive still represents archontic power—the power, that is, to deny access, to arrest meaning, to deny hermeneutic authority to all but a select few, and to withdraw texts from public scrutiny—the novel plays with substitutions, figurations, speculations, translations, and citations. And while the official archive lies in wait for its selected reader, the novel as a staged discursive field allows us to read the intimate struggle of subjects as they poach upon objects or re-present them in ways not sanctioned by official discourse.

CHAPTER THREE

The Politics of Settlement

Historians of the British Empire all too often relegate everyday life and the domestic sphere to the margins of the "main" theater of colonialism—the administration and consolidation of the colony—and in so doing continue to assert that those realms are outside politics. But because colonial power repeatedly broke down distinctions between public and private and redrew the boundaries of cultural, economic, and political production, a historiography of colonial sovereignty can demonstrate the arbitrariness of these modern divisions as well as the uses to which they were put. By looking at texts that explicitly place the concerns normally associated with the private sphere at the center of the colonial enterprise, we see how the separation of private and public often dissimulated political agendas that cut across this divide. In this chapter I will explore the significance of and transformations within everyday cultural spaces of empire by looking at how notions associated with these realms replicated and furthered a politics of settlement in early-nineteenth-century India.[1] As the notion of home increasingly signified for the English in India a place of cultural and biological reproduction that was gendered, racially pure, and free of native influence, the possibility of possessing India permanently was strengthened. But this did not mean that the setting up of English homes in India was a neat task without obstacles. Indeed, the changing formulations of *home* from the 1770s to the 1830s in colonial texts signal that such social spaces had to be reworked constantly as strategies of rule, as well as the relationship between the rulers and the ruled, changed over time.

A historical analysis of changes in representations of domestic and everyday spaces thus shifts the emphasis from a reading of colonial sovereignty as total or absolute in its effects to one that looks at the colonial order's attempts to normalize its operations for its functionaries—whether bureaucrats, soldiers, or officers. If colonial power depended on Manichean oppositions to justify the relationship between the ruler and the ruled, then such power was successful only insofar as it was able to constantly stamp out ambivalence, unevenness, hybridity, and contradictions that worked against these binary oppositions. If we examine home as a gendered social space, a necessary site of cultural and biological reproduction, we see that it often militated against the strict separation between the rulers and the ruled. That is, home continued to pose problems in a colonial order characterized by what Ranajit Guha calls a "dominance without hegemony"—a rule without consent that required a certain amount of isolation of the rulers from the ruled. In an essay that discusses this notion, Guha reveals a lacuna in standard histories of empire, a statist bias with which all anxieties on the part of custodians of colonial law and order are simply read off as fear of a "given object," usually the natives.[2] With his close reading of several memoirs written by colonial functionaries in the field, Guha demonstrates a political ambivalence within those who carry out the work of governance. By disclosing the mixed feelings these subjects experience about domination and conquest in their everyday lives, Guha underscores the subject's potential for resistance and makes the case that no system is fully monolithic or without its ideological weak points.

A particularly useful point of departure for my own analysis of homemaking in empire is provided by Guha's eloquent invocation of home as a site of political ambivalence where the desire to conquer is crossed over by the desire to be at home:

> There is something uncanny about empire. The entity known by that name is, in essence, mere territory. . . . And when all the conquistadors, consuls, and clerks are taken out, there is little left to it other than a vacancy waiting for armies and bureaucracies to fit it up once more with structures of power and designate it again as empire. As such, it *requires* no homes, if only because the authority, the imperium, from which it derives its form, function, and purpose, is easily sustained by forts and barracks and offices. Yet as history shows, empire is not reconciled for long to this abstracted condition. Caravans seek the shade of camps, markets their custom in the garrisons, even religions their flock among war-weary souls. Towns and settlements grow, as empire too is seized by the urge to make a home of its territory.[3]

Guha's larger argument is that the empire generates paradoxical desires—to be an "alien" ruler and to be "at home"—but it can never satisfy the latter because the rulers suffer from an "irreducible and historically necessary otherness." This paradox ensures that an irreconcilable and unsettled mood of "being lost" (an "unhomeliness," or *unheimlich,* as Freud would say) insinuates itself into many triumphal imperialist narratives.[4] What is missing from Guha's analysis of these conflicting urges is a discussion of the materiality of home—of its actual historical implementation within the empire and its success in maintaining or undermining the unquestionable authority of the rulers' "abstracted condition." How does Guha's formulation of this colonial ambivalence as uncanniness materialize within "home" in colonial India? How does the presence of paradoxical desires in the everyday administration of empire act as a theoretical lever for prying open the apparent seamlessness of a regime that seems to work purely by domination, exclusion, and command? I now turn to Homi Bhabha's discussion of the "unhomely" in *The Location of Culture* for an additional avenue of examination into these questions.

Although Bhabha calls unhomeliness a "paradigmatic colonial and postcolonial condition" that accompanies the psychic and geographical dislocations, forced occupation, migration, diaspora, and exile, his discussion in *Location of Culture* focuses mainly on the agency of the colonized: an African American mother who refuses to reproduce for slavery, a Bengali housewife within the nationalist movement, and a South African colored woman in a revolutionary struggle. Bhabha, following Freud, links unhomeliness to the "uncanny," understood here as the recurring symptom of the postcolonial subject's spatial and temporal displacement. Unhomeliness is thus "the estranging sense of the relocation of the home and the world." For Bhabha this structure of feeling is not nostalgia for the lost home (or family, country, history, or culture), but instead a subjective experience that politicizes the subject and reveals future political alternatives, as the intimate "recesses of the domestic space become sites for history's most intricate invasions." In that displacement, Bhabha goes on to say, "the borders between home and the world become confused; and uncannily, the private and the public become part of each other, forcing upon us a vision that is as divided as it is disorienting."[5]

Following Bhabha and Guha, an analysis of these crossover spaces in colonial texts is, on the one hand, a challenge directed toward the social fact of an oppressive structure that tried historically to repress partial and hybrid identities—difference, so to speak. On the other hand, such a reading allows us to assert multiplicity in that history and thereby challenge the continuing power of binary structures today by rearticulating identity in a way that denies it an essential or fixed status. And finally, as the presence of various female figures in Bhabha's analysis suggests, the "unhomely" dramatizes through the figure of woman the very domains and subjective realms that are forgotten in the theoretical distinctions between private and public. A reading of the domestic sphere as the site of reproduction of power may reveal instances when gender difference does not divide neatly between the private and the public. When this sort of an overlap happens, we see how the domestic sphere is not only a place for "normalizing . . . [the] techniques of modern power," but also a site where women are drawn into events as subjects of history as the personal becomes the political, or conversely, as the world becomes the home.[6] When home is revealed to be this in-between space, both inside and outside the system of power, it can provide a standpoint from which women can posit new forms of subjectivity that do not define political power simply in terms of access to public space.

In this chapter, I read a number of texts that imagine home and everyday life as the East India Company consolidated its hold on the Indian subcontinent. These texts include private portraits that capture British immigrant (or Anglo-Indian) domestic life, autobiographical accounts of life in India, handbooks that tabulate everyday life as repeatable routine for potential settlers, and finally, an Anglo-Indian novel that acts as a mnemonic device for archiving collective memory. All these texts were produced during a significant time period—the 1770s to the 1820s, when the territorial consolidation of India through militaristic means was more or less completed and it was possible to talk of British "paramountcy."[7]

In the first of four sections, I discuss selected British portraits of families in Bengal as they reveal home to be a space of overlap where empire signifies contradictory impulses. Here distinctions such as private and public, coercion and persuasion, British and Indian, and Christian and heathen are momentarily displaced in the sexual, reproductive, and domestic practices of everyday life. As the British presence in India moved from military conquest to occupation, the Englishman's home in India gradually became a place for official scrutiny. English culture and lifestyle became reified objects to be possessed and transmitted. To demonstrate this new function of Englishness in India, in the next section I look at guidebooks like Captain Thomas Williamson's *East India Vade-Mecum* (1810), which I read as a pedagogical instrument that inculcates into its readers an appropriate lifestyle for the English in India. In the third section, I extend the discussion of colonial self-fashioning to literary attempts to represent life in India using the figure of the Englishwoman. In Mrs. Monkland's novel *Life in India* (1828), we see how Anglo-Indian society, constantly beset by an awareness of its alienness, gives over to females the role of scripting home in India. Under the Englishwoman's supervision, homes, as sites of sexual contact and of cultural and biological reproduction, allegorize a temporality of empire. The ability to make an English home in India—to sustain it and to protect it from internal as well as external enemies—becomes a test for the empire's own future, its successful continuance. In the final section, I take up the return of unhomeliness and ambivalence in the narrative of settlement. Here, I read the plotting of failure and ideological fractures within *Life in India*'s affective cartography as death, disease, and dishonor beset the women in the colonies.[8]

The Moment of the Sitting: Making Oneself at Home

Figure 2, *The Palmer Family*, was painted by Francesco Renaldi (1786), a European artist visiting India. It is one of several conversation pieces existing from that time; most were commissioned by well-placed English families in Bengal. This painting shows Major William Palmer and his household: two aristocratic Muslim wives, three children, and two (or possibly three) servants. Palmer was Governor-General Warren Hastings's private agent in Oudh from 1782 to 1786, commander of the Seventh Battalion in Calcutta in 1786, and permanent resident at the Maratha ruler's court in 1798. As a high-ranking official and personal friend of the governor-general, in the painting Palmer was evidently recording not a scene of clandestine European sexual deviance but a lifestyle that enjoyed some level of official approval. (The infant son sleeping on the lap of the elder wife, Faiz Baksh, is named Hastings.)[9]

The painting displays the easy domesticity of an Englishman comfortable in an Indian setting, although it carefully maintains that he has not gone native. Palmer, we notice, remains seated in a chair while his family squats on the floor. There are no props or visible markers of Palmer's official status, but his clothing is still formal and European. It asserts his English identity even though the space of the sitting lacks any allusion to European culture. The choice of an inner courtyard, a space that is neither outdoors nor indoors reveals a cultural concession to the women in the picture. It allows the Indian locale to show (the banana and palm trees) without breaking the local norms of seclusion for Palmer's unveiled Muslim wives. These careful cultural compromises aside, the painting's most remarkable aspect is its injection of affective elements into what could just as easily have been a restrained formal scene or a crude depiction of the Englishman as sexual despot.

While there is nothing apologetic about this scene of polygamy, the painting does not cast it within dominant stereotypes of the harem. The painting places Palmer in the center of the picture and at the apex of a

Figure 2. Francesco Renaldi, *The Palmer Family,* 1786, oil on canvas (Oriental and India Office Collections, shelfmark Foster 597; reproduced by permission of the British Library)

domestic triangle. The two ayahs closest to Palmer remain in shadow, faded out so that, in contrast, the faces of the two wives stand out, illumining their connection to Palmer. Palmer's evident ease and pride in this domestic arrangement flies in the face of the ethic of Christian marriage and poses a challenge to English middle-class propriety through its acknowledgment of sexuality. In her recent analysis of this painting, Beth Fowkes Tobin argues that the Palmer portrait depicts a sexual energy often missing from conversation pieces painted of English families in Bengal. Renaldi signals sexual intimacy through the close physical contact between Palmer and his younger wife. They hold hands, and she leans against him with a gaze of great "intensity."[10] If sexuality is one organizing principle for the tableau, biological reproduction is the other. Palmer, the younger wife, and the two ayahs all look toward the senior wife, Faiz Baksh, who draws everyone's gaze even though she is seated on the floor and is placed slightly off-center by the artist. Her symbolic centrality as the mother of the three children gives the elder wife an important place in this arrangement. Palmer's own place as head of the household is momentarily suspended as our gaze follows his to the squatting native wife.

In this multilayered way, the painting creates a multiplicity of positions that depict the two women not as passive possessions of the white man but as his emotional and sexual companions in the private domain. Since the painting explicitly records the domestic life of a well-known English official in a place where English culture is all but absent, where Christian precepts are laid aside and racial intermixture is celebrated, the portrait materializes a historical moment when English homes and private lives were not under official scrutiny. Beth Fowkes Tobin sees these and other paintings of mixed-race domestic settings in the late eighteenth century as evidence of a "remarkable moment in the history of British and Indian relations" when sexual, cultural, and religious boundary crossings were not prohibited by law. In their suggestion that Englishmen could live abroad and carry out the work of empire without Englishwomen, the portraits posed a "serious cultural and moral challenge" to English colonial society as well as to its national self-representation.[11]

While Tobin is convincing when she argues that biracial family portraits advocate alternative values and challenge metropolitan English norms, her larger argument that these late-century portraits represent a transition in the racial attitudes of the British toward India and the Indians injects a determinism into the cultural texts of the empire. Tobin's proposition not only implies a strict causal connection between official policy during Lord Cornwallis's tenure as governor-general and the artistic self-representations of the English, but also levels out the multilayered operations of racial discourses within the colonial state. Race did not simply come into being as a foundational discourse rooted in "a deep distrust of miscegenation," as Tobin, quoting C. A. Bayly, puts it.[12] Although later official policies did advocate racial estrangement at various social and legal levels, practices on the ground reveal more probability than certainty.

The Palmer portrait was painted at the beginning of Lord Cornwallis's rule as governor-general. Between the years 1786 and 1791, Cornwallis set in place statutes that called for the removal of Indians and people of mixed race (Eurasians) from military and civil posts in the British colonial administration. The Europeanization of these services was justified on various grounds, but the most appealing consideration for a British public much exercised by the corruption charges against Warren Hastings's regime was the moral one—the idea that the Indian empire could be maintained only by the honesty and uprightness of Europeans who were free of the taint of the Indian nobility and their despotic, corrupt ways.[13] With these exclusions, skin color came to define suitability for employment or political power. While Renaldi's portrait clearly represents a historical moment before the idea of mixed marriages became moral anathema to Englishmen, the portrait's connection to official British policy may be more refracted. The presence of many portraits of biracial families from 1786 to 1794 (during and after Cornwallis) indicates that official policy and colonial domesticity often did not move in tandem. Especially pertinent to this unevenness in official implementation is the startling portrait painted by Renaldi as late as 1794–1795 titled *A European with His Family*, which shows a European man dressed in the clothes of a Muslim nobleman. Flanked by his two Indian wives and a child, the man expresses the conjugal happiness of having gone native.

Other portraits complicate this chronology further. One family portrait that Tobin discusses as emblematic of the racial and cultural estrangement between the English and Indians is Johan Zoffany's *The Morse and Cator Families* (1784). This painting was executed in Bengal and shows a strict identification with Western classical culture through its use of a Greco-Roman palatial backdrop, elaborate drapery, and columns. However, it was painted before Cornwallis took office and before most of the biracial and India-set portraits Tobin discusses were produced. The choice of a classical setting clearly suggests that the Morses and Cators did not feel at home, or were not reconciled to their Indian life. In an excellent analysis of the painting, Richard Leppert provides an apt caption for the cultural work done by settings like these: "India itself has been absented." Leppert compiles the scene that is foreclosed by the superimposition of the classical one: "trade and labor exploitation, racial separation, bureaucratization, and the brutality of military enforcement."[14] The classical setting erases any possible contamination by the real life the Morses and Cators led in India and forces instead a seamless visual representation of a continuing connection with Britain. Yet home is represented here not through signifiers of English domesticity but rather through an abstracted notion of high culture.[15] In its failure to signify the actual setting of the subjects or to make any references to the subjects' Indian domestic life, this conversational piece may be read as saying that Englishness is reproduced in all its refinement and civilization wherever the British may be.

Taken together, these portraits represent, not a strict chronological plot of negation of India and Indians, but a range of positions available to colonials in the late eighteenth century. The positions run from an extreme identification with Western classical culture, and therefore an anxious denial of Indian cultural influence, to a total identification with native life in the intimate sphere—going native. Reading the paintings merely as reflections of changing official policy erases their complicated cultural role as part of an archive of available self-representations. They attest to the coexistence of various desires that were never fully controlled or manipulated by the colonial state. Indeed, it is well known that Cornwallis's racist policies never stopped sexual contact between the English and the natives. They only denied social or legal legitimacy to such relationships. As late as the twentieth century, the British army in India provided its soldiers managed access to sexual intercourse with native prostitutes attached to cantonments.[16] What we must read in Cornwallis's policies, then, is not the prior existence of race as a "foundational category" that is then implemented, but rather slow steps toward constructing such a category as a foundational one in order to manage the colony through forms of biopower.[17] Therefore, rather than viewing what Tobin terms Cornwallis's "race-conscious" stance as the inevitable result of colonial rule,[18] historiographic analysis must attend to those moments when texts show divergences and gaps in official reason.

For one, racial differences were used to shore up and protect certain hierarchies of rank and class in the colonial state, while they were unevenly implemented in other areas. Such partial maneuvers often posed the danger of overturning the very categorical separations needed to uphold such an arrangement. One way to track the history of this uneven implementation is to follow the fate of the unassimilated mixed-race children. A discussion of this trajectory is not part of the undertaking in this chapter, but suffice it to say that by 1830 continuing "illegitimate" sexual contact between the rulers and the ruled had created a class of vocal and disenfranchised Eurasians. Their collective petition to the British Parliament in 1830, asking for the status of "English subjects," posed the first significant threat to the political absurdity of the colonial state: its attempt to reconcile metropolitan liberalism with colonial autocracy.[19]

The Deployment of the Everyday

Williamson's *East India Vade-Mecum* provides a blueprint of sorts for the uneven implementation that led to the scenario of mixed-race sons asking for inclusion in the political institutions of their fathers. On the one hand, practices of everyday life were cultivated so as to articulate English life and culture apart from native culture. On the other hand, a parallel sexual-social realm was put into place where forms of unscrutinized contact with native women went on in a variety of informal (nonlegal) sexual arrangements throughout the nineteenth century.

Under the undeniable paradigmatic power of liberalism in the nineteenth-century era of reform, the single most powerful justification for the empire after the legitimization crises of the latter part of the previous century was the argument about the superiority of imperial culture. Culture was seen as something one could impart to inferior races: an instrumental or objectified entity locatable not only in books, artifacts, and curricula but also in everyday practices and social rituals that could be imitated by those outside the culture.[20] It became possible at this point to conceive of an archive of behavior, of everyday practices, that was exportable and would signify to the watching native the superiority of English life.

One of the first indicators of the existence of such objectified practices that signified Englishness in the colonies came from the work of Anglo-Indian writers, many of whom, as ex-colonials, revealed a desire to represent and preserve their idiosyncratic life in India. Earlier, writers simply wrote up their past or remembered experiences after returning to England, but now many began to write of their lives as they unfolded in the present. It was as though they were representing a lived reality that would go on interminably into the future. Texts representing experience in this new temporality were different from previous contributions to the colonial archive also in that they focused not primarily on the military and economic campaigns of empire building, but on quotidian life as it was lived in the pores of the colonial state.

Consider, for instance, the different emphasis of the guidebook to India as it sits alongside older formats for representing colonial experience, such as the memoir, the journal, and the travel account. The guidebook describes colonial life and tabulates and organizes information for easy retrieval; reading is a precursor to the subsequent performance of the book's instructions. Captain Williamson's *East India Vade-Mecum* appears, at the level of information, to be a manual or guide for young men planning to go out to India in the service of the East India Company.[21] But when it is read with particular attention to address and delivery, its instructions are a fascinating picking field for new forms of subject constitution. Williamson's text facilitates the self-fashioning of the newly arrived Englishman into a subject who will reproduce, as a daily occurrence, a quintessentially English everyday life in India that breaks down the usual boundary between business and home.

The *Vade-Mecum* translates the autobiographical details of its author's "long residence in Bengal" into a public volume of information. Williamson felt it incumbent upon himself, the preface tells us, to assume the pen to fill in existing gaps in the information network (*Vade-Mecum,* 1:vii–viii). The guide is thus intended for the "great numbers of young gentlemen [who] proceed to India without the smallest idea of the customs &c. peculiar to that country, whither they are adventuring" (*Vade-Mecum,* 1:1). Displaying the explicit transformation of one genre into another, the book takes some of the standard plot details and descriptions of an account of travel to the Indies and reworks them as an inventory of instrumental knowledge.[22] For instance, in the introductory chapter, where one might expect the customary beginning of a voyage narrative—embarkation from England; the bittersweet, anxious moments of impending voluntary exile; and so on—what we get instead is a take-along list: "Instructions to Persons proceeding to India regarding articles to be provided, and the precautions to be adopted." Following that, the usual details and anecdotes about passengers and their mishaps are replaced with a section titled "Matters relating to embarking, and the usual customs on board-ship, sea-sickness, fishing at sea" (*Vade-Mecum*, 1:xiii). In the itemized list of what to take and how much, the account is no longer a narrative in the conventional sense; rather, it is a table with each item arranged serially according to the sequence of presumed necessity. Shirts come first, and then come sheets, hammocks, candles, furniture, servants, and so on.

When memory is reorganized as an inventory or a list, experience becomes pedagogy—instruction for the future. The experience of a retired army man like Williamson is given value, preserved, and circulated as knowledge when it is made into manuals for future generations of colonials. The handbook is thus a projection into a political future; it reveals not only the standardization of colonial experience into a set of guidelines, but also the will to continue colonial control indefinitely. Here is how Williamson's *Vade-Mecum* redoes the usual anecdotal description of a day in the life of a Bengal sahib:

> Rise at daybreak, and ride gently for one hour in the hot season, and two hours in the cold season; make a moderate breakfast, avoiding melted butter, salt meats, salt fish, sweetmeats, &c., good tea or coffee being assuredly the most wholesome; study the language for an hour; attend some office gratuitously, with the view to become acquainted with the accounts, price-currents, markets, provisions, commodities, &c. about two o'clock retire to rest; about an hour before sun-set bathe, by means of three or four large pots of water poured over the head; put on clean linen, and dine moderately upon plain viands, taking care never to exceed four or five glasses of the best Madeira; proceed for two hours with studying the language, and after taking a cup or two of tea, or of coffee, or a crust of bread and a glass of Madeira, go to bed, avoiding to sleep in a strong current of air. (*Vade-Mecum*, 1:176–77)

This is a complicated list. On the one hand, it is the everyday routine that single Englishmen in India must follow in order to become disciplined and orderly officials. On the other hand, it also displays the careful substitutions and alterations that are necessary for survival in alien space. Food that irritates the stomach or produces dehydration is to be avoided. Madeira wine is retained but intake is moderated in the new setting. In the midst of the to-do list for the newly arrived men is the subroutine of mastery: horse riding and the daily learning of the native languages. Elsewhere Williamson cites the case of an old friend who never went to bed until he had learned twenty words of Persian "perfectly by heart," so as to make the language "fall before him in two years." For Williamson the anecdote about language mastery is proof that in India lifestyle can become a calculable formula: "This is an arithmetical demonstration of the powers annexed to preserving regularity, and ought to induce every youth, for that is the season for acquirements, to adopt such a system as should insure the great object in view" (*Vade-Mecum,* 1:179).

The great object in view is, of course, the governance of the empire, and Williamson locates the continuance of that governance in the measure to which the Englishman can transform his home and everyday life into a place of regimented self-discipline. Yet when Williamson ventures into the various elements that constitute the domain of homemaking, a fundamental contradiction opens up in the text. As Williamson begins to list the various sorts of services native servants perform for an Englishman in his home and their titles and expected salaries, the mention of work by female attendants like *dhyes* and ayahs generates an unconscious undercurrent within the text. The inventory of servants and salaries soon gives way to the sexual practices of European men in India. Williamson provides us with this segue: "The attachment of many European gentlemen to their native mistresses, is not to be described! An infatuation, beyond all comparison, often prevails, causing every confidence, of whatever description, to be reposed in the sable queen of the *haram!*" (*Vade-Mecum,* 1:344).

The text now loses its hold on the discussion of an appropriate daily routine for the gentleman in the East and details instead "the private lives and customs of those native women that are secluded from the public eye" (*Vade-Mecum,* 1:346). For the next hundred pages or so the vade mecum puts together a taxonomy of native women with an untidy list of types: ayahs, *meeraseens, dhyes,* nautch girls, prostitutes, slaves, sexual deviants, mistresses, wives, mothers, harem women, Hindu women, Muslim women, aristocratic women, bathing women, jealous women, loving women, and so on. Accompanying the list are descriptions of various female activities:

ornamentation, education, dressing, social rituals, toilette, eating, needlework, housework, travel, child rearing, money lending, worship, entertainment, sexual rituals, marriage ceremonies, conjugal rites, and so forth.

The reason for this textual detour becomes clear halfway through the discussion, when Williamson brings up the issue of native women kept by Englishmen and tells the reader that "plurality" (polygamy) is not "unprecedented" among Europeans. What looked at first to be a mere ethnographic account of native women's everyday lives can now be read as information about lifestyle choices still available to the young men going to the East in the early nineteenth century:

> In regard to the expences attendant upon concubinage in the East, they will depend greatly on the circumstances, and the disposition, of the gentleman, generally speaking; though, after a while, the lady commonly gains a kind of ascendancy, and goes beyond those limits, which, in almost very case, are marked out by previous contract. A certain sum to be paid monthly; the pay of two, or three, female attendants; an allowance for beetle [*sic*], tobacco, . . . shoes, cloaths, and *gynahs,* (i.e. gold and silver ornaments;) are articles in almost every capitulation! Taking a broad outline, we may put down the whole at about forty rupees monthly. (*Vade-Mecum,* 1:414)

Two decades after Cornwallis's tenure, it is evident that sexual contact between European men and native women has not disappeared but is simply distributed across various relationships that substitute for marriage. Women, in Williamson's account, are now "retained," "domesticated," "solaced with," or "domiciliated." In addition to the information that will presumably help newly arrived Englishmen to negotiate native customs in order to acquire a mistress, the guide also provides detailed descriptions of various gold and silver ornaments worn by native women. These ornaments were in many cases part of the financial arrangements made between Englishmen and their mistresses. Though forty rupees per month is an average sum, later in the guide Williamson advises his gentleman readers not to be cheap: "The natives are very scrupulous, and hold it the highest disgrace, for a woman to be retained, without due attendance, suitable cloathing, and a participation of the comforts, if not of the luxuries, of life" (*Vade-Mecum,* 1:415).

Williamson makes a moral case for these sexual arrangements by insisting that native women are not submitting to a "state of prostitution," but that in India a woman "*under the protection*" of an Englishman is "accounted not only among the natives, but even by his countrymen, to be equally sacred, as though she were married to him." Citing various forms of "connubial attachments" ranging from the "formal" to the "very loose," sanctioned, he says, by Muslim law (*Vade-Mecum,* 1:451–52), Williamson goes on to make one of the most notorious defenses of sexual relations between Englishmen and native women in Anglo-Indian literature. It is impossible, he insists, unless "passions are unnaturally obedient," for the "generality of European inhabitants to act in exact conformity with those excellent doctrines, which teach us to avoid 'fornication' and all other 'deadly sins.' There are certain situations, and times, when the law must be suffered to sleep" (*Vade-Mecum,* 1:456–57). Especially detrimental to such conformity, he argues, is the paucity of Englishwomen in India (barely 250 women for almost four thousand European males in Bengal and its dependencies), as well as the huge expense of maintaining an English family in India.

However, although Williamson does not think fornication should be an offense punishable by law, he does support the government's discouragement of Englishmen marrying Indian women. "Matrimony," says Williamson, "is not so practicable in India as in Europe." Citing existing Company statutes that ban the children of such unions from proceeding to England without high security deposits, Williamson argues that legalizing such unions would make the Company responsible for a vast number of "native orphans" in England (*Vade-Mecum,* 1:456–57). Further, it is also clear from his discussion that an official policy of social separation was in place: native wives of even highly placed Englishmen were no longer invited to public assemblies given by the governor-general. But as the vade mecum also points out, there was a curious unevenness in the implementation of such social strictures. Soldiers in India were always allowed to marry, and these marriages were institutionalized through monetary allowances for children that were continued till 1796.[23] It is clear that the banning of mixed marriages among the higher ranks of colonials was motivated by financial considerations. By making an English liberal education a necessary criterion for cadets seeking jobs in the Company while restricting travel to England to "the legitimate offspring of European parents" (*Vade-Mecum,* 1:467), the Company's court of directors minimized the possibility of Eurasian sons claiming inheritances and job privileges from the establishment. The policy also allowed the court to continue a system of patronage that benefited its own class base: the aristocracy and middle classes in England.[24]

In the colony, the type of home colonials could have constituted a class boundary in and of itself. Because the need for domestics, imported clothing, carriages, and spacious accommodations went hand in hand with English brides, already in scarce supply because of the travel restrictions the Company imposed on single women, the English wife was a luxury few could afford. Only one out five Englishmen in India, Williamson points out, had a salary that could make such a lifestyle possible (*Vade-Mecum*, 1:455). And then there were the amounts to be put aside to send the children to England to be educated, as it was customary to do in the absence of institutions of liberal education in India. For these reasons, marrying an English bride of even modest social origins signaled significant economic and class advancement among Englishmen in India. The Englishwoman's appearance at public functions as a valuable object of circulation (if unmarried) or possession (if married) gave her an iconic status almost unheard of in England. There were the Englishmen of the first order who had English homes, English wives, and children with an English education. Lower on the ladder were the Englishmen who kept English homes but without Englishwomen, men who had Indian mistresses, and children who were denied entry into English social circles and civil society. This is Williamson's intended reader for the vade mecum. Finally, there was the class of common soldiers who could marry native women and keep any kind of home they desired but whose diminished class power allowed a kind of policing of them by the state.

In his account, Williamson describes in great detail the institutional homes that coexisted with other kinds of domestic arrangements.[25] Indeed the legal limbo that children of mixed race existed in was contained partly by ensuring that their socialization was completed under strict guidelines in orphanages built for that express purpose. Williamson mentions the "affecting scenes" and the "distress of mothers" when children over the age of three were taken away to the institutions. The language in the guide indicates that the colonial state's compulsory commandeering of children of mixed marriages as "orphans" was justified as being in the best interests of these children. It is clear that by 1810 the biracial homes of soldiers, though not illegal, were already supervised spaces. This form of biopower, which delegates parenting to the Company and the colonial state, is presented as supervision of the children's education and as necessary so that appropriate stations in life can be secured for them. In this we see that a new perception had emerged within colonial power: that the colonial social order could be maintained only by efficient management of, not denial of, the points of overlap in the sexual, racial, religious, and cultural worlds of the rulers and the ruled.

The *Vade-Mecum* enacts a practical resolution of the two contradictory imperatives we have been discussing: the policy of cultural and racial estrangement promoted by the Company in the early nineteenth century and the tendency of English employees to gravitate toward native women for sexual services, intimacy, and domestic comforts. Williamson demonstrates how this crisis is managed through a form of parallel existence in which the everyday English life connected with one's official duties is kept separate from the sphere of interaction with native women. The list of the various forms of "connubial attachments" shows that it was possible for Englishmen to have such domestic arrangements with native women. However, this also meant ensuring that the products of these unions would be culturally indoctrinated to be English, but at the same time kept subordinate by denial of the legal and political rights accorded to British subjects. Through their education in institutions, the Eurasian girls were prepared mainly for domestic work in English households, and the boys for lower-order jobs in the Company's army and its civil establishments.

If racial separation was made into policy in the early nineteenth century, it is clear that that policy's implementation was uneven in terms of class and gender. Englishmen of midlevel ranks, mostly soldiers, often kept primary and secondary homes where native women were wives or mistresses. Later, by mid-century, the Company ensured a more efficient separation of such sexual contacts between soldiers and native women from everyday English life in India, with the regulated use of prostitutes in military cantonments. By recasting the native woman from mistress to prostitute, the army ensured an instrumental use of sex that separated the soldier's home and routine from his "needs." The space where soldiers cohabited with native women was rendered both temporary and renewable as regiments recruited their own prostitutes and housed them in quarters outside the regimental barracks.[26]

Affective Maps: The Literature of Settlement

Literary representations of up-country settlements show us that colonial gender arrangements involving Englishwomen gained in cultural value as sexual relations with native women were increasingly denigrated. More specifically, in the early nineteenth century a phenomenon emerged that today is almost a historical truism—the memsahib's cultural power in the colony.[27] The Englishwoman rose as a valued commodity in the marriage market, and her role signified a gentrified English lifestyle in India. (Contrast this perception with earlier representations from the 1770s and 1790s, when women going out to India were seen only as female nabobs and adventurers.)

Fictional and imaginative texts played a major role in the production of the cultural values underpinning the social mission of colonization. One novel that portrays well-regulated English homes in India, Mrs. Monkland's *Life in India,* replicates through its focus on the domestic sphere the growing interest in the colonial everyday that memoirs had already begun to record. Only when various colonial texts began to represent a quintessential settler culture, which was English even in a foreign setting, did official talk of settlement and colonization also begin in earnest. The longer periods of stay required of civil and army personnel in India indicated not longer periods of exile from England, but prior conditions for imagining permanent rule in India. The articulation of a "superior" European character and set of values grounded in the everyday life of the English in India, in opposition to the so-called degraded and degenerate native culture, helped, in a rapidly democratizing Britain, to justify imperial rule well into the twentieth century.

When William Huggins, an indigo planter from Bengal, authored his monograph, titled in full *Sketches in India, Treating on Subjects Connected with the Government; Civil and Military Establishments; Characters of the European, and Customs of the Native Inhabitants,* the specific listings in the subtitle indicated a new subject position for the Englishman writing of India. As a planter, Huggins was unconnected with the Company's civil or military services. His authority to speak to these aspects of the colonial state derived, as the preface tells us, from his position as a "common observer"—a "free" and "isolated individual" who was not swayed by "passion or party."[28] Connected to India by a long period of residence as a plantation owner, Huggins represented the first set of recognized European settlers, who occupied a subject position untenable before the 1820s because the Company had never allowed private ownership of land to nonnatives.[29] Huggins's preface foregrounds what Benedict Anderson has called the "parallel existence"[30] of the "resident" English in India when he says that the book will describe the "domestic habits and characteristic features of the people who inhabit and reside in our Bengal possessions." Thus he allowed readers to "draw a line of approximation between them [the Bengal inhabitants and residents] and their fellow subjects resident in England."[31] This idea of two resident populations, in Bengal and in Britain, that are both made up of fellow subjects indicates how parallel existence is often the prelude to settler identity formation in a colony. As Anderson has argued, when the continuing link between the settlers and the metropole is beset with discrepancies and inequalities, it provides the necessary condition for the emergence of settler nationalisms. This scenario, we know, never materialized in the Indian case, but in this text of preemergence, we can gather from Huggins's comments that integral to a notion of settler identity is the idea of the settlers' idiosyncratic existence: "domestic habits" and "characteristic features." Thus Huggins offers his book not as a wide survey of the subcontinent such as outlined by nineteenth-century historians like James Mill, but as a different archival project—one that records a colonial everyday that has escaped the historian's eye:

> Without aspiring to the gravity of history, which only animadverts upon great events, and leaves minor ones in obscurity, which only portrays the grand outlines of the picture, and overlooks the numerous inferior etchings necessary to render it complete; a description of the passing events or usages, may be fairly termed a history of the day, and takes up the pencil where general history lays it down.[32]

Huggins, as a historian from below, takes up the pen where "general history lays it down" and sees his work as filling the gaps within the "grand outlines" of a history that already exists. His writing is thus a supplementary gesture that adds to an existing colonial archive and completes the "picture" of India. Yet there is little question that the book is also a personal, or autobiographical, engraving—a "history of [Huggins's] day"—as the writing powerfully extends colonial memory and externalizes it at the same time.[33] When Huggins sees his memories as contributions to the totality of the colonial archive, autobiography is converted into a colonial "history of the day." Here historiography provides the signs of an "activity of organizing knowledge in a new way," as well as of the dispersed, subjective elements of a new power base in the colony.[34]

By 1829 it was clear that official discussions about the future of English rule in India had replaced the language of repressive military force with the language of cultural hegemony. That year, Governor-General Bentinck wrote a minute to the Board of Control in London, initiating one of the first sustained official discussions about European "settlement" in India. In the minute, Bentinck wrote that he was in favor of dispensing with existing Company policies that restricted unlicensed travel of Europeans to India and excluded British settlers from permanent possession of land. He advocated the encouragement of English settlement in India to diffuse "European knowledge and morals among the people," and he posited that effective rule could be guaranteed by inculcating into the natives "the arts and business of life." This minute indicates changes in language of command. The proposed implementation of permanent rule in India was no longer presented as a top-down movement of coercive power. It was now horizontal. Diffusion of "useful knowledge," Bentinck added, would not work unless "we add to the precept, the example of Europeans, mingling familiarly with the natives in the course of their profession, and practically demonstrating by daily recurring evidence the nature and value of the principles we desire to inculcate and of the plans we seek to have adopted."[35] Bentinck's conviction that political control could not be maintained by military force or public rituals of administrative power alone, but only through a pedagogy of recurring examples of everyday Englishness, provided the political charge that intermeshed with the cultural work done by Anglo-Indian novels like Mrs. Monkland's *Life in India.*[36]

In the nineteenth century, one of the important metropolitan cultural forms for representing everyday and private experiences for the express purpose of inculcating morals and values was the domestic novel.[37] In this literary format, plots placed middle-class women at the center of a micropolitics: discussions of domesticity, marriage, and manners made the private sphere into a space of private power. It is not unusual, then, that such a format would soon be exported to an Anglo-Indian context, where the expatriate Englishwoman already enjoyed this cultural role and power to a degree that far exceeded that of her metropolitan counterpart.[38]

Life in India is one of the earliest novels to represent English life in India in a way that imbues this social reality with a certain geographical and cultural autonomy. The novel is set in Calcutta and its outlying English military cantonments, and its curious title suggests an ethnographic imperative that competes with its fictional one. On the one hand, the title suggests that like most travel narratives and colonial memoirs the novel tells of another reality—one that is culturally and geographically different from that of England. On the other hand, a reading of the novel reveals an important departure from those earlier genres. *Life in India* shows the emergence of a new format for narrating Anglo-India; it does away with the self-conscious narrator who constantly reminds readers that the colony is being viewed through the eyes of an exemplary individual on a temporary sojourn from England. Travel narratives for the most part represent the colony as a place for temporary adventure, while epistolary forms based on letters home maintain England as the place of intended return. Writers of both genres still saw colonial India as the habitat of others and not of themselves.

In *Life in India,* the use of third-person narration and the omniscient point of view announces new colonial functions for a style already established in mainstream English literature at this time. The removal of an intrusive authorial presence (the "I" of the correspondent, traveler, or diarist) from the narrative gives the novel's characters and their setting an illusion of relative autonomy. Indeed, their lives seem complicated enough to warrant a plot that follows their actions rather than the other way around, as often happens in memoirs that follow strict calendrical time, or travel accounts that follow tour itineraries. One could also read clear evidence of fictional community formation here in the interplay of the various English characters and in their ability to sustain a narrative determined by social rituals: love, marriage, childbirth, death, misunderstandings, loss, separations, and reunions. The novelistic plot thus produces a different space for these subjects of empire. It replaces the colony that is a space for the lives of the natives with one that is a space for the lives of the English. The English in India now appear as a self-functioning and self-propagating entity, and *Life* as it appears in the title of the novel heralds the beginnings of an immigrant memory that both archives its own existence and memorializes it to produce a successful narrative consolidation of the question of settlement.[39]

After the initial segment of the book, which describes the journey from England, including the customary ports of call along the way and a skirmish with a French warship, the plot of *Life in India* unfolds entirely in India. (Hereafter, Monkland's novel will be cited parenthetically in the text as *Life*.) While the ship's inmates are drawn from various colonial cadres—writers, cadets, assistant surgeons, and Company civil servants—much of the action focuses on the expectations and desires of the six young unmarried women, daughters of British army officers in India going out to join their families after completing an English education. The young army officers on the ship, going back to service after furloughs and sick leaves, form the novel's lineup of future husbands. Unlike Sophia in *Hartly House*, who takes a secret vow to never marry in India, these young women are less prone to invoking England as the home to which they intend to return. The plotting of travel to India as a one-way journey is itself significant, for it signals the changed attitudes toward longer periods of stay by European women. Anxieties about losing English charms, complexion, and beauty are now overridden by a desire to reside in India.

Consider how, as the ship approaches its final destination, the sight of English homes in Calcutta spells for the watching European eyes a colony that is already made over for the newly arrived Englishwomen. But when the ship enters the river channel leading into the port of Calcutta, we get a scene reminiscent of Joseph Conrad's *Heart of Darkness*—disorder and savagery take over: thick impenetrable jungle, ruins of buildings, alligators, howling jackals, man-eating tigers, and hints of human sacrifice. The river, flanked on both sides by a jungle from which "horrible sounds" ensue, seems to grow narrower until unexpectedly it broadens and the ship emerges into what the narrator describes as one of "the finest views in the world":

> Miss Panton pranced about . . . calling upon each by turns to look at the beautiful garden-houses as they drew near Calcutta. They extend seven miles along the left bank of the river, most of them spacious and elegant mansions, seated near the water's edge, at short distances from each other, surrounded by beautiful shrubbery, and verdant lawns shadowed by fine trees. The pillared porticos and verandahs overlooking the river give them an air of Grecian elegance, and convey the idea of a milder clime. (*Life*, 1:121–22)

Traces of classical culture dominate the appearance of these English mansions as they transform India into Europe, and the past-tense narration of the novel gives way to the present-tense descriptions of travel guides. The temporal shift assures the reader of a scene that will continue to exist in the future for other English travelers and emigrants.

After the ship docks, the young women separate to go to their respective local guardians and families. The Percy sisters, Charlotte and Elizabeth, are driven to the mansion of their aunt, Mrs. Russell, the wife of a senior civil servant in the Company. On their way, one of the sisters parodies the words of a "warrior of Khorassan" who is supposed to have said upon seeing Calcutta, "What a charming place this would be to plunder." The newly arrived Miss Percy establishes her distance from this violent history of conquest by exclaiming instead, "What a charming place this must be to live in!" (*Life*, 1:125).

By giving the point of view to these young women, the novel foregrounds the domestic domain and aspects associated with it—marriage, romance, children, and leisure—against an unmistakable historical backdrop provided by references to a bloody frontier war, the British campaigns in Nepal from 1812 to 1815, which act as catalysts and enablers for the various marriage subplots. The military work of empire building seems to take a back seat to a more important task: that of reproducing English culture, a role given to women rather than to men in the novel. In the figure of Mrs. Russell in particular, we see how the Englishwoman gains her authority and status through an association with the concern of domestic fiction—a middle-class culture embodied in notions of honor, taste, and manners.

The centrality of the role given to Mrs. Russell is shown in the way the novel portrays the grand designs of her dinner party, which appears to be a smaller version of the one the governor-general and his wife stage for all of colonial Bengal. These social rituals assume a larger significance as public spectacles of English power. They are presented as evidence of colonial success: even subjugated rulers put in their appearance to validate the power of the new rule. At Mrs. Russell's dinner parties a different responsibility is staged as new arrivals in Calcutta are initiated into the established English community. One of her parties is the first such ritual described in great detail. For almost ten pages, the novel meticulously charts the "indispensable etiquette" characteristic of the English in Calcutta in their private and public dealings with each other. "Well-regulated" society prevents the English from developing excessive "modes of feeling and expression" (*Life*, 1:132, 134).

The "hospitality" Mrs. Russell provides is described as an "intimacy of association" that allows new Company recruits in Calcutta a cultural sphere in which to make themselves (*Life*, 1:136). Here the descriptive detail of the Russell home bespeaks the importance of its cultural function: "Mrs. Russell's rooms were abundantly provided with all the useful helps, which furnish people with occupation, without the trouble of thought" (*Life*, 1:138). Objects such as ivory puzzles, albums, toys, music stands, volumes of French magazines, novels by Walter Scott, books of poetry by Lord Byron, and romances from Paris gain a new significance as they are transformed into "help" for the precariously cultured and the uncultured. With some irony, the novel provides here a catalog of objects that aid in self-making in the colony as Mrs. Russell, "the goddess of the place," makes it her occupation to incessantly create everyday life for her guests. When not in her dressing room, she reclined upon her couch under the punkah and from the "studies of the morning" she "prepared the conversation for the evening" (*Life*, 1:140).

The ironic tone hints of a tension within the novel even as it advocates the acquisition of taste in Calcutta. The novel's portrayal of Mrs. Russell in her dressing room, moving amid "the perfumes of Arabia and the attar of Persia," evokes the image of narcissistic Belinda in Alexander Pope's *Rape of the Lock* (*Life*, 1:140).[40] When this extended description of Mrs. Russell's appearance, manners, and accomplishments ends with the judgment that "the desire of being elegant was all that went beyond her own family," the narrator suggests that she does not fully approve of this figure (*Life*, 1:141). The ideological tension about the social role of colonial Englishwomen is made clearer as the novel shows us a variance of interests between Mrs. Russell and her niece, Elizabeth Percy. Elizabeth's symbolic function is declared when she, alone of all the female characters, is described as being "English, wholly English; a true personification of feminine loveliness and domestic grace" (*Life*, 2:75).

Through Elizabeth Percy the novelist constructs a figure of woman that allows a new territorializing of Anglo-Indian space. As Elizabeth's soldier beau, Captain Bently, lies wounded on the frontier during the Anglo-Nepalese War, he hallucinates:

> Bently experienced them in their full force; his mind formed disjointed and harassing pictures of the events of the past day. Now he fought victoriously while Elizabeth Percy approached to crown him with laurel, bright as her own sunny smiles; then the earth yawned, and he sunk from her sight amid the roar of savage beasts, and yell of fiends in human shape. Again, he was in the good ship Cumberland careering his way over the highest points of the snow-capped mountains, while Elizabeth Percy in vain called upon him to stop or return. (*Life,* 2:21–22)

As Bently lies alone, wounded and delirious in enemy territory on the boundaries of the empire, his vision of Elizabeth Percy is not only palliative. Here, the figure of woman operates in the role of the gendered magistracy of the empire: she acts as its civilizing influence as well as a moderating constraint on male military violence. In one sense at least, Elizabeth's constraining influence is the influence of home as a moral and affective center in the imaginative geography of empire building. Her image draws Bently, lying on the front lines, to the heart of the Indian empire, Calcutta, where love, life, and, by implication, English security and power preside. The novel's plotting of marriage and love thus draws its male characters toward the center where marital rewards await them after their valor on the frontier of the ever-expanding dominion.

Yet within its discussion of women and the upholding of English values in the colonial enterprise, the novel reveals a fracture. The tension is visible at one level in the contrast drawn between Mrs. Russell and other women, like Mrs. Dundas, who, "without personal vanity, or the desire to shine in the eyes of any other person," keeps a house that is "the abode of domestic happiness" (*Life,* 1:167). Elizabeth's marital choice of Bently, a junior officer in the army and a man of modest economic means, mirrors Mrs. Dundas's role as a model companionate wife to her husband. Elizabeth eschews the glory and ostentation of the civil servants in Calcutta and opts for a life in the cantonments. The contradiction between English values and imperial values is suddenly visible in the novel when it is posed as a choice of husbands. Mrs. Russell's disapproval of her niece's choice of a soldier over a civil servant makes this fracture clear and rehearses the tension between new power bases emerging within the colonial state:

> Mrs. Russell said no more, but, in her own mind she pitied the ignorance that could lead to such a choice, and felt that youth, beauty and accomplishments, were thrown away upon a girl who could bestow them upon a Captain in the army, and be contented to inhabit the jungles, live in a bungalow, and ride in a buggy with a single chaprassy to attend her; when she might have been the honoured wife of a Calcutta Judge, blazing in diamonds, and surrounded by silver sticks, moving like a sun, the centre of a system, giving law in the empire of fashion, and shedding light and brilliancy upon all within the sphere of her attraction. (*Life*, 2:93)

Mrs. Russell's idea of army life as socially inferior and the novel's representation of her objections as trivial suggest that her attitudes are lagging behind the times. She has failed to notice what the novel itself advocates with great approbation: the arrival of the soldier as hero in the fiction of empire. (Contrast this, for instance, with the late-eighteenth-century texts discussed in chapter 2, where the virtuous merchant is the upholder of a moral code.)

Mr. Russell, a high-ranking civil servant, attempts a partial bridging of this social divide between the ostentatious administrators who rule India and the soldiers who consolidate its territorial boundaries by citing the common loyalty visible at the public ceremonies in Calcutta. At a ball thrown by the governor-general, he remarks to the company around him: "Soldiers who have extended our territory; merchants whose honour and liberality serve as cement between India and Britain; and civil servants whose wisdom and integrity have exalted European character in the eyes of the natives. Ballrooms are not in general the atmosphere of these things; but on public nights it would be disloyal to be absent here" (*Life*, 1:205). Mr. Russell's observation, coming as it does from a civil servant, testifies to the preeminence of the role of the soldier even as it suggests that empire building requires the joint efforts of the military, the economic, and the administrative units.

Russell declares at one point that there is "no society in the world, of equal compass, which contains a greater proportion of the essentials of domestic happiness and virtue" than Anglo-India. This conclusion, Russell maintains, is supported by the fact that "almost every man" has the ability to find himself in the circumstances to "support a family" and consequently can "marry the woman of his choice without reference to the multitude of foreign considerations which sway people in Europe" (*Life*, 1:204). This ability to marry an Englishwoman, free from class or rank consideration, and to have a home or family is presented as a significant achievement of the English in India. Yet the home that is upheld as the novel's marriage plot unfolds is not the ostentatious one of civil servants like Russell, whose house's interior is always described with a touch of irony. Rather, we see another ideal of home one that was put into place after the consolidation of vast territory and the extension of English power into the interior of the country in the 1820s. In the novel, these military and civil establishments in the up-country and *mofussil* settlements are represented as locations of domestic bliss. Here is the description of the settlement Elizabeth and Captain Bently go to after their marriage:

> Barrackpore, though a large station, presents an air of quiet and retirement like a country village; which joined to its military neatness and propriety, make it one of the sweetest places in India. The bungalows in four lines stand each separated from the others, every one surrounded by its own corn-ground, flower-garden and neat trimmed hedge; while the whole cantonment is at right angles intersected by well kept roads as smooth as bowling-greens, and has the river in front and the parade ground in the rear. (*Life*, 2:125)

The aesthetic transformation of military spaces like cantonments into neighborhoods and the extension of English life into the outlying stations, or *mofussils,* is a fictional cartography that dissimulates a prior inscription: the transformation of rural India into Barrackpore (literally, "city of barracks").[41] In the novel's cartography, created by affect rather than military violence, the bungalow represents an attempt to script new domestic values within the empire. This dwelling evokes not only a kind of life removed from the public ostentation of Calcutta and the classical virtues symbolized in the city's architecture, but also a close connection with rural England. Here we have virtues associated with rustic and rural life reified through the language of the picturesque in which retirement and country cottages are dominant tropes of a shifting canon in taste.[42] The military now seems to provide the basis for this sort of life previously associated with the gentility in England. In India the cantonment bungalow represents something other than class mobility: a sort of moral code where the "up-country" life stands for something that is truly English in appearance but that, in its "military neatness and propriety," also signals its connection to a very specific form of colonial power. The cantonment is a form of power where domestic and private life intersect with military life; where the "sweetest" well-laid-out English garden blends seamlessly into the right angles of roads and the "parade ground in the rear."

In his exhaustive study of the bungalow as a global architectural form, Anthony King traces its migration from rural Bengal to European cities where they became forms associated with modern middle-class lifestyles. King shows how in the first phase of this cultural appropriation, in the early nineteenth century, the simple hut of a Bengali peasant was transformed to meet the requirements of colonial rulers. This Anglo-Indian bungalow, a product of the "cultural and social expectations of its new [English] inhabitants," first came into use against the background of the completion of military conquest of the subcontinent around 1818 (the setting for Monkland's *Life in India*). The bungalow was developed first as the rural and later as the suburban "model dwelling" for the "next political rulers of India." The impetus for the bungalow's development, King shows convincingly, came from the installation and dispersal throughout the subcontinent of two "proto-imperialist" state instruments: the army and the juridical administration. The "officer's bungalow," like that of the magistrate, collector, and commissioner in the districts, became the workplace as well as the residence of these representatives of the new form of colonial power. This power emanated not from Calcutta or the presidencies via the seasonal travel of officials to the interior (in "committees of circuit," for instance) but from a horizontally and spatially dispersed rule, in which the English representatives of law and order set up residences throughout the interior.[43]

In the novel's description of the Bentlys' bungalow in Barrackpore, cited above, the term *bungalow* is no longer in italics; it already represents an exclusively European cultural form. The lack of servants is not presented as a diminishment of the colonial lifestyle but as the enabler of a companionate marriage and the cultivation of affect and sentiment within the English family in India. The continuing association of the bungalow with a sort of settled English life is evident in literature written at the turn of the century. At this point in time, when the threat to the empire's permanence was more pronounced and publicly expressed, the bungalow came to represent the beleaguered empire itself. In Aliph Cheem's poem "The Deserted Bungalow" (1883), for instance, a colonel and his family living in a bungalow at the site of the English army's triumph over Tipu, Sultan of Mysore, find their domestic bliss cut short by cholera.[44] Disease acts as a kind of natural, unspecified revenge that India inflicts upon the British, who are otherwise militarily secure in their cantonment homes. Similarly, in Philip Randell's poem "A Tale of East and West," in a collection titled *Bungalow Ballads* (1910), the "eastern maiden" debauched by the English planter murders him and his new English bride as they sit on their porch.[45] Images of death and destruction dominate the poem's final stanza as the bungalow's "dark, deserted and decaying rooms" evoke the spectral vision of blood splattering across the breasts of the planter and his wife. Here native revenge personified as a murderous betrayed woman interrupts the calm of English everyday life in India.[46]

Unhomely Moments: Redrawing the Limits of Colonial Power

In the late nineteenth century, the tropes of settlement, security, and possession underwent a narrative reversal. These unhomely moments often register as fear and anxiety within colonial subjects as they reflect upon life in India. At such points, the temporality of a never-ending empire is interrupted by images of death and disease. The uncanny place of death within life in India short-circuits the illusion of permanence and introduces ambivalence within the subject's predilection toward mastery. These moments receive their historical fingerprints from the always-present possibility of real native insurgency and struggle against colonial rule. For this reason, a retroactive reading of these tropes in colonial literary texts reveals the historical imprint of a structure of feeling upon the colonizer even if there is no record of actual native struggles. These tropes serve as a colonial archive of sorts in which literary reinscriptions are signifying acts with historical agency.[47] The trope, in other words, is the historical event. The surfacing of fear and anxiety in the colonial text is especially relevant for a historical analysis of coercive regimes, for these structures of feeling signal a political unconscious within a regime; its illegitimacy is signified to the women and men who may otherwise be self-assured about their place and role within the order.[48]

In *Life in India*, the empire's illegitimacy is made visible when the proponents of settled life in the colony imagine their stay as transient and temporary because of the inevitability of human death. Mortality rates were always high for the English in India, driven by unfamiliar climate, precarious lifestyles, and first-time exposure to diseases. In the novel, this real possibility of death is experienced as failure. In the characters' moments of self-reflection, they understand life not as individual tracks they leave in the great field of transplanted civilization, but as a blundering itinerary in an unsettled, uncertain terrain where the characters, removed momentarily from the familiar trappings of their everyday, find their lives to be an alien experience:

> When they left the scene of rejoicing behind them, no breathing thing was to be seen in the streets, but natives stretched out under

> their white sheets, more like dead than the living, sleeping in their open verandahs in perfect security. The night was fine; the moon shone with a splendour only known in eastern climes, shedding a light around, which, but for the extreme stillness, might be mistaken for day. The number of white pillared buildings, ruined mosques and trees even in the centre of native Calcutta, give it a particularly beautiful appearance in a moonlight night when all offensive details are thrown into the shade. (*Life,* 1:253–54)

This is Calcutta at night for Flora Hume, who is watching from a balcony. The usual Manichean distinctions of dirt and darkness that permeate discussions of native India are canceled by the moonlight as it covers over, with its whiteness, the geographical separation of English and native Calcutta. India is beautiful as the natives lie asleep, their "offensive details . . . thrown into the shade." This is a moment not of unity in diversity but of systematic erasure through aestheticization. The natives of Calcutta are "more like dead" in their sleep. Their immobility allows the Englishwoman to enjoy Calcutta with a solitary gaze that appropriates that native space without interruption. But as Flora turns away, her gaze over the rooftops is drawn toward another space that provides a new contrast. Now it is torn between the "mighty city spread out in death-like repose" and the "the enclosure sacred to Europeans, where thickly crowded together, rearing their white tops in the moon-beams, her eye rested upon the monuments of those who slumber their long and their sound sleep in that magnificent and populous city of the silent" (*Life,* 1:255). At this point, the narrative enacts an unexpected reversal. Now the deathlike sleep of the natives is actually life, while the "long and sound sleep" of the English in their cemetery is death—uninterrupted, permanent sleep. Flora seeks to resolve her tumult by turning her thoughts to God, in whose timeline the cemeteries and the entombed English will live "countless ages and boundless infinity" and for whom time is "the same yesterday, today and forever" (*Life,* 1:255).

Michel de Certeau has called history a narrative of the past like the "cemeteries within cities" because historical narrative "exorcises and confesses a presence of death amidst the living."[49] In the above excerpt from *Life in India,* the image of the English cemetery in Calcutta forces Flora Hume to acknowledge the short-lived nature of home in India. However, as a woman intending to marry and settle in India she manages the tear in the ideological fabric of settlement by inserting English mortality into the infinity of a Christian afterlife. This theme is developed more fully later in the novel when Flora's husband, Captain Melville, dies of a fever in the jungle. Abandoned by their native servants, Flora is left alone to bury her husband in the unsupervised native space of the jungle, "far from European assistance" (*Life*, 3:164). The horrific image of the young, pregnant Englishwoman burying a corpse with her bare hands signals the isolation that surrounds the English when they are separated from their familiar spaces. This isolation is made starker by the focus on graves at the end of the novel. When Mrs. Melville, recovered from her ordeal, goes to visit the grave of Harriet Panton, one of the six women who had come out to settle in India, her ruminations render uncanny the various kinds of English homes circulating in the novel:

> "All is past and gone," was the thought which filled Mrs. Melville's mind, as she drew near the quiet spot, after every one had left it. "In this country, every thing changes with appalling rapidity; and leaves nothing behind to show what has been, but a newly covered grave. Such is life in India, and brilliant and beautiful as may often be its path, it ends here:" and tears fell fast on the dark and narrow house of one who had often thought the whole world too little for her own accommodation. (*Life*, 3:188)

"It ends here." The ironic contrast between the "dark and narrow house" Harriet occupies and her initial desire to come out and settle in the great expanse of English-occupied India disrupts the narrative closure expected in a novel of manners. There is no happy tally of wedded couples but instead the constant reminder of Harriet's marital betrayal, which continues to haunt her former companions. Resurfacing thoughts of death, betrayal, and dishonor at the end of the novel remind the reader of the narrative's moral imperative and the precarious balance on which these ideologemes rest.

In the novel, when women bear the burden of representing cultural superiority, they also participate in a patriarchal bargain. The Englishwoman's special status as national and cultural icon implies that all sexual transgressions take on allegorical proportions. The novel displays this rhetorical tendency in the case of the giddy-headed Harriet Panton. As the most impetuous and spoilt of the newly arrived Englishwomen in India, she sets herself up for disaster by marrying for money; her husband is the much older Mr. Marriot, a district magistrate. Their unhappy marriage subsequently threatens the very value system of English life as rumors spread about Harriet's infidelity. When she elopes with another Company soldier, the act has a domino effect on English power in India. Native servants at Marriot's court perceive their judge's humiliation and grief, and their gossip undermines the moral standing of English law. Then Harriet's distracted and guilt-ridden soldier-lover is ambushed in the jungle by bandits, and the Company's revenues, which are being shipped under his protection, are stolen. Dishonorable conduct by a woman, the novel's plot seems to say, undermines the military, legal, and moral superiority that is the basis of English cultural hegemony. In this way the novel displays an anxiety about a narrative bargain: if the figure of a woman as a moral compass serves as a prop for the discourse of cultural hegemony, any immoral or literal behavior could expose the trope operating as truth.

Finally, the novel uses the Englishwomen to erase the presence of other women. First, we have the displacement (and replacement) of the native woman by the Englishwoman through nomenclature. In one scene the novel describes Miss Percy's avoidance of that "languor" that oppresses "Old Indians" (*Life*, 1:133). In the use of the term *Indian* solely as a way to distinguish between the old and the newly arrived English in India, we see what Gayatri Spivak has called the "effacement of specificity and appropriation that one might call violation."[50] Native Indians are made into a nonindividuated mass displaced from its proper habitation. Mrs. Russell reveals a similar appropriation when she is referred to as "burrow beebee" [*sic*], or elder wife, a term usually reserved for the senior wife in a polygamous Muslim household like Major Palmer's (*Life*, 1:132). This poor joke only serves to remind readers about the native woman Mrs. Russell has successfully replaced and continues to keep at bay through her cultural role in the colony.

Though native women are rarely present in the novel except as unnamed servants or as the objects of discussions of gender oppressions inflicted by Hindu culture, the novel excavates a residual anxiety about native women through older figurations. Like Harriet and her lover, who die painful and violent deaths at the end of the novel, a young Muslim woman, Rezia, who as a nautch girl and female *thugee* (bandit) represents a sexual and civil threat to English life, suffers similar justice. As the only native female character in the novel, Rezia is a curious counterpoint to the usual nineteenth-century representations of Indian women as cultural victims. Rezia's death at the end of the novel in an orgy of native-on-native violence exonerates Englishmen and Englishwomen alike from having had a hand in her violent end. It is tempting to touch the political unconscious of this fictional resolution because Rezia is not a secluded Muslim woman to be saved by English social mission, but rather an uncontrollable predator who uses her sexuality to exact revenge when thwarted. But it is clear that the subplot of the native woman who poses a sexual and criminal challenge to English social life is not contrary to the more commonplace descriptions of native women within the novel as victims of social evils like suttee. Both representations deny the place of social agency: in one the woman is a criminal; in the other she is pure victim.

The narrative clearing of space, with India as a scene for domestic romance and manners, marks a new function for the literary representation of the colony. While anthropological and mercantilist writings about India played a crucial role in charting out territory, resources, and people to facilitate administration, novelistic representations of everyday life as self-making activity reterritorialized India into a place of potential settlement. Such fictional plots made it possible to imagine India as a place where the British could feel at home. Yet the imperatives toward reproduction and permanence could not always stave off the ambivalence that registered the Indian empire's own status as a "dominance without hegemony." The novel's political unconscious still signals—through the figurations of native women, infidelity, death, disease, and frontier wars—various impediments to British life in India.

In the next chapter, I flesh out as a historical subject a native woman whose presence in the archival records goes against the grain of the very official discourse that attempted to manage her in the eighteenth century. By going back to a case that existed before the writing of native women for the social mission of imperialism in the nineteenth century, already evident in *Life in India,* I clear a subjective space for some of the women who stare out at us from the family portraits discussed early in this chapter. How does the space of seclusion, in this case that of an elite woman, enter the public politico-economic maneuvers of colonialism?

CHAPTER FOUR

The Rani of Burdwan as Historical Subject

One of the challenges of reading the colonial archive has been the task of identifying topographical changes on its textual surface. It is generally agreed that neither colonialism nor empire are monolithic discourses or formations, but there is little agreement about what is put in place when one dispenses with this supposed solidity. Reading for contradictions or contrapuntal movements breaks up the homogeneity of much of what goes under the name "colonial discourse"; however, such critical moves often stop short of positing the causes or consequences of such dismantlings and displacements.[1] We know that something has happened but not why it has happened. Departing from Michel Foucault's notion of chance shifts in epistemic systems, in this chapter I read the textual surface of the archive to ask why it is rippled in a particular way and why certain tracks lead nowhere while others seem to lead endlessly into other domains. When we read the records of colonial governance, it is clear that not all shifts in the archive are abrupt, inexplicable, or arbitrary. More often than not, we see concerted efforts of many to construct Bengal or India as a manageable and governable object.[2] We also see discourses covering over radical ruptures, which, though enacted militarily (as in the conquest of Bengal), need the ideological backing of theoretical fictions such as "oriental despotism." When these great systemic shifts are under way, we also see the emergence of subject positions that can temporarily allow reversals of power and resistance till the colonial power structures have installed their own legitimizing discourses.

In order to read this cross-relay between the archive and historical reality, I take seriously what has already become the theoretical basis for much of subaltern studies work today—the notion that changes in signification or discursive displacements are intimately connected to historical ruptures and crises, that they are signs of new forces that have gained entry. These forces are especially visible in the records of colonial governance because the various texts are interlinked by their efforts to manage a series of crises involving a reality that is both foreign and difficult to assimilate. Through a reading of the East India Company's records from the late eighteenth century, I catch the nascent empire at a critical moment. The Indian empire was at a point when its later self-assurance was not yet visible, and a series of dispersals and convergences in the textual evidence tells us that the maps of knowledge that had brought the Europeans to what they were about to rule were no longer adequate. New discourses and objects had to be found and new domains identified. Such a historical juncture, it seems to me, holds important lessons for us today.

Several years ago, while speaking at the Center for National Policy in Washington, D.C., a month before the fourth World Conference on Women in Beijing, Madeleine Albright, then permanent representative to the United Nations, listed for her breakfast audience the U.S. delegation's proposed goals for the conference. She ended the wish list with a reminder that "traditional and authoritarian societies" had a long way to go toward becoming societies that were inclusive of women. While preparing for the conference, she was reminded, she said, of an "old Chinese poem" in which a father addresses his young daughter with these words:

> We keep a dog to watch the house
> A pig is useful too;
> We keep a cat to catch a mouse;
> But what can we do
> With a girl like you?[3]

The use of this cultural text as historical evidence suggests that there are two Chinas for Albright and Washington. There is the China that exists as a deviation from a desired norm (capitalist modernity) and that is still conjurable today through an anonymous "old Chinese poem," and there is another China that one deals with on the ground as a business partner. Popular culture and the media warn the public about the China that is catching up, while official discourse exhorts another China to catch up. In this shifting field, women's rights as human rights can become a rhetorical strategy in "Eurocentric strategies of narrativizing history," in which the industrialized West congratulates itself for showing the way without acknowledging any achievements in older social formations.[4] This does not mean we should support older modes of production uncritically, but it does mean that we should be in a position to analyze how certain universalist terms may disguise the specificity of what is actually emerging conceptually in other spaces entering globalization.

Women's history has deconstructive potential when we read the cultures of globalization, especially at a time when women deploy for women new forms of transnationalist thinking and action. Further, we may learn much by revisiting textual sources from the time that first gave such global projects their legitimacy and power—the second half of the eighteenth century, when the great Enlightenment histories were setting up the world into three- and four-step programs, such as Montesquieu's despotism-monarchy-democracy program in *The Spirit of the Laws* (1748) and John Millar's savage-pastoral-agriculture-manufacturing program in *Observations concerning the Distinction of Ranks in Society* (1771, later titled *Origin of the Distinction of Ranks*). This great swath of historiography effectively staged the woman as a measure of a civilization's advancement but excluded her from its modern political configurations. Thus, in my reading of the records of the East India Company and the British parliamentary papers, I pick up the trail of a female subject as she was caught up in a massive Enlightenment experiment in the 1770s. At this time the Company, having just defeated Bengal's local rulers and having acquired the right to Bengal's revenues, was confronted with a choice: should the acquired territory be remade in a normative metropolitan agrarian capitalist image or should it be shuttled back into feudalism, a system already under attack back home by bourgeois radicalism?

The resolution of that dilemma at that historical moment provides a classic case of what Gayatri Spivak has called the "improper imposition of an Enlightenment episteme."[5] The case also demonstrates that the unevenness of European implementation on the ground produces "woman" in the colonial encounter as a complex site of many negotiations. She is never a unilinear movement toward a European norm but is a result of many different configurations and linkages that weave together a subject from various strands of the economic, the political, the sexual, the linguistic, the religious, and so on. As a historical subject, she can be put together today only by a meticulous diagonal reading; a reading that moves both across the body of discourses and up or down the temporal axis. In an attempt to undo Enlightenment historiography's foreclosure of the woman as native and Other, I have deliberately picked as the historical agent in my discussion that story's most pathetic case—the so-called confined or secluded woman of despotic societies.

I pick up the story in the official record when this gendered subject writes to the Company's representatives in Bengal in an attempt to draw attention to her situation and follow the paper trail for almost a quarter-century, till it stops a few years before her death in 1799. The trail of this woman leads us over uncertain and unexpected archival terrain—from Bengal to London, from the zenana to the British Parliament, and from Montesquieu to Marx and Mill. This movement establishes several timelines rather than a single strict chronological order of events. In her archival journey, this female subject also becomes part and parcel of some of the debates that had significant impact upon the politico-economic structure of colonial rule in late-eighteenth-century India. I discuss two occasions that especially pertain to our discussion of the gendered subject: first, the debate over the introduction of English law into Bengal in the 1770s, which uses the figure of the secluded woman as a signifier of despotic laws, and second, John Shore's minute of 1789 that puts the final touches on the proposal for the notorious Permanent Settlement of Bengal, whereby the landscape of Bengal was transformed into a venue of English feudalism.

A Face-Off in the Archive

On 30 December 1774, a petition from the rani of Burdwan arrived at Fort William in Calcutta where the governor-general of India, Warren Hastings, sat in council with four other members: General Clavering, Philip Francis, Colonel Monson, and Richard Barwell. In the petition, the rani informs the gentlemen that she, Bishnukumari, the widow of a recently deceased zamindar of Burdwan, Tilakchandra, and mother of his eight-year-old son and heir, Tejchandra, has suffered "oppression," "treachery," and "injustice" at the hands of the Company-appointed *dewan* (minister) Bridjoo Kishore and John Graham, the chief revenue collector. (The official report in which this and other documents I will be discussing appear will be cited parenthetically as *ER*.)[6] The rani reports her efforts to resist what she perceives to be illegal attempts by outsiders to gain control of her family's traditional privileges. The rani, we deduce from the letter, apparently refused to hand over the zamindari seals—seals bearing her son's name—which were customarily used to authenticate all notices and orders originating from the house. Because she kept them with her in the inner apartments, or zenana, out of reach of the *dewan* and the resident, she was subjected to more punitive measures by the men:

> *Bridjoo Kishore* (the Dewan) used every manner of persecution to get the Seal from me, I did not however yield it up. At last in the year 1797 [*sic*], *Bridjoo Kishore* having brought *Mr. John Graham*

> from *Calcutta* to *Burdwan*, took my son, who was from eight to ten years of age, and got him confined under a guard of Sepoys; and having prevented me from eating for seven or eight days, till I was on the point of death, I found myself without remedy, and gave the Seal into his possession. *Bridjoo Kishore* having thus got the Seal, granted away land . . . and took some lands likewise to himself. . . . All the measures adopted by him are intentionally to ruin me; besides this, he affixes the Seal to Papers, with the nature of which I am unacquainted, according to his pleasure. It never before this happened, that a servant, having got the management of his master's business, engrossed the lands which yield a Revenue. (*ER*, 741)

With this petition to the Company's council, the young widow began her twenty-five-year campaign to keep control of her family's zamindari. (Here I avoid using the word *estate* because of a significant distinction. *Zamindar* translates as "landholder," and the zamindar differs from the feudal landlords in that this person did not own the land but was a revenue collector who paid taxes directly to the state. The zamindar's position could be made hereditary but could also be terminated if public responsibilities to the zamindari's inhabitants were not upheld.)[7] In the 1770s, when the Company had gained ascendancy in Bengal and achieved the right to all its revenues, women managed three of the largest zamindaris. This was not unusual for a number of reasons. A system of patrimonial inheritance and various religious and social rituals required surviving sons, and territorial consolidations through matrimonial alliances encouraged polygamous marriages. The combination of the two often left young widows outliving their husbands for decades and ruling over the landholdings in their sons' names or even getting *sunnuds* (leases) from the state to run them on their own. The Mughal state's priorities were to ensure peaceful governance and the maintenance of its vast civil infrastructure rather than to institute military conscription. Thus, without the requirements of primogeniture or male management at that level, one could say that the state was relatively indifferent to gender when it came to zamindaris.

It is tempting to read the rani as someone who is simply trying to maintain the status quo when a foreign power has appeared in her backyard. But the trail of effects rippling through the records as a result of her petition shows that her presence in the initial records of the Company archive and later in the parliamentary select committee reports is not merely a result of bureaucratic meticulousness. The rani's entanglement with the Company had important consequences. It became the subject of more than one parliamentary investigation and a major catalyst for the dispute between Warren Hastings and the council majority led by Philip Francis, who later became the key instigator of the impeachment hearings against Hastings.[8] It is not unwarranted to surmise that Rani Bishnukumari was one of many unnamed parties in one of the substantial charges against Warren Hastings in the parliamentary trial of 1788—the charge of accepting private presents and bribes. I will spell out in some detail soon how the rani drew Hastings into this quandary, but first, to get our discussion under way, let us look at the zamindari seals that Bridjoo Kishore and Mr. Graham took away from the rani by force.

The seal was an important tool of proxy that did not require the authenticating presence of the person it portrayed. It could be given and held in the name of a child, used by a woman, and even appropriated by a servant or foreigner. Yet its symbolic power is undeniable; the seal not only allowed the zamindar to issue instructions from within the house to various parts of the province, but also prevented the issuance of spurious documents in the zamindar's name. The seal was also a mediating tool in the transfer of power. In the transitional period, the revenue structures of the old Mughal imperial order that the British army had defeated were phantasmally kept in place without being fully replaced. Thus, capital accumulation could go on uninterrupted, as instructions still seemed to issue from a place that connoted the locus of power for the peasantry. The elite zamindari class to which the rani herself belonged was thus not only a collaborating class in alliance with the alien power but also the class that mediated between English capital and native labor, temporarily bridging the radical rupture effected by the transfer of power. The rani was therefore still important for the Company and could not be summarily dismissed, ignored, or mistreated. She was a valuable proxy for the English, who had to rule over a population that was separated from them by language, culture, and religion and that already possessed a complex system of land tenure, revenue, allocation, and distribution that the English did not fully understand and could not change in one swift move.

Now let us look at the response to the rani's petition. The council's minutes, which were later recorded in the Revenue Consultations of Fort William and sent to London, show a very detailed sequence of events.[9] When the petition was read out before the full council, Hastings and his supporter Richard Barwell clearly showed signs of not wanting to pursue it any further. They protested vehemently against the majority's decision to grant the rani's request to be released from the forced confinement within her home and removed to Calcutta, where, closer to the council, she could feel safe from possible harm. Barwell objected, arguing that reversing the orders of "past governments" would give natives the impression that British law could be repealed at any time and would thus endanger British authority in the countryside. Meanwhile, Hastings, referring to the rani as "a violent woman," suspected her motives. He insisted that her charges against the *dewan* and the British resident, if investigated, would "only serve to disturb the peace and quiet of the settlement" and "excite factions among the Banyans and dependants of every person of power or supposed influence" (*ER*, 734). Hastings's second objection is especially significant because it shows the Company's active involvement in keeping the zamindari class as props and proxies:

> I object to her bringing her son with her, because, by a solemn and repeated Act of Government, the charge of her son has been taken from her, and committed to proper guardians, both for the benefit of his education, and to destroy the influence which she possessed with his person. This Act cannot be regularly repealed, but by an express Act of the Administration passed for that purpose; and any resolution taken in breach of it must be publicly considered as an indignity offered to the last Government. (*ER*, 734)

What Hastings is referring to here is the stopgap measure adopted by his administration for cases in which the incumbents of a zamindari were "minors, idiots or females." As considerations of revenue were paramount for the Company in the first two decades of rule in Bengal, the Board of Revenue required certification that proprietors were "capable" of management.[10] But because the Bengal agricultural landscape was being made over in the image of English feudalism with its preservation of private property through male inheritance and primogeniture, the Company was not averse to tinkering with the relative indifference to gender the Mughal state had shown in its award of zamindari leases. Under Hastings, the Company began to intervene in zamindari child rearing. When widows were left with young sons, the sons came under Company stewardship till ready to assume control. At a time when the countryside was dotted with young widows, many with minor sons, the Board of Revenue moved in as substitute householder to appoint tutors and to remove sons from their mothers' influence.[11] In this instance, the rani got her way as the council's majority decided to ignore Hastings's and Barwell's warning and allowed her to proceed to Calcutta with her son.

Meanwhile, after receiving copies of the rani's petition, the council gave the two accused, Bridjoo Kishore and John Graham, the opportunity to reply to the various charges, which included those of manhandling the rani, embezzling from the zamindari treasury, and bribing Company officials. Their replies arrived two days later. Kishore's is short and terse and alleges that the rani is a woman "totally unacquainted with the nature of Accounts, or even of common writing," and is therefore capable of fabricating the charges (*ER*, 742). Graham's response, on the other hand, indicates his years of experience as a Company bureaucrat schooled in the art of correspondence.

Graham's letter is divided into two sections and resembles in format Samuel Richardson's representation of Pamela's response to her harasser Mr. B's prenuptial contract in the novel *Pamela.*[12] Indeed, it seems to me that Richardson's epistolary novel may be of some use to us here as a discursive precursor of sorts. In *Pamela,* we have a graphic representation of the ledger cum contract staged as the transformation of an economic relation into a gendered one, and, by implication, of the social contract into a sexual contract. Mr. B's demands are placed side by side with Pamela's responses, thereby semiotically transforming the nonprivileged representation of sexual relations, where a servant girl has had to steadfastly resist the advances of her employer, into an instrument of power that gives voice to the previously subjugated subject.[13] Below I have provided paragraphs 1 and 7 from Graham's letter as it is reproduced in the Parliamentary record of 1803.[14]

Ranny's Petition

1st. In the Bengal year 1174 Maha Rajah *Tillok Chund* died, and left an infant son, Maha Rajah *Tage Chund,* his heir and successor, appointing *Lalla Omichund* guardian to his son, and sole administrator of his affairs.

Mr. *Graham's* Answer

1st. The Petition, in the beginning of it, asserts the most premeditated falsehood, and bears the complete stamp of human malice. From the death of Rajah *Tillook Chund* all the grievances complained of are said to have commenced: to have told the truth therefore, as to the period of that event, would have been to have invalidated every circumstance that is made to depend upon it, as far as they are applicable to my conduct . . .

Rajah *Tillook Chund* did not die in the *Bengal year* 1174, but in the *Bengal year* 1177, in the

Bengal month of Jeyt, answering (English style) to the month of May 1770.

Vide *Mr. Graham's* Correspondence with the Collector General, 1765 to 1770, inclusive.

Collector General's Reports to the Board.

Mr. *Verelst's*, 1765

Mr. *Russell's*, 1767

Mr. *Becher's*, 1768

Mr. *Alexander's*, 1769

Court of Directors General Letters in 1766, 1767

Lord Clive's Letters. 1766 or beginning of 1767, on leaving the Government.

7th. . . . The necessity of the occasion, as it compels me, so must it apologize for my becoming my own eulogist. And now that I have followed the writer of this petition through the wanderings of falshood [*sic*], I must crave your pardon for trespassing on your time with a few words more.

During the whole of my administration in the Residentships of *Midnapore* and *Burdwan*, the sole and undeviating principles of my conduct were the interests of the Company; the ease, welfare and protection of the country and its inhabitants. The testimonies I could obtain of this, would my time allow me to collect them, are numerous; let the Records of the Company be referred to; let the Records of the *Midnapore* and *Burdwan* Cutcherries be consulted; nay, let the *vox populi* of these two provinces be obtained.

Here in the official records, a kind of self-production is also under way that reverses momentarily the relations of power between the two letter writers. Graham had initially resisted the board's attempts to make him respond to the rani's charges. In a memo that preceded this letter, he had protested the ignominy of having to respond to a person of "such notorious character as the Ranny" and declined to give an answer, saying that he would not do it without being on the "grounds of equality."[15] By pointing out that the rani and her *vackeel* (lawyer) were not British subjects and were thus exempt from the jurisdiction and law of British Acts of Parliament, Graham in effect suggested that they should never meet on the same page.

But they do—because Graham, as we see here, ultimately did reply to the petition. There is some indication in the records about why he underwent this change of heart. Graham was on his way back to London after fifteen years of service in India and expecting to reap, as most former civil servants did, the benefits of this long tenure with a permanent job at the Company headquarters. Aware that the council's minutes were sent to London every week, Graham panicked. His departure was not for another two weeks, and the dispatches (with the rani's petition as an enclosure) could conceivably arrive before him and have his reputation in shambles before his own ship docked. To minimize this lag between accusation and defense, Graham asked that the copies of his letters and his answer to the rani's petition be forwarded in the next packet to the Company headquarters (*ER*, 739).

Though Graham did not recognize a member of the colonized native elite as a signatory to his own social contract, the graphic representation of his response to the rani's petition did enact a momentary reversal of the usual relations between colonizer and colonized. Graham singled out the paragraphs in the rani's petition that mentioned his name or alluded to him in some way and copied them out in his letter to represent a sort of face-off with the rani, whom he had never seen. But Graham was forced to assume the place of the defendant as he counteracted the rani's accusations with his own responses, and he inserted them side by side. To be on the right side of the page was clearly to be at a disadvantage; it put him in the position of having to prove his innocence even before the rani had furnished proof of her charges against him. There is an inescapable irony in Graham's words when he describes his own letter as an exercise in following "the wanderings of falshood" (*ER*, 740). A bureaucrat who reproduced the power of the Company through his official acts of inscription and signature was now no longer the self-possessed subject. His text, as it followed the rani's charges, unraveled the power of his previous subject position.

The rani's appearance on the left side of the page as the initiator of the complaint was also the textual production of a new subject position. By appealing to the council as a previous beneficiary of its decisions (the confirmation of her son's succession to the zamindari, for instance), the rani came before British law without being a British subject. Her appeal depended for its force on the accusation that her two tormentors had also disobeyed the will of the Company. As the space within which the confrontation occurred, the archive became both the guarantor of truth and the place of its production. The rani's words accusing Graham (on the left-hand side) are, at the end of the letter, replaced by Graham's references to archived material that he believed would provide testimony of his conduct over the years. Graham also summoned the archive to establish the rani's lie when he accused her of committing "premeditated" falsehood by lying about the date of her husband's death. "Rajah Tilook Chund," he declared to the council, "did not die in the Bengal Year 1174 but in the Bengal Year 1177" (*ER*, 741).

This counteraccusation by Graham illuminates a difference that can be obscured by the momentary equality enacted by the face-off on the page. What is declared to be a lie was actually a mistake in translation. Three weeks later, when the rani responded to Graham's countercharges, the first point in her letter was this: that in translating the Bengali year into the Christian calendar, her translator had made a mistake. The real date could be verified, she said, by consultation of the Persian copy that accompanied the English translation. The Company's official translation of the rani's petition, by Alexander Elliot, is included in the records and indeed states that the Bengal year of the rajah's death is 1176 rather than the 1174 of the first translation (or 1177 as alleged by Graham) (*ER*, 741). The rani explained the discrepancy of a year as resulting from the zamindari custom of not declaring a year completed till the annual adjustment of revenues was finished (*ER*, 743). The rajah apparently died before this was done and so was regarded as having died in the previous financial year (1177).[16] In the margins of the text, we now notice the act of translation; it shows the precarious nature of the native's speech and writing and the risks of being misunderstood. The rani, however, did not miss a chance to take a swipe at her former tormentor, even as she acknowledged the mistake: "Mr. Graham's pardon upon this occasion I need not ask," she wrote. "He has more than sufficiently made himself amends by the unjust and ungenerous conclusions he has drawn from it" (*ER*, 743).

The verbal assault aside, the rani's most important calculation was the timing of her application to the Company's council in 1774. This act on the rani's part has a timeline that goes back a few years. After Warren Hastings's appointment as governor-general in 1773, unexpected transfers and deaths depleted the council and left Richard Barwell as sole surviving councillor. When Monson, Clavering, and Francis, two soldiers and an ex–war office clerk, arrived in Calcutta in October 1774, the manner and tempo of decision making changed drastically. The newly appointed councillors, who were opposed in principle to Hastings's recently completed military campaigns and what they perceived to be his corrupt administration, blocked many of his initiatives in council meetings.[17] Bitter quarrels soon broke out between the newcomers and Hastings, who was now in the minority with

Barwell. It was in this climate that the rani's petition arrived, barely two months after the council's reconstitution in December 1774. References in the records to earlier meetings indicate that she had failed on two previous occasions to persuade the council to act against the *dewan* and Mr. Graham, both of whom were, incidentally, Hastings's appointees.[18] The resubmission of the petition for the third time in two years seems a deliberate attempt to test the waters with the new council.

The persistent rani's most important maneuver was yet to come, and it was one that would shift in a decisive way her standing with the Company. On getting Bridjoo Kishore's and Graham's responses to her charges, the rani, now probably aware that divisions in the council could be worked to her advantage, was no longer satisfied with a partial victory whereby she effected Bridjoo Kishore's dismissal and was reunited with her son. A whole month passed before the rani finally furnished the proof demanded by the Company. In March 1775, a letter arrived at the council with copies of accounts showing "embezzlements" by John Graham and Bridjoo Kishore. Also enclosed in the letter was another item, one that had not been specifically requested. It is described in the Revenue Consultations as "Enclosure No. 4" and is titled "Account of Monies paid to Cantoo Baboo, the Banyan [accountant] of Governor Hastings" (*ER*, 745). In the accompanying letter, the rani's tone shows considerable change. There is little trace of the subject positions activated in the first petition—those of the helpless widow without protection, the mother deprived of her only child, or the secluded woman of rank whose virtue and honor are threatened by strange men. Instead, we see signs of an emerging strategy to regain full control over the management of the zamindari without the direct supervision of appointed *dewans* or Company officials.

In the letter accompanying the enclosures, the rani appeals to the council as a potential manager whose competence can right the damage done to the Company's revenues by the two corrupt officials. For a woman whose petitions had shown a rather excessive use of formal address, this letter makes its point without much ado: "The Revenue of the Company has suffered much by these alienations; I therefore beg I may be empowered to resume these lands."[19] Her next letter, which arrived a day later, as though she sensed that an uproar would be created by Enclosure No. 4, attempts to minimize her action with these words: "In surrendering the Papers which mention the name of the Governor General, I beg I may be understood to do it in compliance with my duty and a regard to my own safety, I must condemn or be condemned; no alternative is left me" (*ER*, 751). The rani clearly alternated between calculated acts of subterfuge and declarations of submission even as she tried to temper the charge of corruption against the highest-ranking representative of British power in India. The letter ends with this assurance of loyalty: "Whatever favour and indulgence shall be shewn to me and my family will, I flatter myself, be fully repaid to the Company in their Revenues; being well assured that the antiquity of my house will always operate to the Company's advantage, by the influence it will have in establishing that authority over the Ryots [peasants] necessary in the collections, and in securing that obedience which will be chearfully [*sic*] yielded to a family who has so many years presided over them" (*ER*, 751).

This is where I will leave the rani for now—in the subject slot she carved out for herself as a member of the collaborating elite. In exchange for keeping her traditional class and caste privileges, the rani put her family's economic position and familiarity with the peasants to use in harnessing their labor for the Company's revenues for years to come. We will catch up with the rani very briefly at the end of this chapter, when she reasserts her presence after a brief lull. Her attempts to regain control over the zamindari after the Company later made her son the primary manager show that she could not be eased into retirement. The rani curiously escaped a fate that awaited others of her kind: when the Company converted these zamindars into landlords and installed private property in land by 1793 with the Act of Permanent Settlement, female zamindars were removed from the official plans for nineteenth-century Bengal. Why did this happen? The last section of this chapter will address this historical paradox, but as a preamble to that discussion, I look first at the production of the theoretical fiction that facilitated the removal—oriental despotism.

Montesquieu as Discursive Precursor

Let us begin with a hypothesis. When revenue maximization in a large and thriving district like Burdwan meets the Company's objectives, the Company is relatively indifferent to gender as a criterion for selecting zamindars. But as colonial rule fails to maximize revenue according to various physiocratic or free-tradist principles because it meets with resistance in native structures, we soon see the deployment of culturalist arguments about the natives' essential difference. This in turn justifies proposals for far-reaching changes in existing social relations. In the records of governance that are the official archive of colonial rule, this deployment of culturalist arguments is signaled by the explicit entry of secondary material into the rulers' deliberations. Ranajit Guha has made distinctions between various types of colonial writing on the basis of their appearance in time and their filiation. For Guha, primary discourse is marked by its identification with an official point of view, its close proximity in space and time to the events it describes, and its purpose: to urge or direct action of some sort. Secondary discourse, on the other hand, draws on primary or official discourse, is a more processed product, and is often written by former officials well after the occurrence of the events described.[20]

Harry Verelst's monograph *A View of the Rise, Progress, and Present State of the English Government in Bengal,* written in 1772, is a good example from this secondary archive. Verelst, who was governor of Bengal from 1768 to 1771, before Warren Hastings's term, preempted his successor's policy of keeping the British Parliament at bay in Bengal. Like Hastings, he had wanted severe limits on the application of British law in the territories that were administered by the Company. Chapter 5 of Verelst's book is thus unambiguously titled "The Impossibility of Introducing English Laws into Bengal with Some Observations on Native Customs." Because Verelst had read Montesquieu and assimilated his work into his own thinking, law for him was a reflection of the "spirit" of the people. He believed that transplanting British law to the Indies would never work: "As well might we transplant the full-grown oak to the banks of the Ganges, as dream that any part of a code matured by the patient labours of successive judges and legislatures in this island can possibly coalesce with the customs of Bengal."[21]

It is when Verelst investigates what he calls "the domestic relations of private life" to provide instances of the natives' immoral customs that the woman emerges as an important figure in the discussion of law. The biggest obstacles to British law, Verelst argues, are polygamy and the seclusion of women. He sprinkles his text generously with quotes from Montesquieu about the rapid maturing of girls in hot climates, the need to confine them, and the natural facilitation of polygamy. British law, on the other hand, is "formed in a temperate climate, where the charms of women are better preserved, . . . and their reason accompanies their beauty, and all have adopted the natural equality between the sexes."[22] Then, in order to clinch his argument about the total incompatibility of British law with Indian spirit, the secluded woman, or "confined woman" as he calls her, is brought on the scene:

> Shall our writs of liberty unlock these sacred recesses? Shall no reverence be thought due to the honour of a husband? Or shall we disregard the condition of a wife, incapable of governing herself? Shall our courts of justice become the authors of outrage, which the bloody ruffian would fear to commit? Thus, in despite of nature,

> shall we dissolve the ties of domestic life without substituting any government in their place and force the servant, the child and the wife, to renounce their dependence, unable to afford them protection?[23]

Verelst defends the seclusion of women as a necessary precondition for maintaining not only the patriarchal honor of Indian men but also the very forms of civil society (albeit inferior) existing in India. Yet on the other hand, with the typical self-contradiction that characterizes Orientalist discourse, Verelst goes on to assert that under British law and standards almost all sexual intercourse in India is rape:

> Women in the East are transformed with little ceremony and whether they be wives or concubines, their men seldom await their consent. Were our laws of rape and rules of evidence enforced, one half of the males would incur the penalty of death. I mean not to justify their practice, but beg leave to suggest that the sword of justice when too deeply stained with blood may prove but an indifferent corrector of the morals of a nation.[24]

Whereas Verelst first brings the native woman to the fore in his discussion to cast her as the impossible subject of British law (she can never govern herself), in the above excerpt it is the native male who is the impossible subject of the same. As rapist and raped, they are locked in an embrace that is impervious to the liberties of English jurisprudence. In the next chapter we will see how this discourse of cultural difference is transformed by the social mission of imperialism after 1813, when the woman becomes the privileged object of legal, educational, and religious transformation.

My point, however, is not to turn Verelst against himself; rather, it is to demonstrate that even as the rani's petition reached Company headquarters in 1774 and became part of the primary discourse, Company officials in retirement were already creating an archive of secondary discourse. Here the rani could never have access to the subject positions that were available to her in Graham's letter or through the various epistolary engagements with the Board of Revenue and council. On the ground, where revenue maximization was the Company's first priority, it was not Montesquieu but other issues and debates that produced the elite, secluded woman as a subject of history. Yet, in a few years, as British rule initiated its stranglehold on both the elite class and the peasantry and as revenue extraction reached supralevels to pay for colonialist wars elsewhere on the subcontinent, zamindars themselves became obstacles to capital accumulation. They were no longer treated as elites but were regularly placed under guard and confined every time they failed to meet projected revenue amounts. (Later records show that after coming of age the rani's son was put in jail three times by the Company for failing to meet annual revenues.)[25] When this happened, it was Montesquieu who provided the discursive crossover so the theoretical fiction of the secluded woman in despotic societies could replace the real historical subject—the rani of Burdwan. Let us now trace the rani's effacement in the archive as the fate of a generalized category of female zamindars rather than as an individual case.

The arrival of Montesquieu into the monograph of a highly placed former Company employee like Verelst is not to be taken lightly. It shows how new objects were being formed and new domains demarcated in the colonial archive. My reading of this transformation of the archive's surface as a discursive displacement from the secondary to the primary discourse indicates that new deployments and strategies are at work. At one level, when Montesquieu appears over and over as a citation in various testimonies in the records, it indicates the expansion and dispersal of political notions originally derived from Europe's specific encounter with the Ottoman state in the Balkans. Though the Ottoman Empire had been an intimate enemy of Europe since the fifteenth century, its power had passed by 1748, when Montesquieu's *Esprit des lois* was first published. His was the first full-scale comparative theory of despotism, or what Perry Anderson has described as "a general extra-European form of government whose structure was opposed to the principles born of European 'feudalism.'" With colonial exploration and expansion, Persia, India, and then China began to manifest the traits associated with this form of government, and the Enlightenment made sure that "despotism was thus expressly attributed to Asia in the *fons et origo* of all political philosophy in Europe."[26] Some critical theorists have tended to read Montesquieu only for Europe, where he becomes either an expression of the new aristocratic opposition to an increasingly absolutist and alienated monarchy in prerevolutionary France or a revolutionary in historical methods.[27] They miss Montesquieu's role in producing an imaginary map for comparative politics that had great explanatory power as European colonialism spread in Asia.

"Let us therefore leave the Turks and Chinese in peace," writes Louis Althusser, "and focus on the positive image for which this danger is the bugbear. . . . It is absolute monarchy that is Montesquieu's target."[28] But such a reading, that the East is only a "pre-text" for Europe, cannot conceal the obvious: that the discursive displacement Montesquieu effects in his discussion is not accidental but is a sign of other forces. A discussion of Turkey added to the discussion of Europe is establishing the lack within the center. With the demise of the Ottoman Empire, the theme of the historical superiority of Europe started to become central to discussions of the Turkish system.[29] To make the analogy obvious, we can say that the expansion of the conceptual field of despotism into discussions of Bengal suggests that the occasion is yet another shift in signifying systems—here, the replacement of the Mughal Empire with the British. Now the defeated formation too can be drawn into the circle of despotism that stands for the "radical *contrast* between European history . . . and the destiny of other continents."[30]

My intention here is to read Montesquieu as a discursive precursor rather than as a "transparent or motivated repository of 'ideas.'"[31] When Montesquieu arrived on the scene in Bengal, secondary discourse began to remap the terrain; it read the absence of private property in zamindaris and the hierarchical line of liegeships to the Mughal emperor as signs that there was no law as such, only despotism. But the relationship between European discursive production and the axiomatics of imperialism had also changed. Whereas Montesquieu could summon the existing Turkish political system as the limit of politics as such, the Mughal state was an already-defeated formation that did not really exist. The latter was no longer the limit but had to be recast in a new role, in an act that mirrored the movement from dominance to hegemony. The vast British experiment in Bengal—which included the transformation of landholder into landlord, tenure rights into private property, subsistence and sharecropping into revenue farming, and various lines of inheritance into primogeniture—made itself appear as the only way. Thus, primary or official discourse stages what Spivak has termed the "unacknowledged moment" of the "native informant," who is needed by the great texts to account for the other (the native) but is also foreclosed.[32] This is one way to think of proxy, whether of class subjects or gendered subjects. We have already seen how the zamindari class was made into an active collaborator for the new experiments. The woman, on the other hand, while an active collaborator as class agent, also met her limit as the gendered subject because of the imbrication of sexuality with the growing influence of the notion of oriental despotism.

Because law for Montesquieu ultimately emerged from the spirit of the people, and spirit was manifested *through* "manners" and *in* the private sphere, women became central to his discussion of despotism. The ruler's alienation from the people and his resulting despotic traits found an apt metaphor in the harem, a site of European fantasies about depravity and sexual tyranny. The realm of sexuality also provided for Montesquieu the primal pool in which to discover the "intrinsic spirit" of non-European Others and the bases of their political formations: "At all times have we seen in Asia domestic slavery and despotic government walk hand in hand with an equal pace."[33] The woman is paradoxically both the object of and the very figuration of despotic power. The oriental despot's sloth, decadence, and luxury are often symbolized as effeminacy, even as his imprisonment, or confinement, of women is a sure sign of his capacity for patriarchal tyranny in all aspects of life. Thus, in Montesquieu's work the seraglio represents the lawlessness of the Eastern polity and Ottoman Turkey both metaphorically and metonymically. The seraglio's inhabitants, the secluded women, signify negatively the absolute power of their ruler and confirm the abject condition of the powerless subjects under despotism. While the Montesquieu of the West fathered the doctrine of separation of powers and the notion that religion and morality have no right to judge history, for those outside the purview of Western monarchy or the republic, religion and morality were not simply elements within, but the very basis of, their societies. In these places passions ran politics. The question remains: How did this theoretical fiction of the abject, depraved, secluded woman, who metonymically represents all subjects of despotism, move into the primary discourse of colonial rule? Let us catch the discussion on the other side of the world as the rani's charges against Warren Hastings reach the Company's board and a Parliament already jittery about the negative press regarding the colonial wars in North America and English despotism and corruption in the East.[34]

The Rani as Legal Signifier

In 1774, as the rani was warming up for her confrontation with the Company, an act of Parliament established a supreme court of judicature at Fort William in Bengal. Governor-General Warren Hastings's tendency to ignore rules and guidelines for subjecting natives to English law had created a growing tension between the court and the governor, who saw the court's functions as interfering in the task of collecting the revenues of Bengal. There was also more at stake. The supreme court was the single organ that maintained the illusion that the Company was actually subject to the English king and Parliament. It was also a way to ensure, through the uniform prevalence of British law, that there would be no secessionist actions such as those that were already emerging in North America. Given this symbolic power, every act of ignoring the court's instructions was perceived as an affront to the king and Parliament. This explains the strong language with which Mr. Justice

Lemaistre addressed the Burdwan Provincial Council of Revenue president, Mr. Higginson, after reports were made about the rani's forced confinement by officers of the Company:

> A complaint has been made to me against you on behalf of the Ranee of Burdwan, which appears to me of a very serious nature. I apprehend that the late Act of Parliament had particularly in view to protect the natives of this country from all oppressions committed through European influence. The Ranee, who appears to be the widow of one of the most ancient Rajahs, and one of the first families in Bengal, is, it seems with the rajah her infant son, kept in a state of inquietude and duresse by a military force under your orders and directions. . . . The Ranee . . . is thereby rendered no longer mistress of her own house, but obliged to take refuge in her most inward apartments, and prevented (from the fears and apprehensions she is under) from performing her accustomed religious ceremonies. Even her private apartments (by all Europeans hitherto deemed sacred) are, it seems, not considered by you as an asylum.[35]

The justice's reprimand establishes that the rani's epistolary strategies did not start with the petition to the council but that she had also exploited the tension between the commercial and legal wings of the colonial state. The justice's argument that the zenana was sacred or a legal asylum suggests that when it came to the female zamindars, femininity rather than women's rights provided the discursive force that allowed these elite gendered subjects to maneuver in the interstices between two empires. The male zamindar could resort only to honor to stave off possible confinement, and this argument became weaker as the male zamindar's mechanisms of establishing his social standing—family lineage, public functions, religious rituals, and everyday dealings with the peasantry—were now deemed unnecessary by the Company. Having lost his political base, the male zamindar could not ensure that anyone would rise up to defend his honor. The sight of the woman's body forced into public display by foreigners, on the other hand, could still provoke a social reaction.

Thus it is understandable that the creation of the zenana as a protected womanspace was undertaken both by the Company and by those who wanted to curtail its power in India. The incidents leading to the forced confinement of Rani Bishnukumari are utilized first by the supreme court to make the case that it needs to "protect the natives" from the likes of Warren Hastings and his employees. In London, the Company's board of directors and various Company employees testifying before the parliamentary committee were about to make the counterargument that it was British law, insensitive to the cultural mores of the natives and the zamindari class, that was not only hindering the collection of revenues but also endangering the future of British dominion in India. Consider this petition sent from the Company's directors at the India House in London to Parliament in May 1776, requesting amendment of the functions of the judicature. The directors contend that the "exercise of its jurisdiction must inevitably tend to render the Collection of the Company's Revenues impracticable and restrict the power of the Supreme Council":

> Another Consequence to be feared from the exercise of the jurisdiction, is the Alienation of the minds of the Natives; who cannot without great Concern, see a body of laws introduced which clash with their Constitutional peculiarities and with their religious sentiments and prejudices; and who must feel the most sensible alarms on finding themselves exposed to have their persons seized and their laws of property changed by the Orders of a court to whose jurisdiction they were strangers.[36]

Here the petition goes on to list a number of complaints received from zamindars and filed with the governor-general about warrants issued against them from the supreme court. While the reader is told that the petitions "speak for themselves," the board takes care to emphasize one paragraph and some lines in particular:

> The Peons or Officers sent by the Supreme Court to the Zamindar of 7 Annas Tumbook had acted in a most unjustifiable Manner, not only in *prohibiting his Women from Fire and Water* but particularly in entering their Apartments which till That Time had, by all Governments, been held sacred and they express their Hope, that such unwarrantable behaviour will be noticed by the Governor-General and Council in the manner it deserves: As such Acts of Violence and such Violation of the Hindoo Laws must not only disgrace us as a National Body with the natives *but likewise breed a Disgust in their Minds, that may tend to the most serious Consequences,* not to mention the inevitable Loss occasioned to the revenue. (*Petitions,* 83, emphasis in original)

This battle of wills between interests calling for more parliamentary control, on the one hand, and for increased autonomy for the Company and Warren Hastings, on the other, was aptly staged when the House of Commons set up a committee in 1781 to inquire into various petitions that had arrived from India. In what was clearly a preliminary exercise that would lead to the subsequent trial of the governor-general, these petitions included ones from both Philip Francis and Hastings in which they implicated each other in judicial and administrative excesses. The war of words now extended all the way from Bengal to London. The Committee on Petitions' primary focus was to gauge whether Warren Hastings and his council had acted against the supreme court's rules in administering justice in Bengal. Thus, in order to "collect . . . a Body of facts, which might serve as the foundation" for their conclusions, the committee set out to examine a number of witnesses, "all persons minutely conversant in the Affairs of Bengal" (*Petitions,* 83).

This exercise in information gathering is a curious one; it suggests, for one, that the Company's archive was finally limited in its ability to provide a body of facts that all would accept. The select committee seems to have preferred the oral testimonies given under oath with the corroborating presence of the bodies, rather than depositions in writing. The list of witnesses summoned before the committee reads like a who's who of the Company's administration in Bengal. It includes Edward Baber, former resident and chief at Murshidabad; James Rennell, former surveyor general of Bengal; George Vansittart, former council member and chief of Midnapore; Richard Barwell, former council member and friend of Hastings; and Harry Verelst, former governor of Bengal.

Each of them, in his answers to questions posed by committee members, seems to echo the position that Hastings himself had taken over the years. Edward Baber suggested that the jurisdiction of the judges should be carefully limited and properly defined lest the principles of the judicature and the well-being of the Bengal government run "diametrically opposite to each other." Barwell answered that the proceedings of the supreme court judges "appeared to him fair and regular but in many instances detrimental to the revenue" (*Petitions,* 43). Although this set of witnesses seems to have established that it was the supreme court that had been excessive and obstructive rather than Warren Hastings, the committee was also gathering information about the various constraints that might have operated when English law and punishment was being implemented on the zamindars. Most of the witnesses seem to have suggested that the Company was already sensitive to various factors like the caste, class, religious, and gender rules that had to be taken into consideration when attempting to bring zamindars and other native functionaries into line.

One of the more consistent points of evidence provided by the above-listed officials from Bengal is regarding the secluded woman. Baber testified that while he was chief resident at Rajshahi (the largest zamindari in Bengal) he had never seen the zamindar, Rani Bhabhani, who "did not conduct the business herself, but . . . transacted through her agents. . . . She never appeared in public. . . . He never saw the places of her Residence. . . . She lives in great state." When asked how the people would react if she was served a personal process by the sergeant of the Supreme Court of Judicature, he answered that "he should think that they would resist such a process as much as an attempt upon her life" (*Petitions,* 33). When Rennell was asked a similar question, his testimony was recorded as follows: "These women never appeared in public functions of the zamindari, nor on any other Occasion—That under the Country Government, they would not be liable to personal arrest, for it would bring Disgrace upon the whole cast—That the personal arrest of the ranee of Radshi [*sic*] would be considered as one of the grossest Violations of their Customs that could possibly happen" (*Petitions,* 36). When Baber appeared for his second round of testimony, it is clear, Montesquieu was already at hand for him as an authority. He told the committee that "the Connection of the Laws of that Country with its Religion, must render the Introduction of foreign laws peculiarly offensive to its inhabitants." He also offered as a test case of the impossibility of British law in Bengal this example: "To desire to see the wife of a Rajah or zamindar . . . would be conceived of as a ludicrous request" (*Petitions,* 38).

It is clear from the various testimonies that, when the Company closed ranks and asserted the need to run Bengal in the way most conducive to the collection of revenues, women acting as zamindars or as part of zamindari households were rendered objects of protection from the potential violence of laws of the English nation. The protection of this womanspace seems to have emerged as a collaborative project between the native men and the East India Company. It was concluded that neither zamindar men nor zamindar women, but especially women, could be subject to the process served by the supreme court. The requirement of producing the body in public or in court (habeas corpus) seemed to go against the very customs and religions of Bengal, and the best illustration of this point was made by repeated references to the secluded woman as the limit case for English law.

The Unmanageable Space of the Secluded Subject

We return now to the first question, which is also to be our last: If female zamindars held the management of various estates in the 1770s and 1780s, why was there a concerted move on the part of the Company to remove women from these positions by the 1790s?

One of the fascinating aspects of the Company's records is that this vast body of texts moves forward through a system of previous reference so that the very process of accumulation of the archive has built into it an iterative principle that questions the presence of a reported event. The process of citation and repetitive alteration transforms the event into a "function within a larger differential text or tissue," thus undermining the official word on why certain events have happened or must happen.[37] In light of this principle, before we read the official discussions of 1776 and 1789 that recommend the disqualification of female zamindars from positions of management, I first cite instances from the records to show that the rani of Burdwan's was not a singular case. She was one of many ranis who were a source of grief to the Company. The most notorious case, of course, was that of Rani Bhabhani of Rajshahi, who outlived her husband by fifty-eight years and was ruling over a sprawling and thriving district in North Bengal when the English first appeared on the scene. Her efforts to keep her estate away from the forced sales under the farming system made her into a household name in Bengal well into the twentieth century, when nationalist poets took her up as a symbol of resistance.[38] In 1771, this rani foiled an attempt by the Company to sell her *dewry* farms (traditional holdings kept exclusively for the support of women in zamindari households) by publicizing it as an effort to rob her of her "Honour." In a letter to the Council of Revenue, she asserted that a public sale of these lands would deprive her of food, clothing, and servants. When the Company finally decided to ignore her pleas and go forward with the public auction, no bidders turned up.[39] By and by her preferred strategy became the system of *benami* (holding land under title to someone else), whereby she leased portions of the zamindari to her son and other relatives while retaining the control herself.[40]

In the case of the Dinajpur zamindari, also managed by a woman, the Company met with another insurmountable obstacle. In 1781, when the Committee of Revenue adopted a plan to educate the zamindar's minor son, "the obstinacy of the mother defeated it; she would not give up her son to the tuition of his appointed instructors, and resisted all orders and applications for his attendance. He was retained in her private apartments, where instruction was impracticable."[41] The recurring instances of trouble from the secluded women over the years led the Company to reconsider its policy of allowing female zamindars to manage estates, especially as punitive measures against zamindars became the order of the day when revenue collections failed to reach the Company's unreasonable projections. By 1776, when Philip Francis drew up a new plan for Bengal, he proposed that all large zamindaris be divided equally between the sons and that the smaller ones be vested in the eldest son, who was "chargeable with the maintenance of the younger sons." The zamindars who had no heirs of their own could adopt heirs, male of course, and a "court of wards" was to be established for the care of estates of which the incumbents were "minors, idiots or females." In one stroke, primogeniture and patrimonial inheritance English style were to be installed, and all forms of female inheritance or property (such as the *dewry mahals,* for instance) were to be abolished. But the crucial recommendation aimed at unseating female zamindars was this: that in existing cases where women or children were the heirs, a court of wards would be established and the Company would appoint managers.[42]

Francis's plan of 1776 was never implemented in its original form because it was defeated in the newly reconstituted Calcutta council. But the main idea behind it—of fixing the revenue settlements in perpetuity rather than for a few years at a time—was gaining popularity. Finally, in 1793 Lord Cornwallis proclaimed the Permanent Settlement of Bengal, under which the zamindars received new historical functions. With this plan, Cornwallis sought to reform the zamindar by "depriving him of his traditional feudal privileges and . . . convert[ing] him through education and the gift of [private] property into an improving landlord, after the contemporary English model."[43]

We will catch this historical event as it is in preparation in order to understand why in the grand designs for nineteenth-century Bengal the woman zamindar was to be written out. Five years before Cornwallis's declaration, council member John Shore prepared a minute to address the feasibility of a permanent settlement as a preliminary exercise to justify the impending transformation of Bengal agricultural society into a model of England's own prosperous capitalist agriculture. Though John Shore's lengthy minute addresses many aspects of Francis's earlier plan, the recommendation that comes in for an extended explication is the one for abolishing female management in zamindaris. It is important to note that Shore is skeptical that the Bengali zamindar could actually transform himself into an entrepreneur and improver along the lines of the gentleman farmer in England.

In the minute it is clear that what worries Shore most is the Company's forfeiture of its main stranglehold over the zamindars. Once the zamindaris were transformed into private property with permanent settlement, the Company would have fewer prerogatives to intervene in the household management of a zamindar or to remove a zamindar for incapacity or mismanagement. For Shore at this point, the limit case of the Company's ability to intervene in the zamindari had become the female zamindar. But Shore presented the obstacles provided by the ranis' management style as evidence of ignorance, incapacity, fraud, and intrigue:

> In zemindarries, at the head of which minors or females are placed, the mutual contentions of the zemindarry servants, for the direction of the management, scarcely ever subside. In Burdwan the opposition of the zemindar and his mother; in Dinagepoor the representations of the family servants, on behalf of the dowager Ranny and the minor zemindar respectively; in Bishenpore the complaints of the widow of the deceased zemindar against her old servants at one period, and against those nominated on her own representations at another are a few amongst many instances on record.[44]

Shore summoned the list of female zamindars to show the general alienation of the zamindar from the people of the zamindari, the unwarranted power of lesser agents, and the confusion and lack of delineated authority in zamindari functions. Shore suggested that though the court of directors in London had prescribed that "settlements should in all practicable cases, be made with the zamindars," many of them were "disqualified from real interference in the management of the collections from incapacity on account of sex, minority or otherwise."[45] The idea that the female zamindar was incapable was an argument made on the ground of essence and shows that the theoretical fiction of the secluded woman engendered by Montesquieu was now replacing real historical referents like the ranis of Rajshahi and Burdwan, who had satisfactorily met Company revenue projections for many years.

Shore then resorted to this fiction to "suggest the expediency of a rule that they [female zamindars] be declared incapable of holding any management."[46] His arguments were drawn from various contexts, but one paragraph in particular is a very illuminating revelation of beliefs about the problems posed by these women:

> It is well known that women in Bengal are, by laws of their religion and customs, secluded from public society; and that they receive no education to qualify them for the transaction of public business. In

> all suits and causes where they are concerned, it is almost impossible to ascertain whether they are parties to the representations which bear their names, or not; they cannot be produced in the public courts, nor are they accessible to the officers of justice. It is not possible, in the nature of things, that they can be judges of their own interests, or competent to form opinions on the intricate detail attending the management of the revenues. They are mere passive instruments in the hands of their servants; and often perhaps ignorant of the transactions in which they are made to appear as principals.[47]

Here it is clear that much more than incapacity is operating in Shore's arguments against female zamindars, as the discussion moves very quickly from seclusion and lack of education to the impossibility of producing the secluded woman in public. In other words, Shore is attesting to the impossibility of making the female zamindar over as both the subject of private property and the object of the law's disciplinary force. This is the bitter gift that colonialism will bequeath only to the male zamindar.

The secluded woman thus became a perfect example of what Jean-François Lyotard has termed a *differend*—a site of alterity or a subject position that cannot appear within the idioms that regulate the conflict.[48] Although the Company had been willing, during the rani of Burdwan's tussle with the board, to use native legal procedures under which secluded women gave their testimony through a curtain to a native judge, this was no longer a satisfactory scenario. Now, under English law, the female zamindar's seclusion made her a nonwitness because there could be no corroborating presence of her body. Documents with her signature never carried sufficient testamentary force. The voice behind the curtain could never be established as that of a free-willed or consenting subject, and her speech and writing came mediated through *munshis* (secretaries) and translators.

Shore's final recommendation was that the Company should come forward as manager of the female zamindar's household till the minor son was ready to take charge. He also had two proposals about handling the ranis, who might create "difficulties" for implementing the settlement. "The government," he said, "must interpose to over-rule them [the difficulties] or it will be defeated."[49] For ranis who would not listen to "the persuasions of reason," Shore proposed "the separation of mother and son for some time at least." And for the rani who refused to hand over her son for education by Company wards, the solution would be to "compel her to give him up, either by withholding her subsistence until she complied, or by employing women of her own cast to enter apartments and withdrawing him from them."[50] What was happening here was a dismantling of the very womanspace that had been protected in order to limit British law in earlier years. The very actions for which Warren Hastings and the councillors drew censure in 1775 were now being advocated as policy.

The discrepancy between practice and advocated policy is evidence also of the use of a theoretical fiction in bad faith. From 1789 to 1793, when the Permanent Settlement of Bengal was announced, the implementation of John Shore's recommendations began in fits and starts, but it is clear from the records that the incapacity of the secluded woman was only a cover for what was actually going on. The records show that every female zamindar and female farmer came under scrutiny and was either dismissed or, in rare cases, approved by the Company for special reasons. The collectors were given the task of identifying all holdings where a woman was in charge and submitting reports to the Company, which would determine whether any of them had to be considered "exempt" from the "operation of the General Regulations for disqualified landholders."[51] If we consider the fact that the rani of Burdwan held onto her zamindari for several years after the Permanent Settlement, then we can conclude that she was exempt. Why was that so? And what does it tell us about the very evidence of policy that circulates in the archives?

The rani of Burdwan was still in the picture as late as 1794, using a combination of subterfuge and subservience to regain control of the zamindari that had been awarded to her son after he attained majority. In 1794, when Rajah Tejchandra was jailed for not meeting revenues, the rani interceded on behalf of her son and had the zamindari transferred into her name on the promise of meeting the revenues. The Company begrudgingly accepted her plan, since they had no other way to get the defaulted amount. But as soon as the lands were transferred into her name and Tejchandra was released, the rani withdrew from business and "retired" to Amboa, where she was out of the reach of Company officials. The collector soon smelled a rat. After making an unsuccessful attempt to get the son's arrears, he wrote to the council:

> As far as the Rajah's object can be inferred from his conduct in the late transaction, it appears to have been to embezzle as much as he could of the rents and leave Government to look to the Ranny from [*sic*] the balance which would happen in consequence. This would not subject the Ranny to any inconvenience for being by her sex exempted from punishment or coercion of any kind she would remain undisturbed, till the end of the year, while the Rajah

> no longer subject to restraint, would be at full liberty to try every means he might think conducive to the reduction of the assessment on the District.[52]

The Company's suspicion that male zamindars were strategically using the legal loopholes provided by the womanspace or even colluding with their mothers and wives to thwart the Company is a sure sign that the zenana had transformed its possibilities as the Company moved in to discipline the women. The zenana's new function as a space of collusion between men and women is clear in the record of another action taken by the collector of Burdwan in 1788. Acting on the board's instructions, he attached the rajah's furniture and stationed peons over the zenana, where "it has ever been his custom to deposit his most valuable effects."[53]

These events, which appear against the grain of avowed policy declarations in the primary discourse, show that discursive displacements are also strategies of rule. We have seen that despotism as a discourse entered the political economy of Bengal when that territory was at the threshold of being transformed by British law. It became a signifier of the very essence of the native spirit and was thus crucial to both sides of the debate. Despotism was a negative concept that allowed the English rulers to envision the entire world made in their model. In other words, English law, economy, and culture were the models for everyone, but despotism stood in the way of implementation. Similarly, in the nineteenth century when Marx and Engels found that their narrative about the world transformation of capital was blocked by cultural differences, they coined a term that also owes much to Montesquieu—the "Asiatic Mode of Production."[54] It was the refusal to acknowledge a multilinear history of capital that resulted in the production of this Eastern aberration. Grafting this lesson onto the case of the secluded, elite women in Bengal, we can learn another one: When the revenues of Bengal met the demands of mercantilist and free-tradist principles, the woman as a real description of practices on the ground was not an issue. But when revenue expectations were kicked up to levels that were clearly beyond the reaches of the methods of exploitation in place (not agrarian capitalism), then theoretical fictions entered the scene to warrant the transformation of social relations that would make the collection of the higher level of revenue possible. The secluded woman as an incapable agent of a despotic system was the theoretical fiction that ensured the unobstructed penetration of the Company's punitive measures into all spaces.

For a coda to the story of the rani of Burdwan, we could turn to her paradoxical appearance in a footnote in J. S. Mill's celebrated essay "The

Subjection of Women" in 1869. After a long career as an examiner of correspondence for the East India Company, Mill had an encounter with the ranis in the India House archives that allowed him to use the figure of the rani of Burdwan as a different kind of historical evidence. In his essay, she is no longer the degraded and gendered limit case of Western democracy, an object of sexual despotism, but rather the evidence of potential the Englishwoman had yet to achieve. Confronted with the paucity of examples to bolster his argument that women were fit to vote or hold public office, and unable to proceed beyond Queen Elizabeth and Queen Victoria, Mill had to go east for his examples: "When, to the queens and empresses, we add regents and viceroys of provinces," says Mill, "the list of women who have been eminent rulers of mankind swells to a great length."[55] And then the rani arrives as an example, but this time in a footnote, one of only two in the entire essay:

> Especially is this true if we take into consideration Asia as well as Europe. If a Hindoo principality is strongly, vigilantly, and economically governed; if order is preserved without oppression; if cultivation is extending, and the people prosperous, in three cases out of four that principality is under a woman's rule. This fact, to me an entirely unexpected one, I have collected from a long official knowledge of Hindoo governments. . . . When we consider that these princesses have never been seen in public, have never conversed with any man not of her own family except from behind a curtain, that they do not read, and if they did, there is no book in their languages which can give them the smallest instruction on political affairs; the example they afford of the natural capacity of women for government is very striking.[56]

In the footnotes of Mill's text, the rani has become a general example. The rani's appearance exposes the duplicity of discourses that can stage her as evidence of inadequacy at one historical moment but resuscitate her as evidence of natural capacity for government when she is needed to service the argument for her sisters' emancipation in England. This is foreclosure, liberal style.

But the final lesson is this: The rani is not only an aberrant subject punctuating a monotonous, homogeneous landscape written flatly for British improvement; rather, she is the instantiation of a theoretical impasse. To know how to deal with her, the Company officials had to rewrite their discursive precursors as well as the maps whereby they understood the alien culture around them. And just as the rani's battle lines were drawn at a safe distance from the center of the Company's power and her maneuvers from behind the curtain established her power through remote control, various machinations and methods of writing, self-representation, circulation, and archiving had to be put in place so the East India Company's headquarters in London could stand forward as the sovereign power in Bengal. But these forms of mediation also posed limits to such an exercise of power as other subjects of writing occupied the various clearings that opened up in these transactions. It is true that the secluded ranis finally had to give up their leadership by remote control, while the Company at the same time used writing and oral testimonies to give itself the semblance of having its ear to the ground. Reading the archives always gives us another story, one that exposes British rule as a sovereignty maintained primarily through a "network of almost fictitious connections and relationships which were maintained primarily on paper."[57] This exposure could forestall present attempts to rewrite the violence of that historical change as progress.

CHAPTER FIVE

Critical Genealogies

In the late eighteenth century, the figure of the secluded woman moved from the secondary to the primary record from Orientalist histories to the domain of reports and policy making. In the early nineteenth century, the movement of that figure continued, now into official discourses that slowly recast Orientalist tropes and arguments into new versions derived from seemingly scientific and empiricist practices—namely colonial sociology.[1] In this new epistemic regime, discussions of seclusion were secured within investigations into native manners and morals in order to produce a new object of knowledge—Hindu women. Quotations from sources like Montesquieu or scattered speculations from travelogues were no longer the sole guarantees for a truth about this object. Instead, the truth about Hindu women was known primarily through observations and opinions from various expert witnesses—Company employees with field experience in India; missionaries; and, later, informants from the emerging class of Anglicized native elites.[2]

Such empirical exercises about Hindu women had existed in unexpected places in the official records long before the public social reform debates of the 1820s conjured the figure of the Hindu widow as a victim of sati. This prior deployment of a gendered discourse about Hindu women was not, as might be expected, a scenario where "white men are saving brown women from brown men"[3] but rather a deviation and reversal of sorts: here white men were saving brown women from other white men. By reading this lost event from the colonial archive, I hope to insert a crosscurrent into the numerous contemporary postcolonial framings of the 1820s. Such a crosscurrent may reveal what Gauri Viswanathan has called, in another context, the "incalculable borderlessness of cultural developments" within the disparate and heterogeneous nature of colonial formations.[4]

Much of the scholarly interest in the relationship between gender and colonialism in the early nineteenth century has focused on the debates around the social reform spearheaded by the colonialist state in the 1820s—reform that culminated in the 1829 abolition of sati. Scholars have discussed in depth how this legislated moment was a definitive one that has since determined the configurations of subsequent nationalist debates about the woman question or Indian tradition.[5] In this chapter I will look at the historical juncture of the 1820s by framing it as one of three moments in a discursive relay that began in 1813 and ended in 1832. In this relay between the official record and the larger sociocultural context of British Bengal, and between English power and emerging native hegemony, we see the proliferation of representations of Hindu women. While there is little doubt that the vast historical record about sati and the visibility of gendered discourses in the 1820s make the social reform debate into an exemplary case about the battle between colonial and countercolonial forces, channeling all contradictions into this field may occlude various other deviations and ruses operating during this time. For example, because the sati debates crystallize for readers today an official policy of intervention into the culture of the colonized, recasting women's issues of the time as cultural ones has tended to disguise the ongoing work of economic imperialism in the early nineteenth century. There is far less attention given to the continued spread of capitalism, to class formations and class conflict, to parallel or asymmetrical developments in England, to the appropriation of surplus through uneven development, and so on. By looking at an alternative formulation of the woman question in 1813, I will provide one case in which the official discussion of the economic future of India was recoded as a cultural issue, and representations of Hindu women were used to mask this recoding.

I will read a variety of official and unofficial texts from the period from 1813 to 1832, but my primary source is the "Minutes of Evidence," which records testimonies given by East India Company employees before the House of Commons Select Committee on the Affairs of the East India Company in 1813. Other sources include a letter written from the Company to the Board of Control in 1818; some writings of Rammohun Roy, the Indian social reformer involved in the sati debates; and finally, a parliamentary report from 1832 showing Roy's emergence as a privileged native informant and mouthpiece for British rule in India. I argue that the real transferred object in this discontinuous discursive relay was the sign of the Hindu woman, which acted as the vanishing mediator in two instances in order to bring about a third. The Company first used representations of Hindu women in 1813 to make a cultural argument about noninterference in order to protect its trade monopoly from other British interests. This argument did not succeed, and the Company lost its trade monopoly and the power to restrict travel to India. However, the gendered discourse that was set in play during the select committee hearings went on to have powerful and contradictory afterlives. In the 1820s, in contradiction to their initial use by the Company, we see the dispersal of representations of native women in a successful mobilization against sati. This proliferation paved the way for the Company and Britain to present themselves as paternalist protectors of Indian women, and it provided the alibi to initiate a long period of the "civilizing process." At the same time, the figural use of Hindu women as emblems of tradition drew elite Hindu men into an exchange with the colonial rulers and enabled them to establish a native hegemony over the issue of culture. In the third part of this discursive relay, Roy became the representative of a new Anglicized comprador class that sought an alliance with the colonial elite. He was subsequently used by the British liberal imperialists of the 1830s as a testimony of and a native informant for the success of English civilization.

For the last chapter in a book in which I have tried to recast the place of English and Indian women in the history of colonialism, it seems appropriate that I end with a discussion that focuses on those who speak *for* women. The question "Who occupies the place of the informant?" is especially relevant today as contestations over speaking positions about Indian pasts, Indian culture, and Indian women provide a continuing charge in postindependence politics. Moreover, there are important implications for postcolonial studies today. Gayatri Spivak has argued in her most recent work that locating the place of the "native informant" is one way of maintaining a "persistent critique" of the subject positions inhabited by and the problematics taken on by postcolonial and feminist critics today. It is only when we do, she warns, that we can know if what passes as academic critique is actually complicity with neocolonialism.[6]

In the epilogue I outline the power lines and political agenda of Roy's elite economic class as they continue to "animate the present" in postcolonial India.[7] Upper-caste/upper-class patriarchal political groups continue to reformulate the woman question in ways that would allow these groups to occupy the nation for themselves. They do this primarily by using upper-caste and upper-class women to marginalize religious minorities and lower castes; their success lies partly in their ability to disguise economic interests as purely cultural or national ones. Such a dissimulation is also taking place elsewhere. Orientalist tropes continue to make their way into globalization talk in the West as women in the poorer south provide new alibis for development and capital expansion. To begin this genealogy at one end of the timeline, let us now turn to woman's appearance in the official record of 1813.

"THEIR WOMEN"

In 1813, the Select Committee on the Affairs of the East India Company, appointed by the House of Commons, met to examine a number of witnesses before recommending that year's renewal of the Company's charter. The ritual of renewing the charter at regular intervals, since its original granting in 1600 by Queen Elizabeth I, always served as an occasion for various constituencies among the British public to have a say in deciding who was to benefit from Indian trade. Since 1784, when Parliament replaced the crown as the arbiter in this charter ritual, it had slowly allowed various private interests to chip away at the Company's sovereign power and trade monopoly in India. By 1813 many powerful new groups had entered the scene: shipping interests that wanted all ports in England and India open to free trade; British merchants searching for new markets after the disruption of the Napoleonic wars; and missionary societies wanting access to India for proselytization.[8] The Company, wanting to keep India as a base for agrarian-based production rather than for industrial production or marketing, fought these initiatives by insisting on the same tight controls it had enjoyed in the past. But fearing that the select committee would cave in to the mounting pressure from these external interests, the Company's directors played for time by obtaining permission to call witnesses to give evidence. In March and April of 1813, over fifty-one witnesses, mostly retired or current employees of the Company, appeared before the committee.

In the "Minutes of Evidence" printed the same year, the sheer scale of these testimonies—they covered almost six hundred pages in all—reveals a full-fledged exercise in the production of colonial truth. Moreover, these testimonies are evidence of a new modality of truth production. While earlier select committee exercises in evidence collection, in 1811, for instance, used informants or witnesses to answer questions primarily on the basis of their occupational expertise (as customs officials, magistrates, traders, and so on), in the 1813 hearings we see military officers and civil servants, none of whom were scholars of Indian history or culture, being asked questions about native culture. In other words, the testimonies of the various witnesses were not about tax collection, revenue transfers, or military exercises; they all seem to have gravitated toward a new object—a sociology or ethnography of the native. What accounts for this new interest?

Without doubt, such exercises in native ethnography and sociology were not new to Company officials. Many of them had journals, letters, or secondary monographs to prove their interest in such a field. Charles Grant, one of the Company directors, sent his infamous tract "Observations on the State of Society among the Asiatic Subjects of Great Britain" to the India Office in 1797, having extracted bits from previous correspondence by Company employees regarding native "character" and "common life." He prefaced these citations with this remark: "There is a standard to which, for the elucidation of this subject, we may largely appeal—the records of the East-India Company." In his tract, Grant pointed out that the Company's "business" archive was also a collection of accurate "facts" respecting Hindu "character" and "common life" precisely because it was not intended for such a task. Because everyday business transactions in India were recorded in great detail, Grant argued, the natives were themselves "brought upon the stage and heard concerning each other."[9] As the natives spoke in the archive about each other, the reader of the archive needed only to eavesdrop in order to understand them. Grant's observations about the archive providing—among its political, judicial, military, and commercial documents—a hidden story of ethnography that can be rendered visible by a reading against the grain are not very different from my own. What is important to note from Grant's remarks is that even as late as 1797 the Company had never used its written records or its employees for ethnographic purposes.

Thus, in 1813 it was the first time at the highest echelons of the Company and the home government in London that such ethnographically driven hearings were taking place. One way to determine the various interests at play in this unusual scene is to look for patterns and regularities in the utterances. Though the committee's questions seem to have been asked in random order, it is clear that they fall into three main sets, each of which refers back to a group that was bent on depriving the Company of its trade monopoly and sole access to India. There are also instances of overlap and evidence of alliances. For example, on the one hand, trade interests are emphasized when questions are asked about native everyday life and consumption patterns: Who buys British goods? What is the average wage of a laborer or a clerk? How do rich natives live? What do they spend their money on? On the other hand, shipping interests are signaled by questions like these: Should Europeans be allowed to freely sojourn in India? Should sailors and traders be allowed into the interior of the country, away from main ports and settlements? Finally, the missionary interests make their presence felt in questions directed toward ascertaining character and religious beliefs and practices: What is the moral character of Hindus and Mohammedans? How jealous are they of their religion? What are the main social evils caused by the Hindu religion? Sometimes a question can signal a strategic alliance: "Is your Lordship of the opinion that the improvement of their [the Hindus'] civil and moral condition [through the gradual introduction of Christianity] would tend to increase their consumption of . . . various manufactures?"[10] (The "Minutes of Evidence" in which these questions are posed are cited hereafter as ME.)

In the midst of these testimonies, we also see the appearance of a number of scattered and sporadic questions about native women. These questions do not seem to originate strictly from any of these three categories of interests. Few and far between, the questions also do not establish any ethnographic "truth" about Indian women as such—their status as a class, their geographical location, their ethnic background, or their everyday life. Rather, the questions about Hindu women, while seeming to make them into objects of knowledge, actually produce them as figurations that function with tropological force to stitch together the three domains of native ethnography that are produced through the testimonies. Native everyday life, native geographical space in the interior, and native religion are brought together into a single gendered logic by using the woman as a figure for all of these. Let us now track, by means of a careful reading of the testimonies, the textual and discursive turns through which this happened.

We see that the Company was taking no chances at the hearing. First on the list of witnesses was the former governor-general, Warren Hastings, who since his ignominious public trial in 1786 had lived in retirement in England. At eighty-five years of age, rehabilitated and restored to the list of the esteemed colonial rulers of yesteryear, Hastings had become an important figurehead of the empire's origin.[11] He was asked the opening question in the proceedings: "If Europeans were permitted to sojourn in India, according to their own pleasure, and without any restraint, have you, from your long experience in that country, the means of stating to the committee what the effect of that would be?" (ME, 2). Though Hastings's answer to this question was forceful and unambiguous, carrying all the weight of his former authority, it also paradoxically smacked of an older regime of colonial truth that depended almost wholly on Orientalist stereotypes about native mentality:

> Most hurtful and most ruinous, both to the Company's interest, to the Government and to the peace of the country. Nothing could be more opposite than the characters of the Europeans (I will confine it to the English) and that of the natives of India. . . . The native Indian is weak in body and timid in spirit . . . but there are cases in which

> a provocation of general grievance would excite a whole people and even a detached number of them to ferocities of insurrection. . . . The Englishman is quite a different character in India. . . . [Though] the highest idea of a common participation in the sovereignty of the Company . . . possesses the mind of every Englishman in it; this idea in the lower orders of the people rises to despotism and is liable to all the excesses of despotism, where the prerogative attached to it can be asserted with impunity. . . . The aggrieved Indian has no chance with such a disparity. (ME, 2)

While the random sequencing of questions posed to the various witnesses often dispersed noticeable agendas, the first testimony by Hastings marks a point of departure that could not be easily displaced. Hastings's answer to this question set the trend for an imagining of India that would dominate in the proceedings. His representation of the colony as a space of timidity and servitude needing the protection of the Company, especially from the "lower orders" of Englishmen prone to despotism, was a new coding for India, especially given that military campaigns to subdue local powers were still going on.

Read another way, we may see Hastings's testimony as saying that India needed to be protected from trading and shipping interests and from the lower-class English labor that would inevitably infiltrate the colony. Moreover, India also needed to be protected from itself—from the "ferocities" of insurrectionary natives. From this point on in the proceedings, the term *sojourn,* as in "unrestrained sojournment of Europeans," became a code phrase signaling the need to keep tight control over travel to and within India. While such restrictions had allowed the Company to maintain its trade monopoly in the subcontinent, by 1813 it was clear that such a policy was no longer popular.[12] The Company needed new justifications to maintain such restrictions, and it seems to have discovered one in an ethnographic discourse of the native rather than in arguments about fiscal, economic, or political prudence.

Whereas the first question to Hastings staged spatial issues—the consequences of opening ports to shipping and free traders, a question that followed a little farther along in the sequence moved Hastings to a more pointed consideration of the habits and character of the Hindus. This question, translated into the language of interest, reflected the questioners' attempt to know if India was a potential market for British goods: "According to your observation is not the character of the native Indian in its nature stationary and immutable, and not apt to vary from the original habits of the country?" (ME, 4). Hastings, led by the question's Orientalist suggestion agreed completely:

"I believe that the Indians now are in their dress, their manners, and in all habits of life just what they were at the commencement of their juge [*sic*] or age, which is perhaps as far as the history of that country extends" (ME, 4).

The shorthand of Hastings's response is that the natives are so fixed in their habits and everyday life that there is little chance that they can be transformed into consumers with the desire to imitate European "manners and habits." This response thus uses the trope of the timeless, unchanging native to neutralize free traders and merchants who want to export British goods to India. On the question of native missionaries, Hastings is a little more restrained and ambiguous about his position. He does allude, however, to the Vellore Mutiny of 1806, in which rebel native soldiers killed over two hundred British soldiers. By suggesting that such an insurrection might have been caused by aggressive missionary tactics, Hastings's later warning that such activities could be of "great hazard" seems to exclude support to these interests too (ME, 7). All in all, his responses do not provide any openings for the various interests represented on the committee.

What Hastings's various responses do produce in their sequential rendering is a gradual linking of the spatial management of India (protection of its non-British spaces) with native subjectivity. A reading of subsequent testimonies shows how British India, when imagined for a Company monopoly, transformed the older relativistic ideas of native and British character into more sustained investigations of native subjectivity itself. And the committee, paying careful consideration to Hastings's initial warning about likely provocations for native insurrections, then went on to chart the interiority of the native. In questions posed to the next witness, Lord Teignmouth, a retired official from Bengal formerly known as John Shore, the India that is not under British law is termed "the interior" (ME, 10), and the evils of "unrestrained" "intercourse" between Englishmen and natives in this space are alluded to over and over again. Because the native within such discussions is already a protected object, it is little wonder that the various questions and answers describing Englishmen as "penetrating" into the "interior" soon overlay the discourse of spatial management with a gendered and sexualized one.

This gendering is especially apparent when the language of restraints to be placed on uncovenanted Englishmen's movements within British India is mirrored by the discussion of the confined and secluded women. The first explicit question about Hindu women appears during Lord Teignmouth's testimony. The question comes without any lead-in or follow-up, but since it appears within a set of questions directed to Teignmouth about the social evils of caste, religious festivals, infanticide, sati, and other "obstacles to their advancement in civilization," it is clear that if it was meant as fodder for anyone, it must have been the missionaries. Teignmouth was asked, "What is the condition of the female sex among the Gentoos [*sic*] as affected by their religion and prejudices?" He replied, "They are so concealed that we know little or nothing of them; nor is it usual to talk with the gentoos about their female sex: I believe that their state in general is merely that of slaves to their husbands" (ME, 18). The colon that appears in this sentence serves to separate the conclusion from the evidence and thus presents slavery as an explanation for seclusion and vice versa.

A little later, another committee member asked for further clarification of this point: "Is the Committee to understand that the Hindoo women are kept in confinement, shut up?" And Teignmouth replied, "I believe perfectly so; in a perfect state of seclusion" (ME, 19). What was only a rehearsed argument for him in the 1780s, when Teignmouth, then John Shore, argued in the fifth report for the removal of female landholders like the rani of Burdwan, was now absolute and "perfect" historical evidence. Paradoxically, Hindu women were also offered as epistemological blind spots ("We know little or nothing of them"), yet their invisibility to the official eye was a sign not of failed empiricism but of their slave status.

The conflation of the protection of women with the intended protection of the interior took place a little later, when Sir John Malcolm, a former officer in the Company's military service, appeared as a witness before the committee. What was by then a standard question about the dangers of an "unrestrained and unlimited influx" of Europeans into India was followed by a new sort of question: "Do you conceive that those evils [oppression of natives] would be likely to be aggravated in any respect by the manner in which the natives of India consider their women, and persons of the female sex, under their protection, as objects of affection and regard?" (ME, 55). Malcolm's answer resorted to another Orientalist stereotype of the violent, patriarchal Muslim: "Most undoubtedly, and more particularly with the Mahomedans . . . because I think that race of men has . . . a still more violent jealousy of the character of their women than the Hindoos" (ME, 55).

This was a significant moment in the proceedings because in all previous questions and responses alluding to the possible harm to natives that would ensue, the understanding had been that an undifferentiated (ungendered) native would be ill treated by despotic lower-class Englishmen. Now we have the first explicit gendering of the interior also as a sort of womanspace, enacted by gendering the native within that space. Within the interior, native men and women were presumably under a common threat from lower-class Englishmen, but native men were also protecting their women from those Englishmen. Put this way, a sign of the imperiled secluded woman could now circulate in the proceedings so that "penetration" and "unrestrained intercourse" in the interior were coded as illegitimate sexual contact between lower-class Englishmen and native women there. The interior, which was actually nothing but a differentiated space in colonial imaginative geography where native rather than British courts had jurisdiction and where English presence was less noticeable, was now a mysterious feminized space constituted through its association with the embodiment of a secluded woman.[13] The follow-up question to Malcolm makes this new signification even clearer: "Have you known any instances in which it has been necessary to give particular precautions with regard to the conduct of persons in the Company's service going into the interior of the country as to the manner of behaving towards the natives, in respect either to their religious prejudices, their establishments, with respect to the female sex or in any other respect?" (ME, 55).

It should be clear by now that the "female sex" or "Hindoo woman" question had been modified enough to place native women within the interior, which was now transformed from geographical notation, epistemological barrier, ethnic enclave, and protected native space to private space and religious domain: in other words, the domain of native male rights and privileges. The woman could not appear here as a referent but only as a signifier that referred to the subjectivity of the native male. The figure of woman was also thus marked the symbol of his potentially violent psyche—of what it would take to cause him to threaten British rule. The interstitial region between the foreground of British law and control and the background of native everyday life, which drove the notions of coast and interior, where the carefully mapped British India faded back into a potentially uncontrollable space, was now gendered male and female in a hierarchical way. This womanspace was both metonymic, an enclave within Indian men's proper domain and thus under his protection as his property, and metaphoric—the entire native space was coded feminine so that the Company could preside over the natives of India as their overall protector.

Almost forty pages later in the testimony, when Guy Prendergast is asked to specify the kinds of abuses natives were likely to suffer from sojourning Englishmen, we see that sexual violation and rape were already part of the standard response: "Insults to the native women, intrusion upon the houses and pagodas of the natives; all of which will be resented by the natives, and here they would have no authority to apply to, they would have recourse to force" (ME, 95). In this testimony, sexual violence or sexual attentions toward native women are associated with other, nonsexual encroachments into native private space and native religion.[14] The women had become metaphors—emblems of native men's religion and culture and their potential flashpoints. The witnesses testified to the Company's need to protect a caricatured version of Indian rights: culture, women, and religion were ensured to native men, while property rights and political rights for the colonial subjects were rendered unimaginable under colonialism.

Foreclosing Heterogeneity

At places in the testimonies, alternative images of women pressure or challenge the figurations of them as penetrable native space or protected native property. When we attempt to differentiate between women as "interested figurations" and women as historical subjects, all readings involve choices between signification and symbolization. We often exercise this choice by distinguishing between the literal and the figural. While it is impossible for me to reconstruct psychobiographies of the women who were being made over in these proceedings, I can outline the glimpses of other women who were not symbolic constructs, images of women who did not fit easily into the Orientalist storehouse of female tropes. These women appear precisely because some Company officials were playing true to their new role as ethnographic agents and thus were depending on observation and investigation to produce accounts of women they had seen, heard, or known rather than those they had imagined.

First, we have the testimony of Thomas Munro, whose answer to the question "Are the Hindoo women kept in a state of seclusion?" brings about the first favorable comparison with European women: "The Hindoo women, with the exception of one or two tribes . . . have as much liberty, and I imagine more, than the women in Europe." Reading liberty as public exposure, Munro cited the large numbers of "women of all ranks, young and old, bathing every day not only in retired places; but at large garrisons of Europeans" (ME, 127). Munro was the first witness not to use Orientalist tropes of seclusion to draw conclusions about Hindu women. He used the modality of observation: he had seen them. The next question is about her subordination: "Is their state that of slaves to their husbands?" To this Munro countered: "Their state is not that of slaves to their husbands, they have as much influence in their families as I imagine, the women have in this country; I often found them when in charge of the ceded districts, very troublesome tenants as farmers; I have frequently known women of respectable families who kept their husbands, and sons grown up, at home and came to the cutcherry to debate about their rents" (ME, 127). Here Munro reversed two interpretations of rural India already in play: rural India as a signifier of native men's privacy (the interior) and rural India's association with the seclusion or slavery of Hindu women. Through the evidence provided by his observation, he reworked the interior into a place of women's public activity, whether economic or everyday. However, it is an indication of the power of alien discourses that write native women's subjectivity that later in his testimony Munro referred back to his earlier statement by saying that his speaking of the women's "bathing in public" should not leave "an unfavourable impression of their demeanour" (ME, 169).

Thomas Sydenham provides yet another instance of gender heterogeneity in the witnesses' perceptions. Unlike other witnesses, Sydenham, as the Company's resident at the Mahratta Court, had access to an interior that Orientalism only provides as a fantasy: upper-class Indian households. Thus, when he was asked if "Hindu women are kept in a state of slavery, degradation or seclusion," his answer, which drew on empiricism and observation, added one more layer of complexity and contradiction to earlier versions of the secluded woman:

> I have never observed that the Hindoo women are kept in a state of slavery, degradation or seclusion; I believe that they are permitted to go abroad whenever they chuse upon their domestic concerns; and frequently for the mere purposes of exercise and amusement; they are to be seen in every town and village of the country. While I was resident at Poonah I had frequently occasion to transact business with the ministers of the Mahratta court in the private apartments of their dwellings; on most of those occasions I have seen their women, and they have sometimes been present at the transaction of ordinary business between the minister and myself. The only degradation amongst the Hindoo women with which I am acquainted is the state of the widow after the death of her husband, the widow has the hair of her head shaved, and is obliged to do all the menial offices of the family. I have known many Hindoo women however in this state, when her children had not been of age, conducting the business of the family, having the management of the estate belonging to the family, employing agents and attornies at the Mahratta court, and in short, doing everything in the direction and management of the family which women in similar circumstances in Europe do. (ME, 321)

This long answer provides a classic example of how a civil servant who was faithful to the oldest form of colonial information gathering, what Bernard Cohn has called the "observational or travel modality,"[15] could displace the tropological operations of Orientalist stereotypes, where the expert never had to reveal how he knew what he knew. In Sydenham's testimony, the place of seclusion was transformed into a place of economic deliberation, property management, and legal subjectivity. Sydenham's description did split midway though, as he balanced the account of female agency with a reminder about the oppressed widow. He also complicated this subject position by subsequently adding to his account women like the rani of Burdwan—young widows with minor sons, who, liberated by the deaths of their husbands, showed a penchant for management. Yet neither of these two accounts, Munro's or Sydenham's, found its way into the Company's final summary, which I will discuss later. Whatever heterogeneity was offered here did not contribute in any way to the "truth" of Hindu women. Instead, the version that won out was the one established by Teignmouth's initial testimony—Hindu women were invisible women who were completely possessed by native men.

The tendency to ignore varied evidence about Indian women is emphasized further when another testimony, by a scrupulous act of differentiation, reveals momentarily in the proceedings the staged perspective of a poor, subaltern woman. For the Company, keeping European labor out of India ensured that the Indian peasantry could be mined at superexploitative levels. At the end of the eighteenth century, the East India Company had supervised rapid deindustrialization in its Bengal territories so that a vast reserve of population could be left "free" in the countryside to churn out handloomed cloth and raw materials for export to Europe. Subsequently, India was imagined in the metropole as a vast undisturbed countryside where natives worked in semifeudal arrangements. Thus, there was little interest on the Company's part in introducing mechanization or in bringing to the colonies the industrial revolution that was transforming England.

Now we see another woman being scripted into the Company's narrative for a deindustrialized India. It seems that as time went on it became clear to many witnesses, as well as to those on the committee upholding the Company's position, that a gendered subject could play an important role in almost any argument. In one of the penultimate testimonies of the hearing, Mungo Dick, a former Company employee from the commercial department, testified about the condition of "native manufacture"—handloom weaving in Bengal. When Dick showed a reluctance to admit that the injection of English capital, or mechanization, could be advantageous to this class of workers, a committee member asked if he "wants to keep the weavers poor." Dick responded by providing an account of the thread-spinning stage of cloth production and described how thread was "prepared generally by the female population at large, by the poorer classes of females." He emphasized this process as a key source of employment for "the females of the families of cultivators" and ended with a clincher: if this resource failed them, he said, "it would be more difficult in India than in any other country in the world, to turn to any profession to which they have not been brought up" (ME, 559).

Now the poor rural woman was operating as an alibi for continuing deindustrialization in the colony and for continuing exploitation of the male peasantry through a rather astute use of the notion of gendered work. Committee members were maneuvered into a false choice: supporting either the only employment that secluded Indian women would ever get or the public mode of factory work that would benefit only men. It is clear that references to Indian women operated in contradictory and self-negating ways throughout these testimonies and that the only unity granted to them categorically was that of their ability to simultaneously serve the arguments used to oppose all of the various interests. First, we have the convergence of the spatial with the gendered body through a sexual connection—that of Englishmen helping themselves to women in the interior—being used against shipping interests and merchants who would bring seamen and traders into the interior. The figure of the imperiled woman forced a class division among Englishmen—the elite and middle-class men, who ran India, and the lower orders, who as a result of the freeing up of trade would bring their sexual and moral intemperance into the colony. Second, the Indian woman was an emblem equated with religion and culture, so that any attempt by missionaries to save her would set off insurrections among native men. Third, she was labor that the British had to protect by keeping India in agrarian feudalism. The woman facilitated these moments of exchange between the Company and those who opposed it, but she rarely came forward as a real referent. She was more than anything else the evocation of an activity that circulated between various groups of Englishmen.

Scholarship in recent years has addressed the various ways in which upper- and middle-class biases against the growing working and manufacturing classes in Britain took mainly two forms. On the one hand, there were cultural representations in which images of degeneration and dirt were often used to allegorize members of the laboring class as racial Others.[16] Britain was often conceived as two nations of opposite character in much the same way that Hastings saw British India.[17] On the other hand, there was the discourse of social reform in Britain too—of the moral regeneration and rehabilitation of the working class—spearheaded, coincidentally, by the same forces that were clamoring for a moral role in ruling India: the Evangelicals and the Methodists.[18] In the casting of the "lower orders of Englishmen" as a potential threat to the stability of British India, we see a classic example of how "regulatory mechanisms of the colonial state were directed not only at the colonized" but also against those seen as "internal enemies" of Europeans.[19] We learn through the testimonies that the "lower parts," or lower-class Europeans, needed to be "kept in order" by "severe restraints of the government" (ME, 68); that "lower classes" acquired "habits" in India that made them reluctant to leave after having resided there for some time (ME, 70); that "seamen, tradesmen and artificers" were morally "intemperate" (ME, 75); and, most importantly, that presence of the lower classes would result in the "degradation" of European character in front of the natives (ME, 35). Racial superiority, already a justification for colonial rule, would be threatened, Company employees insisted, by the presence of the noncovenanted British underclasses in India (ME, 91). The testimonies show us how representations of native women were used to preside over this kind of regulation in the metropole and the colony at the same time. It was in their name that the degeneracy of the working class was invoked, though the anxiety that circulated was centered on fears not of miscegenation but of native insurrection.[20] Despite all the shapes this discussion took, the Company's gendered allegory for protecting India from trade penetration and the English working class did not work.

Discursive Dead Ends and Reemergences

Historian Nicholas Dirks has remarked that "colonial texts did not always mean what they seemed."[21] This is a useful reminder, especially for a researcher who is looking at six hundred pages of official testimony that ultimately prove a historical dead end. The Company's concerted effort to disallow free trade in India failed, and the new charter of 1813, voted in by Parliament, added clauses to permit more flexibility in the issuance of licenses for Europeans to proceed to and reside in India. Shipping ports were laid open and British goods could be sold in India. Also added was a "Pious Clause" that said, "It is the duty of this country to promote the interests and happiness of the native inhabitants of the British Dominions in India."[22] In 1818, five years after the failed effort, we see that the Company's court of directors was still trying to persuade the Board of Control to ignore the newly legislated provisions. In a letter to President of the Board George Canning, the chairman and deputy chairman of the East India Company, John

Jebb and James Pattison, argued that many of the applications the Company had received since the enactment of the new charter appeared to be "wholly unfounded," while others "have been preferred in a spirit of adventure by persons of ruined fortune and questionable character." The chairmen went on to express regret that the board continued to overrule their refusals and warned Canning that "evils are likely to arise from the large influx of Europeans in India." What is striking about this letter is that the chairmen rehearsed many of the arguments made by the witnesses in 1813 and actually begged leave to refer to the "valuable mass of authentic testimony" collected during that time. Here in the letter we see the Company's own summary of that exercise and its concluding propositions, though they never made it to the final committee report. Many years later, it is the closest we can get to an idea of what the Company interpreted as its most powerful arguments from that massive oral archive of employee testimony. When the chairmen outlined the main propositions of 1813, this was the first item on the list: "That the natives of India, though generally speaking weak in body and timid in spirit, are very susceptible of resentment and of peculiarly quick sensibility in all that regards their religion and women."[23]

Indian women are disproportionately present in the summary by the chairmen. Although they had appeared only intermittently and briefly in the mass of testimonies, here they became part of the Company's main proposition to keep India closed to European traffic. They were also hitched to the most authoritative source among the testimonies, Warren Hastings, thus giving the impression that native women had originally been part of his evidence. The quotation marks are missing, but the first part of the sentence in question is word for word from Hastings's opening response. Despite this narrative grafting, the proposition is also an accurate rendering of the awkward and contradictory place given to native women in the official discourse that used them. They were "natives," but at the same time they were excluded from that category when attached to the possessive pronoun *their*. As "their" women, Indian women, here read primarily as Hindu women, could not also logically be part of the first category of natives, for there the native men occupy their place—"weak in body and timid in spirit." When native men were feminized, native women were excluded from the former's place and became the mirroring supplement—a potential catalyst for the men's remasculinization in that they reflected native-male powerlessness.

We see that whatever heterogeneity existed in the evidence of native women was voided at the level of the propositions. Women were reduced to a persistent chronotope in the official discourse: that of unchanging possessions of the native men through their religious and cultural "rights."

As mediators between the foreground of British rule and the background of native existence, women also served as a shifting temporal boundary to designate native men's simultaneous existence in the time zones of tradition and modernity: native men were reconstituted in the proceedings not only as despots (religious fanatics and sexual tyrants) and captive labor in feudal structures, but also as free, woman-owning Hindu or Muslim householders in modernity. I will address the temporal aspects of such gendering later, but I want to end the discussion of these testimonies by looking briefly at oral testimonies, the narrative structure through which information was gathered at the proceedings. Let us begin by retracing the steps from the chairmen's failure to persuade the board.

After the Company's letter reached him in March 1818, George Canning took almost five months to reply and then represented the reply as a mere formality. In their letter, the two chairmen had referred to the "valuable mass of authentic testimony" of the "Minutes of Evidence" taken in 1813 and asked Canning to consider their contents. Canning's response to that suggestion as well as to the list of propositions the Company arrived at is worth noting:

> [Your] letter recapitulates the recorded maxims of old and able governors and magistrates of India, and refers to the opinions of those eminent servants of the Company who were examined before the committee of the House of Commons on the renewal of the Charter in 1813. But it must not be forgotten, that all these arguments and authorities against laying open India to the influx of uncovenanted Europeans, were manifestly and notoriously brought forward to prevent the opening of the trade. Parliament not in consonance to these arguments and authorities, but in spite of them, decided to adopt this measure.[24]

There is little doubt that Canning was rejecting not only the content of the testimonies as biased in favor of the Company but also the very modality of the knowledge production that was being staged—oral testimonies instead of written records. It is worth asking what epistemic considerations operated in the use of oral testimonies and what their failure tells us about the relationship between the format of the official record and the changes in the politico-economic function of the East India Company.

For a system of governance that had long depended on various formats of written communications in its deliberations, the six hundred pages of viva voce demanded attention. It is likely that the Company used these witnesses in person not only to lend the weight of public luminaries like Hastings and Lord Teignmouth but also to give the impression of unmediated and authoritative access to British India through the self-presence of voice and body. Yet there is something unusual about this set of witnesses. Most of them were retired from Company service. Cowper, Teignmouth, and Hastings had not been back to India for twelve, fourteen, and thirty years respectively. If this was the extent of their temporal distance from India, what exactly was their expertise?

The native is supposed to be constituted as an ethnographic object through the use of empiricist methods, but the witnesses in these proceedings traditionally resorted to reports, hearsay, and personal experience. Paradoxically, it was the assertion that the native was "unchanged" since the beginning of Indian history that allowed the disparity between time of service and knowledge of a contemporaneous India to go unchallenged.[25] In other words, such a motley crew could be assembled for a sociology of native manners only because Orientalist discourses were still exerting their residual power at the scene of empiricism. It is remarkable how few of them referred to published scholarship for their observations on Indians. It is almost as though a new storehouse of information based on hearsay, gossip, rumor, and tropes had become the common basis of knowledge for the bureaucrats and officers of the Company. Interestingly enough, Hastings was one of the few witnesses to refer to the Company's official record, but he did this merely as an exercise to prove his own consistency over the years. Hastings asked the committee to consult his old letters in the Company's archive to ascertain that his opinions had not changed. The archive would guarantee, he insisted, that he was under no "bias of attachment to the East India Company" (ME, 4).

The testimony seemed to undo its own grounding assumptions as the proceedings got under way. The very congruence of various individual testimonies shook the appearance of random viewpoints of experienced people from the field. As the same tropes were repeated in various responses and as the patterns of questions and answers began to indicate the positions and interests at stake in them, the experimental format of colonial truth became colonial nonsense—a wasted effort of many months for the Company. The very people whose words were unquestionable fact when arriving as written dispatches from India to the Company's office, and whose observations became the fundamental basis of policy making in the metropole, were now dismissed in Canning's letter as stagers of manifest and notorious bias.

It is clear from Canning's dismissal of the chairmen's letter that the Company's gradual loss of political and economic power had rendered its official knowledge channels simply one more conduit of what-shall-we-do-with-India talk. Perhaps it was this very knowledge, that the loss of real power had also diminished the potential of rational arguments and logical premises, that led the Company through its functionaries and well-wishers to resort to arguments based on a sexual allegory—a sexual allegory whose main players were a figure of simmering native insurrection (the Hindu man), a figure of potential violation (the Hindu woman), a figure of sexual depravity (the working-class Englishman), and a figure of benevolent protection (the Company). It was assumed that the audience would know how to read the allegory, that their need for deep reassurances about the various class, race, and sexuality contests going on in England at that time would ensure a plotting that was just the way the Company needed it to be.

Although the exercise failed, there is no doubt that the Company and the select committee were rehearsing tropes that would only grow in power and a sexual allegory that could be reworked in time into a new script with new players. Though the policy intentions of this exercise ran their official course, we can still track the figure of the Hindu woman as it goes on to other sites and afterlives. The 1813 arguments for protection and noninterference were made at the highest and most public sites of British power. The colonial administration established through these discussions and through the widely circulated documents from the proceedings a figuration of the Hindu woman as the final frontier of colonial rule. As the protected object in the colony, the Hindu woman also served as a metaphor for Hinduism, its cultural practices, and the private sphere of Hindu subjects. This would have far-reaching implications for shaping the woman question in subsequent colonialist social reform legislation, nineteenth-century nationalist agendas, and postcolonial struggles. I will not address all the lineages of this discourse but will touch briefly on the most significant rendering of this figure in the 1820s—as the Hindu widow in the sati debates. Even as the Company was getting its knuckles rapped by Canning in 1818, Rammohun Roy was already formulating the next stage of this figure's afterlife.

Woman as Sign of Tradition

It is only a short thematic journey from the official record made up in London to the unofficial discussions by Hindu men in Bengal as they took on the task of rearticulating native tradition as well as their own subjectivities as upper-caste, zamindari, and *bhadralok* (urban middle-class) subjects by recasting the Hindu woman's place in relation to theirs. The rearticulation of woman as a sign for tradition, albeit a tradition disempowered and objectified, enabled the later "re-empowering of different groups of elite men as the transcendental social critics of that tradition."[26]

The appearance of Rammohun Roy, the son of the rani of Burdwan's lover, Ramkant Roy, and perhaps the most famous reformer of nineteenth-century British India, allows us to connect the power lines from that earlier scene to this one. His case may be a metonym for the nexus between the zamindari class and British colonial rule. Rammohun Roy became notorious as an apologist for that rule, and his well-publicized trip to England to appear before the 1831 Select Committee of the House of Commons on the Affairs of the East India Company is an ironic coda to the 1813 exercise that began this chapter. The select committee's use of Roy enacts the last act in the long script of an allegory of empire, revealing the roles played by expert witnesses and native informants who appeared in colonial discourse at various historical moments to herald new configurations of power.

In 1818 Rammohun Roy published an English translation of his first tract on widow burning, titled *A Conference between an Advocate and an Opponent of the Practice of Burning Widows Alive.* The opponent begins by arguing that widow burning is "forbidden by the Shasturs [*sic*] and by every race of men."[27] The advocate responds by quoting from saints and various ancient scriptural texts that seem to condone or celebrate the practice. The opponent agrees that the quoted passages are indeed "sacred law" but goes on to quote other ancient texts that presumably supersede the authority of the ones used by the advocate. The Vedas and Manusmrti, the opponent insists, do not advocate widow burning; they suggest either that the widow must live an ascetic life or at least that sati is a matter of personal choice.

At first glance, Roy's act of making ancient texts give up lessons for widows' liberation may seem like an exercise in oppositional reading. Yet, as Lata Mani has argued convincingly in her path-breaking study of the sati controversy in nineteenth-century British India, making the widow into a discursive site for scriptural debates often left the real suffering of women as satis marginal to the debate's central concerns. Moreover, the widows were discussed either as heroines or victims—positions that precluded the possibility of a complex female subjectivity.[28] In Roy's *Conference,* such a displacement of women is performed when Hindu women are hitched to national honor and tradition. Here is the opponent of sati making a final exhortation to the advocate: "By forsaking prejudice and reflecting on the Shastur, what is really conformable to its precepts may be perceived, and the evils and disgrace brought on this country by the crime of female murder will cease."[29] Roy tied amelioration of Hindu women's position to the restoration of the legitimacy of the community and tradition they were part of, and the goal of such a restoration was already mapped out in the ancient Hindu scriptures. In 1829, when Roy drafted an address to Governor-General Lord Bentinck after sati was prohibited, this point was developed further to incorporate new domains into a gendered nexus.

In the address, Roy thanked Bentinck for the "invaluable protection" that his government had "afforded to the lives of the Hindoo female part of [his] subjects" and for his "humane . . . exertions in rescuing [Hindu men] from the gross stigma hitherto attached to [their] characters as willful murderers of females, and zealous promoters of the practice of suicide."[30] The residual power of an earlier discourse is visible in Roy's words: the colonial state and the governor-general were protectors of Hindu women. But in that the status of Hindu women was tied to the character of Hindu men, the latter were also rescued from cultural disgrace by the rearticulation of the place of the former. A hierarchy was established in the differentiated native as Hindu women slipped away to the margins so their reform or their rescue from Indian men was replaced by the real issue—that of saving Hindu men from themselves.

What is undeniable in the language of the address is the now ubiquitous place of religion and the ancient scriptures. In Roy's earlier tract of 1818, the Shastras operated as early sources for finding the legitimate authority on sati. Now we get a sense that Hindu women's status in a broader context was also being derived from the religious domain. As Roy extols the virtues of the prohibitory act he says, "The lives of [his] female Hindoo subjects should be henceforth more efficiently protected; that the heinous sin of cruelty to females may no longer be committed, and that the most ancient and purest system of Hindoo religion should not any longer be set at nought by the Hindoos themselves."[31]

In a fundamentally unequal and gendered way, religion was now given the task of writing women's subjectivity. In the address, Roy also argued that the system of "female destruction" was a recent "degradation" of Hindu religion "followed in defiance of the most sacred authorities"—the Upanishads, the Vedas, the Bhagavad Gita, and the Manusmrti. These ancient texts were now installed as the primary authorities on women's status. Thus, when Roy suggested a more general return to Hinduism in its "most ancient and purest system," it was clear that this dredging operation was to be conducted primarily for Hindu women rather than for Hindu men. Now Roy's readers were to think of Bengali upper-caste women in their most ancient and pure form. When the woman was scripted through the various versions of religious texts, her original undegraded figuration became the proper meaning—everything else was degraded trope. There is inescapable irony here: Roy was able to make this argument precisely because the colonial rulers had already created the conditions for such an ahistorical articulation of religious and cultural identity. This was done through their own systematic creation in the 1770s of what they believed to be a fundamental archive of Hindu law and religion—a paradoxically modern endeavor.[32] It reminds us of the unacknowledged genealogy of what people today often glibly identify as religious fundamentalism, thus reflecting the mistaken idea that such ideological formations are surviving remnants of premodern thought or culture.

The sati debate telescoped through the work of Roy shows us that the figure of the Hindu woman replicates itself within a constellation of meaning not very different from that of the 1813 discussions. Only the speaking positions have been rearranged, and in this round it is the Hindu woman who has no history and must remain unchanged for all time. The so-called degradation of the Hindu woman's status also affected the status of the Hindu male: when she became victim of male violence, he was recoded as murderer, and saving the Hindu woman became part of the larger project of saving Hindu men, and by extension India, from disgrace. The figure of the Hindu woman thus facilitated the emergence of a new, urban, politicized class through her metonymic and metaphoric function. As part of that tradition she is a *Hindu* woman and, as a substitute for it, the emblem of tradition and nation. Because her existence was scripted through ancient texts and religious discourses, she quickly became the antimodern chronotope that is often identified today as being part and parcel of nationalist discourse. Anne McClintock has described this phenomena as a "temporal anomaly" within nationalism: the "veering between nostalgia for the past and the impatient, progressive sloughing off of the past . . . is typically resolved by figuring the contradiction in the representation of *time* as a natural division of *gender*."[33] Thus the Hindu woman represented the authentic tradition of Hinduism and Indian culture, the embodiment of cultural autonomy, purity, and national essence, while Roy and other men like him represented the "progressive agents of modernity" and its transformative, onward drive into the future—here the common horizon of English civilization.

Roy has allowed us to move from the colonizer-colonized binary to questions of native hegemony. It is already well established that the Bengali upper-caste elite, or the *bhadralok,* emerged out of the 1793 Permanent Settlement in Bengal, when a class of largely absentee landlords was created. This settlement deprived female landholders of a future place in the Company's designs but allowed other Bengalis, like Roy's father, Ramkant Roy, to consolidate their position as members of the new class, which worked in close collaboration with the English. A genealogy of this class will establish its power lines to the 1820s. We have already seen that Roy became a new kind of informant: not to give testimonies about the natives, as the Company servants did in 1813, but to *be* the testimony itself. He was both speaking subject and mouthpiece for his culture, religion, and class. Not only that, Roy was also a testimony to the success of British rule, of its ability to make the natives over into imaged products of English civilization.

In 1830 Roy sailed for England, where his role in the sati debate, his journalistic and cultural writings in the vernacular press, and his interaction with the active segment of missionaries had already created unprecedented publicity for him. Sophia Collet, an Englishwoman who chronicled his life in the late nineteenth century describes his visit from 1831 to 1833 as a "dramatic culmination" of his half-century of public service.[34] Forces of liberalism that had energized the first reform bill and had set the stage for the slow transformation from a closed oligarchy to a democracy needed a new argument for the empire. Roy's arrival, no doubt, helped stage what Uday Singh Mehta has termed, in a different context, "the liberal justification for empire." Liberal and progressive forces could now speak of the "temporary necessity and foreseeable prolongation" of the empire.[35] Thus Collet's description of Roy as India "incarnate" and as "the noble and precocious type of the New India that had been growing up under British rule," though belated, is still an accurate rendering of one way in which Roy was being scripted into metropolitan dominant ideologies.[36] He embodied literally for the British public their first exposure to Indian intellect, but that was not a transparent position either. Roy also presented, as an admirer and ally of English rule, a new signifier for the liberal imperialists—the past success of British rule and the reason it should continue.

In 1832, Rammohun Roy's name was entered into the appendix to the *Report from the Select Committee of the House of Commons on the Affairs of the East India Company*. As the committee and Parliament began their deliberations over the imminent renewal of the Company's charter, the ghost of an earlier debate was coming back with great ferocity. Encouraged by the relaxation of travel and residency requirements in India, English indigo planters from Bengal were now calling for new laws that would allow them to actually own land in India. Previously, the Company had restricted them to long-term leases. India was being reimagined: from a Company jurisdiction to a permanent settler colony for the English. Capitalizing on Roy's presence in England, the select committee summoned him as a witness. In the appendix to the report, published in 1832, there is a memorandum titled "Remarks by Rammohun Roy on Settlement in India by Europeans." I discussed in chapter 3 why an official discussion of settlement and colonization had to wait till the 1830s. It is significant that its debut in the official records was presided over by the figure of the enlightened native nodding assent to the takeover of his land by an alien power. Though Roy plays the pros and cons of colonization in his memorandum, his closing words are unambiguous, and they parrot the Company officials' long-standing class bias: "On mature consideration, therefore, I think I may safely recommend that educated persons of character and capital should now be permitted and encouraged to settle in India without any restriction of locality or any liability of punishment."[37]

We have already seen how conjuring the figure of the Hindu woman was an important way for the native bourgeois elite to exercise its presence to itself as a class and to the British authorities as a potential source of collaboration or conflict. What is often less known is the role of print and the vernacular press in consolidating the position of this elite. The emergence of the vernacular press coincided with the beginning of the sati debate; its role in facilitating a textual interplay between colonizer and colonized is visible when we look at the final report by the committee. While it was true that Roy's physical presence in England made it possible for the Company to stage him as the ideal native subject, the technology of print and the circulation of his writing finally ensured his preservation in the colonial archives in ways Roy could not fully anticipate. In a memorandum commissioned by the Board of Control and inserted into the final report of 1831–1832, we see that the board was united with Parliament in supporting local interests clamoring for colonization. A segment from a speech given by Roy in Calcutta on 15 December 1829 and subsequently printed in the *Asiatic Journal* in 1830 was now carefully excerpted into the new script of British colonization.

Roy is the only source quoted directly, and to his name are added embellishments such as "an illustrious native" and "an authority of great weight." All native opinions from the vernacular press contesting the change in British policy are mentioned in a general statement in the memorandum about charges made by "native writers" in the "Indian press." None are excerpted in the report. Even Roy himself has been flattened to erase any contradiction. The one negative charge he had made before the board, about the ill effects of British rule on the *ryots*, or sharecropping farmers, was neutralized by the writer of the memorandum, who followed Roy's remarks to this effect with a statement from an earlier speech in which Roy praised the indigo farmers for keeping their laborers "better clothed and better conditioned."[38]

By entering the official record as an expert witness, Roy signaled the new phase of colonialism as liberal paternalism. In place of Company officials playing ethnographers, we have the privileged native informant, not in his older role as translator or scribe or religious authority, but as the new elite class that nods assent toward the center of imperial power.

Recon(figuring) Woman

In this book, I have tried to breach the divide between feminist historiography and feminist literary analysis by rethinking the relationship between the symbolic constructs of women and women's role as social agents. By reading these symbolic constructs not only in their more usual domain—in literary and cultural texts—but also in spheres of social ordering where women are less visible as historical subjects, I have attempted to demonstrate how these social spheres are gendered. I have made the case that by eschewing the need for individualized historical subjects to provide quantitative proof of participation we may actually see hidden agendas more clearly. Where women are all but absent, we may still see their presence as politically interested figurations when agendas that may not affect them directly are carried out in their name.

Joan Scott has argued that gender seems to have been a "persistent and recurrent way of enabling the signification of power in the West, in the Judaeo-Christian as well as the Islamic tradition."[1] This means that in general sex-related differences were constantly summoned as testimony to social relations and phenomena that had very little to do with sexuality.[2] I have not ascribed such representational practices to cultural tendencies solely in specific traditions, for doing so would ignore the power of figurative language in all language use. Recasting various political and economic interests through modes of figurative speech—indeed recoding them allegorically as sexual relations—adds to their ideological power. Because gender, like race, is still one of the primarily recognizable or visible ways of organizing difference, where arbitrary explanations often appear as natural, self-evident, and commonsensical, such allegorical recodings are often political attempts to disguise these processes. The two cases of strategic recoding in the last chapter, one by the Company and the other by Rammohun Roy, show us how the act of changing a proper or literal meaning into a rhetorical or figurative one, or vice versa, is a contestatory act that is part and parcel of social and political struggle.

In a recent essay written jointly by feminist scholars Susie Tharu and Tejaswini Niranjana, we read that the use of women as alibis for new political configurations is alive and well. The authors place the term *women* in quotation marks every time they refer to the gender mobilizations of upper-caste and upper-class Hindu political groups in contemporary India, showing us an activist assertion of literal meaning against symbolic constructs. The essay begins with the startling declaration that "suddenly 'women' are everywhere," but the authors do not make this visibility fully into "an index of the success of the women's movement." Instead, Tharu and Niranjana assert that a wide range of issues rendered critical by feminism are now "being invested in and annexed by projects that contain and deflect that initiative."[3]

Such hegemonic appropriations, Tharu and Niranjana argue, are characterized by the hidden structuring of feminist subjects as unmarked and neutral, even as their agendas carry all the markings of class, caste, and community. Thus, on the one hand, we get the neonationalist middle-class subject that "proclaims its Indianness even as it internationalizes itself." On the other hand, there is the middle-class woman recruited as an "icon of purity and idealism" in order to effect an othering of lower-caste men as a collective threat to her "honor."[4] Such fractures of class, caste, and religion within gendered struggles only help consolidate the restructuring work of globalization as middle-class women are recruited into economic agendas seen as feminist. A reconfiguring of feminism is especially urgent, Tharu and Niranjana assert, as middle classes help make poor women into alibis for projects cited by development experts, population planners, and economists. Here, the task of feminists resisting such appropriations in postcolonial or neocolonial spaces clearly intersects with that of feminists in the First World, where forces are spearheading globalization, also in the name of women.[5]

It is significant but not surprising that in Tharu and Niranjana's discussion of contemporary gender politics a moment of historical memory asserts itself: "The marking of 'women' as middle class and upper caste has a long genealogy that, historically and conceptually, goes back into nationalism as well as social reform. Marked thus, 'women' are seen as morally pure and uncorrupted—hence the significance of their protest, which becomes a 'disinterested' one since they have no place in the organized political process."[6] The opening of the past into the present in this excerpt provides an important lesson for feminist critics and historians. To articulate the past historically means, to borrow a phrase from Walter Benjamin, nothing less than seizing hold of a memory "as it flashes up at the moment of danger."[7] This book, I hope, will serve such a purpose in the present. On this side of the neocolonial divide, here in the United States, postcolonial scholars and scholars of the eighteenth and nineteenth centuries could begin critical excavations into the history of their own preferred significations. Such critical genealogies must track the forces that continue to animate the markings of women of the South as cheap labor, objects of population control, bearers of ecological burden, veiled victims of fundamentalism, and premodern subjects.

NOTES

Introduction

1. Elizabeth Hamilton, *Translations of the Letters of a Hindoo Rajah,* 89. *Shastra* is Sanskrit for any of the sacred texts of the Hindus.

2. For a discussion of some of the important Enlightenment comparative histories of women in eighteenth-century France and England, see Sylvana Tomaselli, "The Enlightenment Debate on Women," 101–24. The work of many political economists shows the growing importance of women as objects of historical inquiry and their use as simple abstractions within long swaths of historical observations. In the latter half of the eighteenth century, several "histories" of women appeared along with extended accounts of women's economic and legal status that traced their originary roles from the "beginning of time" until their arrival into the companionate marriage of western Europe. See especially John Millar, *Observations concerning the Distinction of Ranks in Society,* and William Alexander, *The History of Women, from the Earliest Antiquity, to the Present Time; Giving Some Account of Almost Every Interesting Particular Concerning that Sex, Among All Nations, Ancient and Modern.*

3. Lora Wildenthal, *German Women for Empire, 1884–1945,* 1. For various elaborations of the feminism-imperialism nexus, see especially Gayatri Chakravorty Spivak, "Three Women's Texts and a Critique of Imperialism"; Jenny Sharpe, *Allegories of Empire: The Figure of Woman in the Colonial Text;* Ann L. Stoler, *Race and the Education of Desire;* and Lata Mani, *Contentious Traditions: The Debate on Sati in Colonial India.*

4. See Betty Joseph, "Gendering Time in Globalization: The Belatedness of the Other Woman and Jamaica Kincaid's *Lucy,*" and Suzanne Bergeron, "Political Economy Discourses of Globalization and Feminist Politics." Naila Kabeer's *Reversed Realities: Gender Hierarchies in Developmental Thought* tracks the use of comparative gender analysis in post-1970s theories of development and United Nations projects. For a general outline of the liberal formulation of the woman question under past and contemporary formations of globalizing capital and a Marxist critique of this projection, see Gayatri Chakravorty Spivak, " 'Other Things Are Never Equal': A Speech."

5. See especially Rosemary Marangoly George, *The Politics of Home: Postcolonial Relocations and Twentieth-Century Fiction,* chapter 2.

6. Elizabeth Fox-Genovese, "Placing Women's History in History," 7, 15.

7. For this point in relation to historiography, see Gayatri Chakravorty Spivak, "Subaltern Studies: Deconstructing Historiography," 219.

8. Gayatri Chakravorty Spivak, *Outside in the Teaching Machine*, 159, and Fox-Genovese, "Placing Women's History," 29.

9. Hélène Cixous, "Laugh of the Medusa," 252.

10. For a succinct discussion of Cixous put to use for imagining a new decolonized subject, see Spivak, *Outside in the Teaching Machine*, 282, 158–60.

11. *The New Shorter Oxford English Dictionary*, 1993 edition, s.v. "archive."

12. James Mill, letter to Dumont, 13 December 1819, quoted in Uday Singh Mehta, *Liberalism and Empire*, 8.

13. See George Birdwood, *Report on the Old Records of the India Office*, 3–5.

14. See William Foster, *A Guide to the India Office Records, 1600–1858*, i–vii.

15. See especially C. H. Philips, *The East India Company, 1784–1834*, 261–68, for an account of Lord Ellenborough's attempts to improve the board's control over the Indian government after the new governing structure was put in place. He did this primarily by introducing a streamlined system of correspondence and copying for all written communication between London and India.

16. For a general history of this trend, see Ian Haywood, *The Making of History*.

17. See Jacques Le Goff, *History and Memory*, 86–88.

18. See the comments made as late as 1889 by F. C. Danvers, Registrar and Superintendent of Records, in Birdwood, *Report*, 7.

19. Bengal Baptisms, Marriages, and Burials.

20. Suresh Chandra Ghosh, *The Social Condition of the British Community in Bengal, 1757–1800*, 58.

21. "Marriages in Calcutta," in Bengal Baptisms, 1:149.

22. See the discussion of climatic theories and sexuality in Felicity Nussbaum, *Torrid Zones: Maternity, Sexuality, and Empire in Eighteenth-Century English Narratives*, 7–14. For figurations of country-born women, see Sophia Goldsborne [pseud.], *Hartly House, Calcutta: A Novel of the Days of Warren Hastings*, 16, 204, and Thomas Williamson, *The East India Vade-Mecum; or, Complete Guide to Gentlemen Intended for the Civil, Military, or Naval Service of the Hon. East India Company*, 1:458.

23. Bengal Baptisms, 1:159.

24. Bengal Wills, 1774–79 and 1780–1783.

25. Equally significant are provisions made by Company employees to have their illegitimate, "half-caste" children sent to England to be educated. That such acts of paternal concern would constitute a threat at the century's end, when racism became part of the logic of governance, is evident in later legislation. In 1792, Lord Cornwallis banned biracial children from the Company's service. Almost simultaneously, schools were started in Calcutta to educate "military orphans," thus preventing their passage to England. See Percival Spear, *The Nabobs: A Study of the Social Life of the English in Eighteenth-Century India*, 63.

26. See especially Lennard J. Davis, *Factual Fictions: The Origins of the English Novel*, and Ian Haywood, *Making of History*.

27. Nicholas Dirks, a historian of South Asia, provides a case in point: "It is all too often the case that the historical experience of colonialism . . . gets lost in the elegant new textualism of colonial discourse studies. While our readings of colonial texts have been reanimated by the recent efflorescence of interest in colonialism, we must realize

that the contexts for interrogating these texts are multiple, and necessarily, historical" ("From Little King to Landlord: Colonial Discourse and Colonial Rule," 175).

28. For this point and the novel's place in eighteenth-century racial discourses, see the excellent reading in Roxann Wheeler, *The Complexion of Race: Categories of Difference in Eighteenth-Century British Culture,* 158–67.

29. Wheeler, *Complexion,* 161.

30. *The Lady's Drawing Room,* 101–2.

31. Davis, *Factual Fictions,* 142.

32. Davis, *Factual Fictions.*

33. For the historical emergence of this phrase, see ibid.

34. Consider this sentence from *The Missionary:* "It was evening when [Hilarion] reached the vale of Cashmire." The footnote at the bottom of the page tells us, "According to Forster, the utmost extent of this delicious vale from S. E. to N. W. is scarcely 90 miles; hither travellers assert it to be but 40 miles from east to west and 25 from north to south." Lady Morgan (Sydney Owenson), *The Missionary,* 1:131–32.

35. *Lady's Drawing Room,* 100.

36. Single women from Europe were not allowed to proceed to India without a license. These were awarded only if financially stable families sponsored them and ensured their upkeep.

37. See Nancy Armstrong, *Desire and Domestic Fiction: A Political History of the Novel.*

38. Michel Foucault, *The Archaeology of Knowledge,* 130–31.

39. Edward Said, *Orientalism,* 42.

40. For similar arguments in the African context, see Christopher Miller, *Blank Darkness,* and V. Y. Mudimbe, *The Invention of Africa.*

41. For an overview, see the chapter "Disorienting Orientalism," in Robert Young, *White Mythologies: Writing History and the West.* Whereas Said has argued that the colonial archive was a body of knowledge or know-how that actually worked, other scholars privilege the fantastic, or what Said terms the latent, aspects of this know-how. In these cases the archive is a fetish, a substitute for what is not really attainable—an image of complete control and unity that substitutes for the actual difficulty of unifying a discontinuous mass of people and territory, even as it provides pretexts and reality effects for the everyday running of the empire. See Thomas Richards, *The Imperial Archive: Knowledge and Fantasy of Empire,* 3–5.

42. Young, *White Mythologies,* 129.

43. Said, *Orientalism,* 94.

44. Tejaswini Niranjana, *Siting Translation: History, Post-Structuralism, and the Colonial Context,* 37–38.

45. Gauri Viswanathan, *Masks of Conquest: Literary Study and British Rule in India,* 2.

46. Ibid., 12.

47. Priya Joshi, *In Another Country: Colonialism, Culture, and the English Novel in India,* 7–8.

48. Gaurav Desai, *Subject to Colonialism: African Self-Fashioning and the Colonial Library,* 4–5, 7, 17; for discussion of the African informant's text, see chapter 3 (145–61).

49. Gayatri Chakravorty Spivak, "The Rani of Sirmur: An Essay in Reading the Archives," 249.

50. Ibid., 270.

51. Ibid., 270–71.

52. For this and similar questions, see Asha Varadharajan's discussion of the essay in *Exotic Parodies: Subjectivity in Adorno, Said, and Spivak*, 100–106.

53. Ibid., 106.

54. Srinivas Aravamudan, *Tropicopolitans: Colonialism and Agency, 1688–1804*, 11, 6, 8, 15, 12 (emphasis in original).

55. Ibid., 310, 313, 315.

56. Ibid., 315, 319–20.

57. Ibid., 70, 308, 323.

58. Spivak, "Rani of Sirmur," 253.

59. Sharpe, *Allegories of Empire*, 61.

60. See chapter 1 of Nussbaum, *Torrid Zones.*

61. Sharpe, *Allegories of Empire*, 7.

62. See Mani, *Contentious Traditions;* Sangeeta Ray, *En-Gendering India: Woman and Nation in Colonial and Postcolonial Narratives;* Partha Chatterjee, *The Nation and Its Fragments;* and Kum Kum Sangari and Sudesh Vaid, *Recasting Women: Essays in Colonial History.*

63. Ernesto Laclau and Chantal Mouffe, *Hegemony and Socialist Strategy: Towards a Radical Democratic Politics*, 108.

64. Ranajit Guha, "The Prose of Counter-Insurgency."

65. For this discussion of tropes as truth, see Gayatri Chakravorty Spivak, *A Critique of Postcolonial Reason: Toward a History of the Vanishing Present*, 147.

66. Raymond Williams, *Marxism and Literature*, 121, 122, 123.

67. See Michel Foucault, "Two Lectures," 202.

68. Michel Foucault, "Nietzsche, Genealogy, History," 83–84. See also "Two Lectures," 203.

69. For a large-scale story of European middle-class formation taking place at home and abroad using the woman as a sexual and cultural boundary, see Ann L. Stoler, *Race and the Education of Desire.*

70. Cixous, "Laugh of the Medusa," 252.

71. J. S. Mill, "The Subjection of Women," 170–71.

Chapter One

1. Edward Said, *Culture and Imperialism*, 51.

2. For a useful discussion about the problem of locating early "Third World" responses to colonialism, one that problematizes the use of the colonial archives for this purpose, see Gayatri Chakravorty Spivak, "The Rani of Sirmur: An Essay in Reading the Archives," 249.

3. For an excellent discussion of the Orientalist sources of Defoe's heroine, see Katie Trumpener, "Rewriting Roxane: Orientalism and Intertextuality in Montesquieu's *Lettres Persanes* and Defoe's *The Fortunate Mistress.*"

4. For a discussion of various eighteenth-century cultural comparisons, see Sylvana Tomaselli, "The Enlightenment Debate on Women," and Felicity Nussbaum, *Torrid Zones: Maternity, Sexuality, and Empire in Eighteenth-Century English Narratives.* Important discussions of the feminism/imperialism nexus include Gayatri Chakravorty Spivak, "Three Women's Texts and a Critique of Imperialism"; Jenny Sharpe, *Allegories of Empire: The Figure of Woman in the Colonial Text;* Ann L. Stoler, *Race*

and the Education of Desire; Lata Mani, *Contentious Traditions;* and Lora Wildenthal, *German Women for Empire, 1884–1945.*

5. The phrasing is Gayatri Chakravorty Spivak's. See her cautions about feminism under globalization in *A Critique of Postcolonial Reason: Toward a History of the Vanishing Present,* 176–77.

6. Daniel Defoe, *Roxana the Fortunate Mistress;* Records of Fort St. George, Diary and Consultation Book of 1721.

7. Maurice Godelier, quoted in Joan Wallach Scott, "Gender: A Useful Category of Historical Analysis," 170.

8. Scott, "Gender," 173.

9. See Gayatri Chakravorty Spivak, ed., *In Other Worlds,* 215–19, and Jenny Sharpe's use of this principle in *Allegories of Empire,* 7.

10. In an interview published in the *Oxford Literary Review,* Gayatri Spivak takes to task the nativist feminist's attempt to argue for an opposition between "feminism" and "rights of woman": "I think it is also important that you recognize that the concept of human rights, individual rights, has a deep complicity with the culture of imperialism. If you say this then some anthropological search will isolate and find some native text where something can be translated as 'right.' . . . Again this is a very politically important gesture to say, 'no, we had it all along.' But none the less gesture politics and the production of knowledge are not the same thing. You cannot fight something if you do not acknowledge that what is poison has also historically been medicine" ("Neocolonialism and the Secret Agent of Knowledge"). Spivak is arguing the impossibility of a separate history for the Indian feminist who speaks up for rights while rejecting the conceptual framework of Western feminism. Ignorance of the history that "secures one's position" and creates the law under which one is making one's claim cannot, for Spivak, be equated with self-determination in knowledge production. For an example of elite feminist articulation of such an "independent self-view," see Madhu Kishwar, "Why I Do Not Call Myself a Feminist."

11. See Madeleine Kahn, *Narrative Transvestism,* and Nancy Armstrong, *Desire and Domestic Fiction: A Political History of the Novel.*

12. Armstrong, *Desire and Domestic Fiction,* 9–10, 14.

13. Kahn, *Narrative Transvestism,* 93.

14. For a wonderful elaboration of this argument, see Janet Sorenson, " 'I Talk to Everybody in Their Own Way': Defoe's Economies of Identity," 77.

15. For a thoughtful discussion of the evolution of these concepts, see C. B. Macpherson, *The Political Theory of Possessive Individualism.*

16. See Gayatri Chakravorty Spivak's argument to this effect in "Theory in the Margin: Coetzee's Foe Reading Defoe's Crusoe/Roxana."

17. Armstrong, *Desire and Domestic Fiction,* and Carole Pateman, *The Sexual Contract.*

18. We can, for instance, see *Roxana* as situated within these debates by looking at some of the organs of publicity, such as the *Spectator* or *Rambler.* In 1712, a letter in the *Spectator* responded to another letter in which a man had complained about the misuse of his money and status by a wife who enforced the common-law custom of pin money to support her lavish habits and immoral practices: "Separate Purses, between man and Wife, are, in my Opinion, as unnatural as separate beds" (*The Spectator,* 53). This connection between sexuality and separate property is made even more forcefully in Samuel Johnson's letter to the *Rambler* in 1751: "Two thousand pounds in the last age, with a domestick wife, would go farther than ten thousand in this. Yet settlements

are expected, that often, to a mercantile man especially, sink a fortune into uselessness; and pin-money is stipulated for, which makes a wife independent and destroys love, by putting it out of a man's power to lay any obligation upon her, that might engage gratitude, and kindle affection" (Samuel Johnson, in *Rambler* 97, 158).

19. Armstrong, *Desire and Domestic Fiction*, 3.

20. Terry Eagleton, *The Rape of Clarissa: Writing, Sexuality, and Class Struggle in Samuel Richardson*, 4–5.

21. Jacques Derrida, *Acts of Literature*, 36.

22. Peter Fitzpatrick, *The Mythology of Modern Law*, 81.

23. This argument is an extrapolation of Eagleton's reading of *Clarissa* in *Rape of Clarissa*, 60.

24. In her study *Ends of Empire: Women and Ideology in Early Eighteenth-Century English Literature*, Laura Brown traces the profusion of narrative conjunctures of empire and the figure of woman in eighteenth-century British literature. Her argument that the "logical conclusion of the extension of the ideal of mercantilist capitalist profit to women is a brutal and uncontrollable violence, a violation of the supposedly natural and benevolent forces of trade" (154) asks that we see Roxana's hatred of and cruelty toward her children as a displacement of the violence that originates within and permeates male mercantilist, colonialist trade practices. Brown's reading of displacement is useful to show how female subjects are often proxies for power, but it cannot adequately explain the narrative logic of the conjuncture of mothering and paternalism as stand-ins for female individualism and colonial trade.

25. See Betty Joseph, "Mutations of the Imperial Contract."

26. See Daniel Defoe, *The Fortunate Mistress; or, a History of the Life of Mademoiselle de Beleau, Known by the Name of Roxana.*

27. See Daniel Defoe, *The Fortunate Mistress; or, a History of the Life and Vast Variety of Fortunes of Mademoiselle de Beleau . . .*; Daniel Defoe and Isaac Taylor, *The History of Mademoiselle de Beleau; or, The New Roxana. . . .*

28. See Joseph, "Mutations of the Imperial Contract," 45–46.

29. For this summary I have depended on Maximillian Novak's introduction to Daniel Defoe, *The Manufacturer.*

30. Defoe, *The Manufacturer*, 1 (30 October 1719).

31. Ibid., 3.

32. Ibid., 1.

33. Defoe in *Review* 8 (3 June 1712): 751, quoted in Bram Dijkstra, *Defoe and Economics: The Fortunes of Roxana in the History of Interpretation*, 43.

34. Fitzpatrick, *Mythology of Modern Law*, 107.

35. Records of Fort St. George, Diary and Consultation Book of 1721.

36. Frances Ferguson, "Rape and the Rise of the Novel," 88, 98, 91.

37. Robert Chambers, *A Course of Lectures on the English Law, 1767–1773*, 1:406, quoted in Ferguson, "Rape," 91.

38. Quoted in Ferguson, "Rape," 89.

39. Michael Ryan, "Self-Evidence," 7.

40. The social rather than individual nature of this violence, which is seen as endangering caste purity rather than individual property in the person, is also visible in the ancient legal institutes, the Laws of Manu from the second century A.D.: "For by [adultery] is caused a mixture of the castes [*varna*] among men; thence [follows] sin, which cuts up even the roots and causes the destruction" (*The Laws of Manu*, 8:352). For reasons of maintaining caste purity, a number of "adulterous" acts that caused

"defilement" and "mixture" were seen as synonymous with rape: speaking with female members of another caste, touching, offering ornaments, and so on. The punishments levied for these crimes were higher if there was no consent from the victim, and they were highest when the act neared the greatest levels of caste transgression. In some of these intercaste rapes, for instance, consent was statutorily immaterial because the caste rules against cohabitation forbade anything nearing consensual intercourse. There is little evidence about a source of "native law" in the case of the Bashwar woman. To assume that the caste council or the woman's relatives were appealing to ancient law is a fallacy. My reading of this early text is merely to indicate that there was some cultural variation in the reading of rape, even as money was becoming the universal standard of judgment.

41. See Arthur Berridale Keith, *A Constitutional History of India, 1600–1935.*

42. This is clearly a rebuttal of a number of board members who gave it in writing that they were not willing to consider the woman's testimony over that of a loyal employee of the Company (Diary, 37–41).

43. Even ancient Hindu texts do not show evidence that women were disallowed testimony on the grounds of incredulity. Women were able to testify in all cases involving women and in those cases where they had personal knowledge of an act committed in the interior apartments of a house or in a forest, or of a crime causing loss of life, even if the dispute was an intercaste one involving men. Testimony was disallowed on grounds of incredulity to infants, aged men, and the mentally deranged. See Dwarka Nath Mitter, *The Position of Women in Hindu Law,* 174–76, and *Laws of Manu,* 8:75.

44. Just as women must be figured literarily in Defoe's texts as participants in the fabric of liberal rights, so that the narrative can effectively consign them to appropriate places (rather than simply banish them), in colonial India a similar gesture was undertaken to install relations of private property. Land holdings over which peasants had customary cultivation rights were transformed into private holdings and then appropriated by the British for tax revenue with the help of "contracts" and newly installed landlords. See Ranajit Guha, *A Rule of Property for Bengal: An Essay on the Idea of Permanent Settlement.*

45. These fines can be seen as resulting from the judgment of robbery: they represent compensation or restitution for stolen goods. What is up for speculation is the extent to which the fines were invented for this particular situation. *The Laws of Manu,* for instance, never indicates the proper recipient of the fines imposed for sexual crimes and adultery. The understanding is that if no recipient is named, the fines are to be paid to the king. While loss of property is compensated by a fine imposed on the thief, the only named recipient of a fine for rape is the father of a "maiden," who may accept a "nuptial fee" if he is willing to let his daughter marry the accused. The Company, by accepting a part of the fine, is already taking the place of the higher overseers and assuming the displaced authority of the king.

46. General letter from Fort St. George to the Company, 12 November 1721, in Records of Fort St. George, Despatches to England, 1719–1727, 68.

47. Ibid.

48. Records of Fort St. George, Despatches from England, 1721–1724, 52.

49. Records of Fort St. George, Despatches to England, 1719–1727, 89.

50. Madras, the city surrounding the fort, grew continually after the initial grant was made in 1639. For a brief history of its founding and development patterns in the eighteenth century, see Norma Everson, *The Imperial Metropolis,* 1–15; and Percival

Spear, *The Nabobs: A Study of the Social Life of the English in Eighteenth-Century India*, 1–22.

51. See Spivak, "The Rani of Sirmur," and Homi Bhabha, "Of Mimicry and Man: The Ambivalence of Colonial Discourse."

52. Gayatri Chakravorty Spivak, "Subaltern Studies: Deconstructing Historiography."

53. Derrida, *Acts of Literature*, 191.

54. See Bram Dijkstra's *Defoe and Economics* for an account of various public debates surrounding Defoe's *Roxana*. Even the law of the text, its authorship and its wording, did not remain in place. *Roxana* underwent a number of literal rephrasings as self-appointed coauthors changed the text to make the heroine more palatable or more pleasing. On the other side, of course, are nativist scholars from India who succeed in making the ancient Hindu texts surrender rights for women where it was previously believed none existed.

CHAPTER TWO

1. J. G. A. Pocock, *Virtue, Commerce, and History: Essays in Political Thought and History, Chiefly in the Eighteenth Century*, 49–50.

2. See Markman Ellis, *The Politics of Sensibility: Race, Gender, and Commerce in the Sentimental Novel*, 17, 139.

3. Tobias Smollett, *The Expedition of Humphry Clinker*, 38–39.

4. Helenus Scott, *Adventures of an East-India Rupee: Wherein Are Interspersed, Various Anecdotes Asiatic, and European*, 23.

5. Robert Markley, "Sentimentality as Performance: Shaftesbury, Sterne, and the Theatrics of Value," 210–12.

6. See Felicity Nussbaum, *Torrid Zones: Maternity, Sexuality, and Empire in Eighteenth-Century English Narratives*, 1, 20.

7. For a list of the various official accounts, see Brijen K. Gupta, *Sirajuddaullah and the East India Company, 1756–1757: Background to the Foundation of British Power in India*, 73. Captain Tooke, a factor who took part in the fighting, wrote a voluminous account of the Black Hole, but it is mostly hearsay, for he is believed to have deserted the fort on 19 June—before the night of the Black Hole. For this argument, see Iris MacFarlane, *The Black Hole; or, the Makings of a Legend*, 215–17. Then there is the testimony made by John Cooke before a select committee of the House of Commons in 1772. But this testimony was given almost sixteen years after the incident, by which time his recollection had been supplemented with various other versions of the story. This leaves us with Holwell's narratives and reports and Captain John Mills's text as the only other eyewitness accounts by survivors of the Black Hole written close to the time of the events described. Captain Mills supposedly kept a notebook during the event, but his version is identical word for word with that of a George Grey and seems to have been copied from the latter. So we have the ridiculous situation of an eyewitness's account that is actually based on a hearsay account. See Gupta, *Sirajuddaullah*, 73–74, 146–55, for a word-for-word comparison of the two versions and the argument about the fabrication of the Mills version.

8. Holwell, John Zephaniah. *A Genuine Narrative of the Deplorable Deaths of the English Gentlemen, and Others, Who Were Suffocated in the Black-Hole in Fort-William, at Calcutta, in the Kingdom of Bengal, in the Night Succeeding the 20th*

Day of June, 1756, in a Letter to a Friend, 2–3. On subsequent references, this work will be cited parenthetically in the text as *Narrative*.

9. For the various forms of impressions that make up the archive, see Jacques Derrida, *Archive Fever: A Freudian Impression*, 2, 25–26.

10. For the discussion of eighteenth-century novelistic conventions that moved across the continuum of fact and fiction, see Lennard J. Davis, *Factual Fictions: The Origins of the English Novel*, 161.

11. For this point, see Nancy Armstrong and Leonard Tennenhouse, "The American Origins of the English Novel," 393, and Christopher Castiglia, *Bound and Determined: Captivity, Culture-Crossing, and White Womanhood from Mary Rowlandson to Patty Hearst*.

12. Davis, *Factual Fictions*, 141–43.

13. For a related discussion of the body as a "signifying system," see John Mullan's *Sentiment and Sociability: The Language of Feeling in the Eighteenth Century*, 232.

14. Seid-Gholam-Hosain Khan, *The Sëir Mutaqherin*.

15. For a list of Holwell's versions and the "official" lists used by historians who have corroborated Holwell's account, see S. C. Hill, *List of Europeans and Others . . . at the Time of the Siege of Calcutta*, 6–10.

16. See Saiyid Amin Ahmad, *The Black Hole of Calcutta*, 19–21. Also see Iris MacFarlane, *Black Hole*, 227 n. 1, for her argument about the relationship between Holwell's itinerary after his release from the Black Hole and the timing and location of the appearance of various versions of the events.

17. John Zephaniah Holwell and Friends, *India Tracts*, 180–81.

18. MacFarlane, *Black Hole*, 230.

19. Quoted in Ahmad, *Black Hole of Calcutta*, 39–40.

20. Subsequent British rulers in India were ambivalent about the incident of the Black Hole in later decades. Only Holwell seems to have merged his life into a planned futurity with it. Holwell later became governor of Calcutta, and around 1760 he built a monument in memory of the sufferers at his own expense. Inscribed with the names of the dead, it stood as a testament to the "tyrannic" and "Horrid Act of Violence" by Sirāj-ud-Dawlah while triumphantly proclaiming how he was "deservedly revenged . . . by his Majesty's Arms." For the full text of the inscription see the diagram of the monument in Holwell's *India Tracts*.

The monument stood on the spot assumed to be the mass grave of victims, but the site was also next to the Writers Building, where Company employees could see it every day on their way to work. The memorial soon fell into disrepair with Holwell's departure and was demolished in 1821 to make way for a customs house. There is some speculation that the governor-general, the marquis of Hastings, demolished it because its message was inappropriate for his time. It is possible that he believed that it would offend native sensibilities during a period when the rule of force was being replaced by the rule of consent, or worse, that it would remind the natives of a "defeat of the British arms." For an account of the fate of the monument, see Ahmad, *Black Hole of Calcutta*, 7–9.

21. Dominick LaCapra, *Writing History, Writing Trauma*, 23.

22. See especially chapter 6 in Gillian Skinner, *Sensibility and Economics in the Novel, 1740–1800*.

23. See Chris Jones, *Radical Sensibility: Literature and Ideas in the 1790s*, 83, quoted in Skinner, *Sensibility and Economics*, 144.

24. Robert Bage, *Mount Henneth,* 119. All further references are to this edition, which will be cited parenthetically in the text as *Mount Henneth.*

25. Mary Louise Pratt, *Imperial Eyes: Travel Writing and Transculturation,* 74.

26. Long before Karl Marx asserted that primitive accumulation played approximately the same role in political economy as "original sin plays in theology," Adam Smith had already acknowledged the existence of a "previous accumulation," an accumulation that was not the result of the capitalist mode of production, but its point of departure. In the eighteenth century, one classic fable of how people accumulated wealth was that of the solitary man (Robinson Crusoe) creating use value on an island through his own labor and invention. But these anecdotal narratives about the past are always an attempt to defend property, as Marx argues: "As soon as the question of property is at stake, it becomes a sacred duty to proclaim the standpoint of the nursery tale as the one thing fit for all age-groups and all stages of development. In actual history, it is a notorious fact that conquest, enslavement, robbery, murder, in short force, play the greatest part. In the tender annals of political economy, the idyllic reigns from time immemorial. Right and 'Labor' were from the beginning of time the sole means of enrichment. . . . As a matter of fact the methods of primitive accumulation are anything but idyllic." Karl Marx, *Capital,* 1:874–75.

27. Ibid., 917.

28. See Uday Singh Mehta's helpful discussion of the Burkean moment in *Liberalism and Empire,* chapters 2 and 5.

29. Jenny Sharpe, *Allegories of Empire: The Figure of Woman in the Colonial Text,* 2.

30. Sara Suleri, *The Rhetoric of British India,* 49.

31. Ibid., 60.

32. Reprinted in M. Dorothy George, *English Political Caricature to 1792: A Study of Opinion and Propaganda,* plate 79, pp. 192–93.

33. Suleri, *Rhetoric,* 61.

34. I have borrowed the term *moral barometer* from Sylvana Tomaselli, "The Enlightenment Debate on Women." For an excellent discussion of how women gained such a position within metropolitan discourses of sensibility in the late eighteenth century, see Skinner, *Sensibility and Economics,* chapter 6.

35. Sarah Scott, *The History of Sir George Ellison,* 164.

36. Henry Fred Thompson, *The Intrigues of a Nabob; or, Bengal the Fittest Soil for the Growth of Lust, Injustice, and Dishonesty.*

37. Mariana Starke, *The Sword of Peace; or, A Voyage of Love: A Comedy in Five Acts.* The play was first performed at Haymarket Theater on 9 August 1788.

38. Mrs. H. Lefanu, *The India Voyage.*

39. See Nancy Armstrong, *Desire and Domestic Fiction: A Political History of the Novel,* 4.

40. Sophia Goldsborne [pseud.], *Hartly House, Calcutta,* 4.

41. Janet Todd, *Sensibility: An Introduction,* 110–15, 119.

42. Nussbaum, *Torrid Zones,* 181, 190.

43. Todd, *Sensibility,* 129.

44. Ernest Renan, "What Is a Nation?" 11.

45. Homi K. Bhabha, "DissemiNation: Time, Narrative, and the Margins of the Modern Nation," 310.

46. G. J. Barker-Benfield, *The Culture of Sensibility: Sex and Society in Eighteenth-Century Britain,* 216–24.

47. G. F. Barwick, introduction to *Hartly House, Calcutta.*

48. Ibid.

49. William Foster was the last in a series of energetic superintendents of records appointed beginning in 1884 to head the central Registry and Record Department who exercised wide control over both current and historical records. Under Foster and his predecessors, the department carried out a wide-ranging program of sorting, listing, binding, and publishing that opened the pre-1858 records to the world of scholarship. Foster's publication *A Guide to the India Office Records, 1600–1858* was the culmination of this reorganizing. Prior to 1947, all records after 1858 were unavailable for public access unless a special application was made for them. Only after 1947 and Indian independence were those files freely accessible to the public. For information about Foster's tenure, see a later guide by Martin Moir, *A General Guide to the India Office Records,* xiii–xiv. In this guide we see that Foster himself enters the archive after his death in 1951. His notebooks can be found under *L/R/5 Compilations and Miscellaneous Records, c. 1868–1945* (Moir, *General Guide,* 206).

50. William Foster, "Who Wrote *Hartly House*?" 28.

51. See Monica Clough, introduction to *Hartly House, Calcutta,* xvi.

52. Foster, "Who Wrote *Hartly House*?" 28–29. To Foster's disappointment, John MacFarlane changed his mind a little before his death and suggested the author could be a woman after all, one who was recollecting, through a fading memory, a previous trip to India.

53. Ibid., 110. Writing in the 1980s, A. L. Basham, another historian-turned-critic, also does not depart from this privileging of male self-evidence. For him, Sophia's veiled criticism of recent East India policies regarding wars with local rulers is sufficient to signal that the author has crossed the gender bar—a crossing that only men can do. His conclusion, though based on different evidence, is the same as that of his predecessor Foster: "The above comment [on East India policies] might be taken to suggest that the author of *Hartly House* was in fact a man, for in the eighteenth century few women took any interest in politics" (15). The irony is of course clear when the novel reverts back to the excessively sentimental language of "feminine" affect. Basham then suggests that such stresses on femininity are the result of the hyperbolic requirements of "literary tranvestism" on the male author—a practice he exemplifies with the work of Defoe and Richardson. (A. L. Basham, "Sophia and the 'Bramin,' " 25).

54. For the various categories, see Moir, *General Guide,* 216.

55. See Isobel Grundy, " 'The Barbarous Character We Give Them': White Women Travellers Report on Other Races," 75, 85 n. 15.

Chapter Three

1. While I use *home* mainly in its narrowest spatial denotation as private or domestic space, its extended signification as a larger geographic unit like a country, or nation, is also important for the general argument of the chapter. For an excellent discussion of the shrinkage and pliability of the term *home,* see Rosemary Marangoly George, *The Politics of Home: Postcolonial Relocations and Twentieth-Century Fiction,* chapter 1. The term *everyday* goes beyond the topographical reference to home, even though the domestic and private social activities associated with the home often fall within its purview. The critical task the term executes is that of exploring recurrences and repetitions in labor, leisure, habits, timekeeping, and so on—the practices through

which human subjects reproduce themselves as social beings. See Henri Lefebvre, *Everyday Life in the Modern World,* chapter 1.

2. Ranajit Guha, "Not at Home in Empire," 485.

3. Ibid., 482.

4. Ibid., 482, 484; Sigmund Freud, "The Uncanny," 370.

5. Homi K. Bhabha, *The Location of Culture,* 9.

6. Ibid., 10–11.

7. See Francis Hutchins, *The Illusion of Permanence: British Imperialism in India,* for a discussion of the shift from rule to reform in early-nineteenth-century debates about India. For the political backdrop of this shift, see Eric Stokes, *The English Utilitarians and India,* xiii–xvi. Stokes points out that in the period from 1798 to 1818, British power, through a series of conquests and annexations, gave the political map of India its "recognizably modern shape." The coastal settlements of Bombay and Madras became the two great new presidencies that, by joining the Bengal presidency, extended British territorial control over the whole peninsula: south of the Krishna river, in the Ganges valley, to the foothills of the Himalayas, and over the entire coastline. By 1818, the power of the Mahrattas, the single formidable challenge to the English after the Mughals, had been extinguished, and no other enemies seemed to challenge British paramountcy as a relatively quiet and assured rule continued till 1857.

8. Mrs. Monkland, *Life in India; or, the English at Calcutta.*

9. See Beth Fowkes Tobin, *Picturing Imperial Power,* for a detailed discussion of this painting. I have depended on her excellent reading as well as on Mildred Archer's *India and British Portraiture, 1770–1825,* 282–83, for most of the biographical information. Recently the British Library has reattributed this work to painter Johann Zoffany (1733–1810). The library catalogue's description also suggests that only one of the women in the painting is Palmer's wife. I have followed Archer's reading of the painting's execution.

10. Tobin, *Picturing Imperial Power,* 114.

11. Ibid., 114, 116.

12. Ibid., 117.

13. See Hutchins, *Illusion of Permanence,* 14–15; Percival Spear, *The Nabobs: A Study of the Social Life of the English in Eighteenth-Century India,* 62–65; and C. A. Bayly, *Imperial Meridian: The British Empire and the World, 1780–1830,* 149–50.

14. Richard Leppert, "Music, Domestic Life, and Cultural Chauvinism: Images of British Subjects at Home in India," 67–68 and 78–80.

15. Leppert has argued that since Zoffany was rather fond of executing portraits with Indian themes, landscapes, and motifs, the erasure of such references must have been by special request or in response to the "preferences of his sitters" ("Music," 88).

16. See Kenneth Ballhatchet, *Race, Sex, and Class under the Raj.*

17. I have borrowed this phrasing from Gaurav Desai, *Subject to Colonialism: African Self-Fashioning and the Colonial Library,* 12.

18. Tobin, *Picturing Imperial Power,* 117.

19. See the text of the East Indian Petition of 1830 and of various documents relating to its presentation in both Houses of Parliament, included as appendixes in Thomas Edwards, *Henry Derozio,* 223–76.

20. Gauri Viswanathan, *Masks of Conquest: Literary Study and British Rule in India,* provides an account of nineteenth-century cultural indoctrination through English education for natives.

21. Thomas Williamson, *The East India Vade-Mecum; or, Complete Guide to*

Gentlemen Intended for the Civil, Military, or Naval Service of the Hon. East India Company. On subsequent references this work will be cited parenthetically within the text as *Vade-Mecum.*

22. The best known and most comprehensive guide after Williamson's is John Gilchrist's, *The General East India Guide and Vade Mecum: For the Public Functionary, Government Officer, Private Agent, Trader, or Foreign Sojourner, in British India, and the Adjacent Parts of Asia Immediately Connected with the Honourable East India Company.* In 1845, Emma Roberts published *The East India Voyager or the Outward Bound,* which, unlike earlier guides that only cater to men, includes an entire section for the outfitting of ladies. This new readership attests to the increase in the number of women going out to India.

23. Williamson cites amounts as high as five rupees and as low as three given out monthly for each child born to a European soldier, irrespective of whether the soldier was in the regular employ of the Company or part of the "non-commissioned" ranks (*Vade-Mecum,* 1:463).

24. For a chronology of the Company's discriminatory policies regarding Eurasian children from about 1786 on, see Suresh Chandra Ghosh, *The Social Condition of the British Community in Bengal, 1757–1800,* 83–84. For a later attempt by the Company to be more efficient about racial markers, see Gayatri Chakravorty Spivak's discussion of a Company document from 1822 in *A Critique of Postcolonial Reason: Toward a History of the Vanishing Present,* 165–69. The document provides these details: the Company's standing order denying Eurasian children's entry into the Company's services was first enforced on the basis of "chromatism." The Eurasian offspring were subjected to an "examination" for "exhibited signs of native origin in their colour" (165). However, as lighter-skinned children passed as European to gain entry into the services, the "race" of the rulers was subsequently revised in 1822 to include other criteria: three generations of undiluted European blood, marriage and baptismal certificates, and a European liberal education (166).

25. In 1783 the Military Orphan Society was founded in Bengal, funded through monthly deductions from all officers' pay. The home soon enlarged its scope by taking in children of noncommissioned personnel. The separation of children of officers from those of the NCOs in the "upper" and the "lower" orphanages indicates that the fathers' military rank was nonnegotiable, even when racial purity was compromised! See Ghosh, *Social Condition,* 84.

26. Ballhatchet, *Race, Sex, and Class,* 42–44. See also Elizabeth W. Andrew and Katherine C. Bushnell's *The Queen's Daughters in India* for an illuminating account of how British social-reform feminists intervened at the turn of the century and called for the abolition of "brothel slavery" in Indian army cantonments.

27. For a diverse set of historical arguments about the role of Englishwomen in empire building, see Margaret Strobel, *European Women and the Second British Empire;* Nupur Chaudhuri and Margaret Strobel, eds., *Western Women and Imperialism: Complicity and Resistance;* Jenny Sharpe, *Allegories of Empire: The Figure of Woman in the Colonial Text;* and Pat Barr, *The Memsahibs: In Praise of Women of Victorian India.*

28. William Huggins, *Sketches in India, Treating on Subjects Connected with the Government; Civil and Military Establishments; Characters of the European, and Customs of the Native Inhabitants,* v.

29. In the 1770s, after the Company took over land revenues in Bengal, sporadic debates began about permanent settlement of Europeans in India. Fearing conflicts of interest and threats to its trade monopoly, the Company forbade its employees to own

land, and it restricted private individuals' travel to India. After the opening of India to private trade in 1813, settlement debates increased. In 1821, the annual number of licenses given to private British settlers doubled from the previous year. In council in 1829, Governor-General William Bentinck yielded to public support and allowed European indigo planters, like the coffee planters before them, to hold lands in their own names. See "Minute of the Governor-General," 30 May 1829.

30. The phrase is Benedict Anderson's. See his *Imagined Communities: Reflections on the Origin and Spread of Nationalism,* for a discussion of creole communities that imagine a "parallel existence" with the mother country.

31. Huggins, *Sketches,* iii.

32. Ibid., v.

33. Ibid.

34. Jacques Le Goff, *History and Memory,* 62. See especially his discussion of the "broadening of collective memory" in the eighteenth century: the publication of encyclopedias, building of cemeteries and monuments, secularization of festivals, opening of museums, and, finally, the creation of great archival depositories in Turin, St. Petersburg, Vienna, Warsaw, Venice, Florence, Paris, and London between 1720 and 1838 (85–89).

35. "Minute of the Governor General," 274. The first official, high-level discussion of colonization as possible policy is documented in an 1832 Select Committee Report of the House of Commons, in the appendix of which appears a subsection on the "Settlement of Europeans in India." This discussion, we surmise, arose only because English indigo planters in Bengal, like the coffee planters before them, had begun to agitate for permanent occupancy of land, prompting Governor-General Bentinck to send a minute to the Company's Board of Control in London. Bentinck advocated the cause of the planters by tying the need for British permanent rights to land to a general need for colonization, or the settlement of English in India. In this move, Bentinck was radically challenging the prevailing official view that India was already fully peopled and that all available land was worked or held by natives.

36. For a succinct discussion of the pedagogical in identity formation and nation building, see Homi Bhabha, "DissemiNation: Time, Narrative, and the Margins of the Modern Nation."

37. See Nancy Armstrong, *Desire and Domestic Fiction: A Political History of the Novel.*

38. In her brilliant analysis of late-nineteenth-century home management guides written for Englishwomen in India, Rosemary George shows how these books had both a prescriptive and an entertaining function. They defined a generic authoritative Englishwoman who had to run her home like a military cantonment, but they also extended to their obedient readers the pleasure of a subject position that was gendered but had racial and class power and national status in a way never possible in the metropole. The guides reveal that any construction of the domestic and the home presupposed a scripting of women as members of the citizenry, and they show the extent to which gender became the unspoken category of analysis in debates about culture, territoriality, and race in the nineteenth-century British imperial state. See George, *Politics of Home,* chapter 2.

39. A number of works, both fictional and journalistic, that make Anglo-Indian society into an object of description and discuss it as an expatriate community were published from the 1820s onward. Here is a sampling of titles: the anonymous *Life in India 1, Six Sketches Illustrative of Life in India;* Charles Marsh, "Society in India";

William Brown Hockley, *The English in India, A Novel;* Emma Roberts, *Scenes and Characteristics of Hindostan with Sketches of Anglo-Indian Society;* and Augustus Prinsep, *The Baboo and Other Tales Descriptive of Society in India.*

40. Alexander Pope, *Rape of the Lock,* canto 1:121–48.

41. See, for instance, the narrative cum guidebook of an army wife, Mrs. Major Clemons, published as *The Manners and Customs of Society in India.* The title page includes this long subtitle: "including scenes in the Mofussil Stations; interspersed with characteristic tales and anecdotes and reminiscences of the Late Burmese War to which are added Instruction for the guidance of cadets and other young gentlemen during their first years' residence in India." The parceling out of smaller and dispersed Indias is evident both in the promised novelty of the *mofussils* and in the book's inclusion of a map that shows not all of the Indian subcontinent, but only the southwestern territory of the Carnatic, including the cities of Madras, Mysore, and Bangalore

42. For a discussion of the country cottage, associated with gentility, and cultural trends of the picturesque and the Romantic movement, see Adrian Tinniswood, *Life in the English Country Cottage,* chapter 4. For an aesthetic discussion of Indian landscapes that was part of the ongoing colonization debates, see Emma Roberts, *Hindostan: Its Landscapes, Palaces, Temples, Tombs; the Shores of the Red Sea and the Sublime and Romantic Scenery of the Himalaya Mountains.* In her preface, Roberts alludes to a travel narrative by Captain Skinner to show why her work will open the "prospect of the continuance and prosperity of our empire." Like Skinner's journal, it too will attest to the potential of the Himalayas for European settlement: "There is every reason to suppose that the Himalaya mountains will, by affording a climate suited to European constitutions become the principal residence of those colonists who are desirous of carrying British capital and British science into India" (1).

43. Anthony King, *Bungalow: The Production of a Global Culture,* 14, 23–24. King points out that bungalows were used mainly for the army: "Though references are occasionally found to 'collector's' and 'judge's' bungalows, most civilian officials still relied on tents for accommodation" (35). King also shows how the very construction of the bungalow reveals the relations that existed between the ruler and the ruled. Bungalows were often set apart from native towns, situated within the military cantonments from which they derived their protection, or in isolated large plots far away from native dwellings in the case of civil servants and plantation owners. The horizontal spread of the single-story dwellings over several acres of land demonstrated the ability to command and appropriate large spaces in the rural areas and also provided a spatial separation that had not existed in the towns and cities (34–35). Yet, as King argues, there was also something distinctly modern about this dwelling in the way it resembled the formats for nuclear family dwellings in the metropole (3). Servants now slept on the verandah outside the dwelling, where most business with natives was conducted. This enabled a sort of privacy for the English family that neither the extended-family dwellings of natives nor the more open servant-run mansions of European families in the cities could allow.

44. Aliph Cheem, "The Deserted Bungalow," in *Lays of Ind.* Quoted in King, *Bungalow,* 39–41.

45. Philip Randell, "A Tale of East and West." Quoted in King, *Bungalow,* 64.

46. The replacement of thatched bungalow roofs by corrugated iron ones after the 1857 mutiny shows us earlier, in architectural form, the general anxiety visible in the literature at the turn of the century.

47. For a succinct discussion of the tropological work of the literary in eighteenth-century literature, see Srinivas Aravamudan, *Tropicopolitans: Colonialism and Agency, 1688–1804*, 9–16.

48. Guha, "Not at Home in Empire," 485–86.

49. Michel de Certeau, *The Writing of History*, 87.

50. Gayatri Chakravorty Spivak, "Feminism and Imperialism," 524.

CHAPTER FOUR

1. See for instance, Edward Said's idea of "counterpoint," in *Culture and Imperialism*. He offers it as a strategy of reading that emphasizes intertwined histories and interdependence that could break down the Manichean divisions of West and East that lead to a "politics of confrontation and destruction" (18). Said does not say what determines the contrapuntal movements in the cultures of imperialism except to suggest that the double movement results from the desire on the part of imperialists to totalize and the corresponding desire on the part of the native and the "discrepant" subject (the exile, the migrant) to resist this takeover. My own reading is interested in both of these aspects of colonial discourse, but I believe it is possible to read for counterpoints almost anywhere in the archive as the inescapable play of any discourse that exceeds its own limits and pushes into alien domains where it has to reveal its own working in order to adapt.

2. See Gayatri Chakravorty Spivak, "The Rani of Sirmur: An Essay in Reading the Archives," an essay from which I draw many of my methodological premises, including the argument that a reading of the colonial archive demonstrates the "fabrication of representations of historical reality" (271). Yet it should be noted that Spivak's essay and mine read different subject positions for the ranis concerned. For Spivak, there is no real rani of Sirmur to be found; for me, the disciplinary satisfaction of finding the wide array of crises the rani of Burdwan sets off in the archive leads to the restoration of her status as a historical subject.

3. Madeleine Albright, "Charting Further Gains in the Status and Rights of Women," remarks delivered at Center for National Policy breakfast, Washington, D.C., 2 August 1995.

4. Gayatri Chakravorty Spivak, *A Critique of Postcolonial Reason: Toward a History of the Vanishing Present*, 91.

5. Spivak, *Critique of Postcolonial Reason*, 239. For a more thorough discussion of the experiment in Bengal, see Ranajit Guha, *A Rule of Property for Bengal: An Essay on the Idea of Permanent Settlement*.

6. Representation to the Nabob, Governor General, and the Gentlemen of the Council, in *Eleventh Report from the Select Committee on the Administration of Justice in India, 1783*, 741–42. Hereafter this report will be cited as *ER*.

7. For an account of the zamindar's imperial functions under the Mughals and the transformation of these under the English, see John R. McLane, *Land and Local Kingship in Eighteenth-Century Bengal*, 8–15.

8. For a concise account of the trial and its main players, see David Musselwhite, "The Trial of Warren Hastings."

9. The rani's petition and other papers relating to the case are reprinted as appendix O in a section titled "Papers Respecting the Ranny of Burdwan," in *ER*, 733.

10. John Shore, Minute of 18 June 1789, in *The Fifth Report from the Select*

Committee of the House of Commons on the Affairs of the East India Company, 1812, 2:71, 74.

11. In 1776, Philip Francis drafted a minute that outlined the guidelines under which the Company would play ward for each of the three categories of incapable zamindars, but at this point he was extremely sympathetic to the rani and rallied to her cause. See extracted discussion of Francis's Minute in *Fifth Report*, 2:74.

12. I have not seen Graham's original letter and am not aware if it still exists, but the *Bengal Revenue Consultations*, 6 January–15 February 1775, has the letter copied in this format. All five council members have signed underneath the text of the letter, thereby attesting to its status as a true copy and permitting it to be forwarded to the court of directors in London.

13. Nancy Armstrong, *Desire and Domestic Fiction: A Political History of the Novel*, 111–13.

14. "The Burdwan Ranny's Petition Dissected and Answered by Mr. Graham," *ER*, 737–40.

15. Letter from Graham to the council, 6 January 1775, *ER*, 735.

16. The coexistence of two timelines is itself a sign of the epistemic upheaval. In usual proceedings, Company servants use the Bengali calendar to record local revenues and transactions with the natives but use the Christian calendar for all their general communications with each other.

17. See P. J. Marshall, *The Impeachment of Warren Hastings*, 5–7.

18. See letter from the resident Charles Stuart at Burdwan to Warren Hastings complaining about the rani's refusal to hand over the zamindari seals, 10 May 1772, and Hastings's reply to the resident approving the removal of the rani's son from her quarters, 15 May 1772. *Bengal Consultations*, 1771–1772, 266–68.

19. Letter from the rani of Burdwan to the council, 10 March 1775, *ER*, 746.

20. Ranajit Guha, "The Prose of Counter-Insurgency," 47.

21. Harry Verelst, *A View of the Rise, Progress, and Present State of the English Government in Bengal*, 134.

22. Ibid., 137.

23. Ibid., 141.

24. Ibid.

25. See Samuel Davis's letter to the president and members of the Board of Revenue, 31 January 1794, about Tejchandra's imprisonment as a "defaulter" to government, in Ranajit Guha and A. Mitra, eds. *West Bengal District Records (New Series): Burdwan Letters Issued, 1788–1800*, 98–99.

26. Perry Anderson, *Lineages of the Absolutist State*, 400, 463.

27. Althusser's reading of Montesquieu as the initiator of the new method of universalist history is worth noting: "Never before him had anyone had the daring to reflect on *all the customs and laws* of all the nations of the world." Louis Althusser, *Montesquieu, Rousseau, Marx: Politics and History*, 19 (emphasis in original). He also argues that the real object of Montesquieu's work is law; that despotism is misrecognized as Eurocentrism and that it was merely an "oriental myth" that allowed Montesquieu to posit what could happen to monarchy gone wrong in Europe: "It is the limit government, and already the limit of government. It is easy to guess that the example of real countries is only providing Montesquieu with a pretext" (75). This is a puzzling deflection in what is otherwise a brilliant reading of Montesquieu's abdication of politics itself.

28. Ibid., 82.

29. Anderson, *Lineages*, 399.

30. Ibid., 401 (emphasis in original).

31. Spivak, *Critique of Postcolonial Reason*, 3.

32. Ibid., 4.

33. Charles de Secondat, baron de Montesquieu, *The Spirit of the Laws*, 256.

34. The accusations against Warren Hastings show the influence of Montesquieu—in the idea, for instance, that Hastings's "despotism" is a violation of the long-established customs and laws of the country. Yet Hastings did not depart from Montesquieu either when he countered that he was following the long-held customs of India. Edmund Burke's take on this position was that evil was evil everywhere, irrespective of geography. While Hastings's supporters quoted cultural relativism, Burke went to the idea of divine and human law where the morality that made despotism evil was not geographical. Even Francis used Montesquieu in 1777 in a letter to Lord North listing the deplorable effects of British policy in Bengal. In it he said that a prince should not be a merchant and that ruling powers should not be proprietors but that there should be separation of powers. For these various points see F. T. H. Fletcher, *Montesquieu and English Politics, 1750–1800*, 214, 217.

35. Quoted from the introduction to *Fifth Report*, 1:cclxiv.

36. Letter from Board of Directors, 19 November 1777, *Report from Committee on Petitions*, 8 May 1781.

37. See Michael Ryan, *Marxism and Deconstruction: A Critical Articulation*, 40–41.

38. Guha, *Rule of Property*, 54–55.

39. Letter from Rani Bhabhani to the Council of Revenue, 16 September 1771, in *Letter Copy Book of the Supervisor of Rajshahi.*

40. Guha, *Rule of Property*, 55.

41. Minute of John Shore, in *Fifth Report*, 2:77.

42. For the main provisions of Francis's plan, see the appendix in Guha, *Rule of Property*, 218–24.

43. Guha, *Rule of Property*, 182–83.

44. Minute of John Shore, in *Fifth Report*, 2:45.

45. *Fifth Report*, 2:71.

46. Ibid., 2:72.

47. Ibid.

48. Jean-François Lyotard, *The Differend: Phrases in Dispute*, 9.

49. *Fifth Report*, 2:77.

50. Ibid.

51. See letter from J. Rawlins to the acting collector of Burdwan, 26 October 1791, in Guha and Mitra, *West Bengal District Records*, 194. For queries regarding the status of various female zamindars identified by the collector, see pp. 35, 95, 195, 219, and 290.

52. Letter from the collector of Burdwan, 27 February 1794, in Guha and Mitra, *West Bengal District Records*, 106–7.

53. Quoted in Guha and Mitra, *West Bengal District Records*, lxx.

54. See Karl Marx, "The British Rule in India."

55. J. S. Mill, "The Subjection of Women," 170–71. I am grateful to Lora Wildenthal for pointing this out to me.

56. Ibid.

57. Ruth Perry, *Women, Letters, and the Novel*, 71.

Chapter Five

1. See Nicholas Dirks, "Colonial Histories and Native Informants: Biography of an Archive," 310.

2. For an example of a "transitional text" that uses travel literature, Montesquieu, and Company employees, as well as the modality of investigative ethnography, see Charles Grant's "Observations on the State of Society among the Asiatic Subjects of Great Britain, Particularly with Respect to Morals." Grant sent this tract to India House in 1797 with a letter asking that it be considered on the same footing as the many "Papers of Business" with which "the records of [the] East Indian governments have been furnished" (4). The section on the abject condition of Hindu women appears in chapter 2. The entire tract was attached to the select committee report of 1831–1832 as a key document to corroborate the need to open India to settlement by Europeans. For a textual example of the discursive shift I am describing, see Lata Mani's discussion about the reissuance of William Ward's 1811 tract, *Account of the Writings, Religion, and Manners of the Hindoos,* as "ethnographic writing" in 1822 (Lata Mani, *Contentious Traditions: The Debate on Sati in Colonial India,* 133). Mani also discusses Ward's belated preface, which recast the monograph as an analysis of Hindu religiosity's dire consequences for women (129). For a related point, made with regard to representations of Hindu women in imaginative and missiological literature of the early nineteenth century, see Gauri Viswanathan, *Outside the Fold,* 28–31. Finally, see Ratnabali Chattopadhyay and Tapati Thakurta, "That Woman Perceived: The Changing Visual Iconography of the Colonial and Nationalist Period in Bengal," for a compelling study of Company paintings of Indian women in the early nineteenth century, paintings that transformed them from the category of the "Oriental" to that of the "native."

3. This phrase is borrowed from Gayatri Chakravorty Spivak, *A Critique of Postcolonial Reason: Toward a History of the Vanishing Present,* 285.

4. Viswanathan, *Outside the Fold,* 43.

5. For a sampling of these arguments, see Mani, *Contentious Traditions,* 2; Partha Chatterjee, *The Nation and Its Fragments,* 116–21; Rosalind O'Hanlon, "Issues of Widowhood: Gender and Resistance in Colonial Western India," 78; and Jasodhara Bagchi, ed., *Indian Women: Myth and Reality,* 1–3.

6. Spivak, *Critique of Postcolonial Reason,* 4.

7. The phrase is from Michel Foucault, "Nietzsche, Genealogy, History," 81.

8. C. H. Philips, *The East India Company, 1784–1834,* 181–93. For a brief summary of the role played by missionary interests in 1812–1813, see Ainslie T. Embree, *Charles Grant and British Rule in India,* 269–75.

9. The section quoted is in Grant, "Observations on the State of Society," 25.

10. "Minutes of Evidence Taken before the Whole House and the Select Committee on the Affairs of the East India Company (Public)," 18. On subsequent references, these minutes will be cited parenthetically as ME.

11. For an account of the acclamations Hastings received from the House of Commons during his appearance in 1813, see Thomas Babington Macaulay, "Warren Hastings," 400, 510–11.

12. See E. J. Hobsbawm, *Industry and Empire: From 1750 to the Present Day,* 49.

13. Maps of the British Empire too often obscured the lived reality of colonial rule and its relation to the total space of the native. If one were to map a nineteenth-century British India unmarked by native habitation, British rule would probably show only as a patchy presence. Settlements and port cities governed entirely by the British would

remain minuscule dots in a vast territory, and mostly concentrated along the coast and in the hill stations.

14. For the use of examples of violence against women in other witnesses' testimonies, see John Stracey (ME, 293) and John Malcolm (ME, 408).

15. Bernard Cohn, *Colonialism and the Forms of Knowledge*, 6.

16. See Anne McClintock, *Imperial Leather: Race, Gender, and Sexuality in the Colonial Contest*, 75–180.

17. See Patricia Ingham, *The Language of Gender and Class: Transformation in the Victorian Novel*, 24. For a discussion of class terminology, especially variants like *lower ranks* and *lower orders*—the two most prevalent in the 1813 testimonies—see pp. 6–10.

18. Lawrence Stone, *The Family, Sex, and Marriage, 1500–1800*, 422–23.

19. Ann L. Stoler, *Race and the Education of Desire*, 96.

20. Also happening at this time, but nowhere in the discussions, was the actual ongoing regulation of sexuality in the colonies. Kenneth Ballhatchet has charted in his classic study the numerous communiqués sent off to the Company headquarters by army commanders and surgeon generals in India during this period complaining about the uncontrollable breakout of venereal disease among British soldiers. Thus the danger of potential sexual contact raised in 1813 was actually a dissimulation of the problematic sexual contact that was already taking its toll on English soldiery in India. See Kenneth Ballhatchet, *Race, Sex, and Class under the Raj*, 12–13.

21. Nicholas B. Dirks, "From Little King to Landlord: Colonial Discourse and Colonial Rule," 175.

22. Embree, *Charles Grant*, 270.

23. Letter from John Jebb and James Pattison to George Canning, 255–57.

24. Letter from the Right Hon. George Canning to the Chairman and Deputy Chairman of the East India Company, 267.

25. See Hastings's initial remark. Here is Thomas Munro's production of an Orientalist trope through an investigative method: "I do not think from all I have been able to observe personally, or to learn from reading, that there is a probability of any essential change being produced. . . . The natives of Hindostan seem now in their state of society, and in all their customs, to be in much the same state as they were when we first heard of them in history" (ME, 124).

26. O'Hanlon, "Issues of Widowhood," 76.

27. Rammohun Roy, *Translation of a Conference between an Advocate and an Opponent of the Practice of Burning Widows Alive*, 2.

28. Mani, *Contentious Traditions*, 72–77.

29. Roy, *Translation of a Conference*, 28.

30. Rammohun Roy, "Address to Lord William Bentinck," 483.

31. Ibid., 485.

32. See Mani, *Contentious Traditions*, 68–71; Rosane Rocher, "British Orientalism in the Eighteenth Century," 229; and Tejaswini Niranjana's discussion of the ideological underpinnings of William Jones's work in *Siting Translation: History, Post-Structuralism, and the Colonial Context*, 13. For the imperialist designs of early Orientalists like Jones, see Garland Cannon, ed., *The Letters of Sir William Jones*, 2:795.

33. McClintock, *Imperial Leather*, 358–59.

34. Sophia Collet, *The Life and Letters of Raja Rammohun Roy*, 118.

35. Uday Singh Mehta, *Liberalism and Empire*, 2.

36. Collet, *Life and Letters*, 118–19.

37. Remarks by Rammohun Roy, on Settlement in India by Europeans, 14 July 1832.

38. Ibid., 348, 365–66.

EPILOGUE

1. Joan Wallach Scott, "Gender: A Useful Category of Historical Analysis," 169.

2. Maurice Godelier, "The Origins of Male Domination," 17. Quoted in Scott, "Gender," 170.

3. Susie Tharu and Tejaswini Niranjana, "Problems for a Contemporary Theory of Gender," 494–95.

4. Ibid., 501, 503.

5. Hillary Clinton's official support for microcredit agencies during the 1995 United Nations World Conference on Women is worth quoting here: "I think of women in a village in Bangladesh, a village of untouchables—women were Hindus—who invited to their village for my visit Moslem women from the neighboring village. I think of how these women sat together under a lean-to—Hindus and Moslems together in one of the poorest countries of the world, but so many of those women telling me how their lives had been changed because they had become borrowers and were now part of the Grameen Bank microenterprise effort" (Hillary Rodham Clinton, "Remarks to the NGO Forum").

6. Tharu and Niranjana, "Problems for a Contemporary Theory of Gender," 502.

7. Walter Benjamin, "Theses on the Philosophy of History," 255.

Ahmad, Saiyid Amin. *The Black Hole of Calcutta.* Patna: United Press, 1935.

Albright, Madeleine. "Charting Further Gains in the Status and Rights of Women." *UN Fourth World Conference on Women Press Kit.* Washington, D.C.: U.S. Department of State, 1995.

Alexander, William. *The History of Women, from the Earliest Antiquity, to the Present Time; Giving Some Account of Almost Every Interesting Particular Concerning that Sex, Among All Nations, Ancient and Modern.* London: W. Strahan and T. Cadell, 1779.

Althusser, Louis. *Montesquieu, Rousseau, Marx: Politics and History.* London: Verso, 1982.

Anderson, Benedict. *Imagined Communities: Reflections on the Origin and Spread of Nationalism.* London: Verso, 1983.

Anderson, Perry. *Lineages of the Absolutist State.* London: NLB, 1974.

Andrew, Elizabeth W., and Katherine C. Bushnell. *The Queen's Daughters in India.* London: Morgan and Scott, 1899.

Aravamudan, Srinivas. *Tropicopolitans: Colonialism and Agency, 1688–1804.* Durham, N.C.: Duke University Press, 1999.

Archer, Mildred. *India and British Portraiture, 1770–1825.* London: Sotheby Parke Bernet, 1979.

Armstrong, Nancy. *Desire and Domestic Fiction: A Political History of the Novel.* New York: Oxford University Press, 1987.

Armstrong, Nancy, and Leonard Tennenhouse. "The American Origins of the English Novel." *American Literary History* 4, no. 1 (1992): 386–410.

Bagchi, Jasodhara, ed. *Indian Women: Myth and Reality.* Hyderabad: Sangam Books, 1995.

Bage, Robert. *Mount Henneth.* In *The Novels of Swift, Bage, and Cumberland.* Vol. 9 of Ballantyne's Novelist's Library. London: Hurst, Robinson and Co., 1824.

Ballhatchet, Kenneth. *Race, Sex, and Class under the Raj.* New York: St. Martin's Press, 1980.

Barker-Benfield, G. J. *The Culture of Sensibility: Sex and Society in Eighteenth-Century Britain.* Chicago: University of Chicago Press, 1992.

Barr, Pat. *The Memsahibs: In Praise of Women of Victorian India.* London: Century Press, 1976.

Barwick, G. F. Introduction to *Hartly House, Calcutta: A Novel of the Days of Warren*

Hastings, by Sophia Goldsborne [pseud.]. 1789. Reprint, Calcutta: Thacker, Spink and Co., 1908.

Basham, A. L. "Sophia and the 'Bramin.'" In *East India Company Studies: Papers Presented to Sir Cyril Philips*, ed. Kenneth Ballhatchet and John Harrison, 13–30. Asian Studies Monograph Series. Hong Kong: Asian Research Service, 1986.

Bayly, C. A. *Imperial Meridian: The British Empire and the World, 1780–1830*. London: Longman, 1989.

Bengal Baptisms, Marriages, and Burials. Part 1. 1755–1779. Oriental and India Office Collections, British Library, London.

Bengal Consultations, 1771–1772. Shelfmark P/2/1. Oriental and India Office Collections, British Library, London.

Bengal Revenue Consultations, 1775. Shelfmark 1OR/Z/P/662 1775. Oriental and India Office Collections, British Library, London.

Bengal Wills, 1774–1779. Shelfmark P/154/40–55. Oriental and India Office Collections, British Library, London.

Bengal Wills, 1780–1783. Shelfmark Z/L/AG/34/29/4–184. Oriental and India Office Collections. British Library, London.

Benjamin, Walter. "Theses on the Philosophy of History." In *Illuminations*. New York: Schocken Books, 1969.

Bennett, Agnes Maria. *Anna; or, Memoirs of a Welch Heiress: Interspersed with Anecdotes of a Nabob*. London: W. Lane, 1785.

Bergeron, Suzanne. "Political Economy Discourses of Globalization and Feminist Politics." *Signs* 26, no. 4 (2001): 986–1006.

Bhabha, Homi K. "DissemiNation: Time, Narrative, and the Margins of the Modern Nation." In *Nation and Narration*, ed. Homi Bhabha, 291–322. London: Routledge, 1990.

———. *The Location of Culture*. London: Routledge, 1994.

———. "Of Mimicry and Man: The Ambivalence of Colonial Discourse." *October* 28 (1984): 125–33.

Birdwood, George. *Report on the Old Records of the India Office*. London: Eyre and Spottiswood, 1890.

Brooke, Henry. *The Fool of Quality; or, The History of Henry, Earl of Moreland*. London: W. Johnston, 1766–1770.

Brown, Laura. *Ends of Empire: Women and Ideology in Early Eighteenth-Century English Literature*. Ithaca, N.Y.: Cornell University Press, 1993.

Busteed, H. E. *Echoes from Old Calcutta, Being Chiefly Reminiscences of the Days of Warren Hastings, Francis, and Impey*. Calcutta: Thacker, Spink, 1882.

Cannon, Garland, ed. *The Letters of Sir William Jones*. 2 vols. Oxford: Clarendon Press, 1970.

Castiglia, Christopher. *Bound and Determined: Captivity, Culture-Crossing, and White Womanhood from Mary Rowlandson to Patty Hearst*. Chicago: University of Chicago Press, 1998.

Certeau, Michel de. *The Writing of History*. Translated by Tom Conley. New York: Columbia University Press, 1988.

Chambers, Robert. *A Course of Lectures on the English Law, 1767–1773*. 2 vols. Edited by Thomas M. Curley. Madison: University of Wisconsin Press, 1986.

Chatterjee, Partha. *The Nation and Its Fragments*. Princeton, N.J.: Princeton University Press, 1993.

Chattopadhyay, Ratnabali, and Tapati Thakurta. "That Woman Perceived: The

Changing Visual Iconography of the Colonial and Nationalist Period in Bengal." In *Indian Women: Myth and Reality*, ed. Jasodhara Bagchi, 147–67. Hyderabad: Sangam Books, 1995.

Chaudhuri, Nupur, and Margaret Strobel, eds. *Western Women and Imperialism: Complicity and Resistance.* Bloomington: Indiana University Press, 1992.

Cheem, Aliph. "The Deserted Bungalow." In *Lays of Ind*, by Aliph Cheem. Calcutta: Thacker and Spink, 1883.

Cixous, Hélène. "Laugh of the Medusa." In *New French Feminisms: An Anthology*, ed. Elaine Marks and Isabelle de Courtivron, 245–64. New York: Schocken Books, 1981.

Clemons, Mrs. Major. *The Manners and Customs of Society in India.* London: Smith, Elder and Co., 1841.

Clinton, Hillary Rodham. "Remarks to the NGO Forum." *Remarks by First Lady Hillary Rodham Clinton: United Nations Fourth World Conference on Women, September 5–6, 1995, China.* Washington, D.C.: Executive Office of the President, 1995.

Clough, Monica. Introduction to *Hartly House, Calcutta: A Novel of the Days of Warren Hastings*, by Sophia Goldsborne [pseud.]. London: Pluto Press, 1989.

Cohn, Bernard. *Colonialism and the Forms of Knowledge.* Princeton, N.J.: Princeton University Press, 1996.

Collet, Sophia. *The Life and Letters of Raja Rammohun Roy.* London: Harold Collet, 1900.

Davis, Lennard J. *Factual Fictions: The Origins of the English Novel.* New York: Columbia University Press, 1983.

Defoe, Daniel. *The Fortunate Mistress; or, a History of the Life and Vast Variety of Fortunes of Mademoiselle de Beleau, afterwards Call'd the Countess of Wintselsheim, in Germany. Being the Person Known by the Name of Lady Roxana, in the Time of King Charles II.* London: E. Applebee, 1740.

———. *The Fortunate Mistress; or, a History of the Life of Mademoiselle De Beleau, Known by the Name of Roxana.* 2 vols. 1745. Reprint, Boston: Dana Estes, 1904.

———. *The Manufacturer.* 1719. Reprint, Delmar, N.Y.: Scholars Facsimiles and Reprints, 1978.

———. *Roxana the Fortunate Mistress.* 1724. Reprint, London: Penguin, 1982.

Defoe, Daniel, and Isaac Taylor. *The History of Mademoiselle de Beleau; or, The New Roxana: The Fortunate Mistress, afterwards Countess of Wintselsheim.* London: F. Noble . . . and T. Lowndes, 1775.

Derrida, Jacques. *Acts of Literature.* Edited by Derek Attridge. London: Routledge, 1992.

———. *Archive Fever: A Freudian Impression.* Translated by Eric Prenowitz. Chicago: University of Chicago Press, 1996.

Desai, Gaurav. *Subject to Colonialism: African Self-Fashioning and the Colonial Library.* Durham, N.C.: Duke University Press, 2001.

Dijkstra, Bram. *Defoe and Economics: The Fortunes of Roxana in the History of Interpretation.* New York: St. Martin's Press, 1987.

Dirks, Nicholas B. "Colonial Histories and Native Informants: Biography of an Archive." In *Orientalism and the Postcolonial Predicament*, ed. Carol A. Breckenridge and Peter van der Veer. Philadelphia: University of Pennsylvania Press, 1993.

———. "From Little King to Landlord: Colonial Discourse and Colonial Rule." In *Colonialism and Culture*, ed. Nicholas B. Dirks. Ann Arbor: University of Michigan Press, 1992.

Eagleton, Terry. *The Rape of Clarissa: Writing, Sexuality, and Class Struggle in Samuel Richardson.* Minneapolis: University of Minnesota Press, 1982.
Edwards, Thomas. *Henry Derozio.* 1884. Reprint, Calcutta: Riddhi-India, 1980.
Eleventh Report from the Select Committee on the Administration of Justice in India, 1783. In *Reports from Committees of the House of Commons, 1775–1801.* First series, vol. 6. London: House of Commons, 1803–1806.
Ellis, Markman. *The Politics of Sensibility: Race, Gender, and Commerce in the Sentimental Novel.* Cambridge: Cambridge University Press, 1996.
Embree, Ainslie T. *Charles Grant and British Rule in India.* New York: Columbia University Press, 1962.
Everson, Norma. *The Imperial Metropolis.* New Haven, Conn.: Yale University Press, 1989.
Fay, Eliza. *Original Letters from India (1779–1815).* London: Hogarth, 1986.
Ferguson, Frances. "Rape and the Rise of the Novel." *Representations* 20 (1987): 88–112.
The Fifth Report from the Select Committee of the House of Commons on the Affairs of the East India Company, 1812. 3 vols. Edited by Walter Firminger. New York: Augustus M. Kelley, 1917.
Fitzpatrick, Peter. *The Mythology of Modern Law.* London: Routledge, 1992.
Fletcher, F. T. H. *Montesquieu and English Politics, 1750–1800.* London: Edward Arnold, 1939.
Foster, William. *A Guide to the India Office Records, 1600–1858.* London: India Office, 1919.
———. "Who Wrote *Hartly House?*" *Bengal Past and Present* 15, pt. 2, no. 30 (1917): 28–29.
Foucault, Michel. *The Archaeology of Knowledge.* New York: Pantheon Books, 1972.
———. "Nietzsche, Genealogy, History." In *The Foucault Reader,* ed. Paul Rabinow. New York: Pantheon Books, 1984.
———. "Two Lectures." In *Culture/Power/History: A Reader in Contemporary Social Theory,* ed. Nicholas Dirks, Geoff Eley, and Sherry Ortner, 200–222. Princeton, N.J.: Princeton University Press, 1994.
Fox-Genovese, Elizabeth. "Placing Women's History in History." *New Left Review* 133 (May–June 1982): 5–29.
Freud, Sigmund. "The Uncanny." In *Collected Papers,* vol. 4. Translated by Joan Riviere. London: Hogarth Press, 1925.
George, M. Dorothy. *English Political Caricature to 1792: A Study of Opinion and Propaganda.* Oxford: Clarendon Press, 1959.
George, Rosemary Marangoly. *The Politics of Home: Postcolonial Relocations and Twentieth-Century Fiction.* Cambridge: Cambridge University Press, 1996.
Ghosh, Suresh Chandra. *The Social Condition of the British Community in Bengal, 1757–1800.* Leiden: E. J. Brill, 1970.
Gilchrist, John. *The General East India Guide and Vade Mecum: For the Public Functionary, Government Officer, Private Agent, Trader, or Foreign Sojourner, in British India, and the Adjacent Parts of Asia Immediately Connected with the Honourable East India Company.* London: Kingsbury, Parbury and Allen, 1825.
Godelier, Maurice. "The Origins of Male Domination." *New Left Review* 127 (1981): 3–17
Goldsborne, Sophia [pseud.]. *Hartly House, Calcutta: A Novel of the Days of Warren Hastings.* 1789. Reprint, Calcutta: Thacker, Spink, and Co., 1908.

Grant, Charles. "Observations on the State of Society among the Asiatic Subjects of Great Britain, Particularly with Respect to Morals; and on the Means of Improving It." General appendix no. 1 to Report from the Select Committee of the House of Commons on the Affairs of the East India Company, 1832. In *Irish University Press Series of British Parliamentary Papers. Colonies: East India,* 5:3–89. Shannon: Irish University Press, 1970.

Grundy, Isobel. " 'The Barbarous Character We Give Them': White Women Travellers Report on Other Races." *Studies in Eighteenth-Century Culture* 22 (1992): 73–86.

Guha, Ranajit. "Not at Home in Empire." *Critical Inquiry* 23 (spring 1997): 482–93.

———. "The Prose of Counter-Insurgency." In *Selected Subaltern Studies,* ed. Ranajit Guha and Gayatri Chakravorty Spivak, 45–86. New York: Oxford University Press, 1988.

———. *A Rule of Property for Bengal: An Essay on the Idea of Permanent Settlement.* 1963. Reprint, Durham, N.C.: Duke University Press, 1996.

Guha, Ranajit, and A. Mitra, eds. *West Bengal District Records (New Series): Burdwan Letters Issued, 1788–1800.* Calcutta: Sree Sraswaty Press, 1955.

Gupta, Brijen K. *Sirajuddaullah and the East India Company, 1756–1757: Background to the Foundation of British Power in India.* Leiden: E. J. Brill, 1962.

Hamilton, Elizabeth. *Translations of the Letters of a Hindoo Rajah.* 1796. Reprint, Ontario: Broadview Press, 1999.

Haywood, Ian. *The Making of History.* Rutherford, N.J.: Fairleigh Dickinson University Press, 1986.

Hill, S. C. *List of Europeans and Others . . . at the Time of the Siege of Calcutta.* Calcutta: Office of the Superintendent, 1902.

Hobsbawm, E. J. *Industry and Empire: From 1750 to the Present Day.* 1968. Reprint, Harmondsworth, Eng.: Penguin, 1983.

Hockley, William Brown. *The English in India, A Novel.* London: Printed for W. Simpkin and R. Marshall, 1828.

Holwell, John Zephaniah. *A Genuine Narrative of the Deplorable Deaths of the English Gentlemen, and Others, Who Were Suffocated in the Black-Hole in Fort-William, at Calcutta, in the Kingdom of Bengal, in the Night Succeeding the 20th Day of June, 1756, in a Letter to a Friend.* London: A. Millar, 1758.

Holwell, John Zephaniah, and Friends. *India Tracts.* London: T. Becket, 1764.

Huggins, William. *Sketches in India, Treating on Subjects Connected with the Government; Civil and Military Establishments; Characters of the European, and Customs of the Native Inhabitants.* London: John Letts, 1824.

Hutchins, Francis. *The Illusion of Permanence: British Imperialism in India.* Princeton, N.J.: Princeton University Press, 1967.

Ingham, Patricia. *The Language of Gender and Class: Transformation in the Victorian Novel.* London: Routledge, 1996.

Johnson, Samuel. Letter to *Rambler* 97 (1751). In *The Yale Edition of the Works of Samuel Johnson: The Rambler,* ed. W. J. Bate and Albrecht Strauss, 3 vols. New Haven, Conn.: Yale University Press, 1969.

Jones, Chris. *Radical Sensibility: Literature and Ideas in the 1790s.* London: Routledge, 1993.

Joseph, Betty. "Gendering Time in Globalization: The Belatedness of the Other Woman and Jamaica Kincaid's *Lucy.*" *Tulsa Studies in Women's Literature* 21, no. 1 (2002): 1–17.

———. "Mutations of the Imperial Contract." In *On Your Left: Historical*

Materialism in the 1990s, ed. Ann Kibbey et al., 35–68. *Genders* 24. New York: New York University Press, 1996.

Joshi, Priya. *In Another Country: Colonialism, Culture, and the English Novel in India*. New York: Columbia University Press, 2002.

Kabeer, Naila. *Reversed Realities: Gender Hierarchies in Developmental Thought*. London: Verso, 1994.

Kahn, Madeleine, *Narrative Transvestism*. Ithaca, N.Y.: Cornell University Press, 1991.

Keith, Arthur Berridale. *A Constitutional History of India, 1600–1935*. New York: Barnes and Noble, 1969.

Khan, Seid-Gholam-Hosain. *The Sëir Mutaqherin*. Translated by Nota-Manus. 1789. Reprint, Lahore: Oriental Publishers, 1975.

Kindersley, Mrs. *Letters from the Island of Teneriffe, Brazil, the Cape of Good Hope, and the East Indies*. London: J. Hourse, 1777.

King, Anthony. *Bungalow: The Production of a Global Culture*. London: Routledge and Kegan Paul, 1984.

Kishwar, Madhu. "Why I Do Not Call Myself a Feminist." *Manushi* 61 (November–December 1990): 2–8.

LaCapra, Dominick. *Writing History, Writing Trauma*. Baltimore: Johns Hopkins University Press, 2001.

Laclau, Ernesto, and Chantal Mouffe. *Hegemony and Socialist Strategy: Towards a Radical Democratic Politics*. London: Verso, 1985.

The Lady's Drawing Room. London: M. Cooper, 1744.

The Laws of Manu. Translated by Georg Bühler. New York: Dover Publications, 1969.

Lefanu, Mrs. H. *The India Voyage*. London: G and J Robinson, 1804.

Lefebvre, Henri. *Everyday Life in the Modern World*. Translated by Sacha Rabinovitch. New York: Harper and Row, 1971.

Le Goff, Jacques. *History and Memory*. Translated by Steven Rendall and Elizabeth Claman. New York: Columbia University Press, 1992.

Leppert, Richard. "Music, Domestic Life, and Cultural Chauvinism: Images of British Subjects at Home in India." In *Music and Society: Politics of Composition, Performance, and Reception*, ed. Richard Leppert and Susan McClary, 63–104. Cambridge: Cambridge University Press, 1987.

Letter Copy Book of the Supervisor of Rajshahi at Natore. Oriental and India Office Collections, British Library, London.

Letter from John Jebb and James Pattison to George Canning, 27 February 1818. In general appendix no. 5 to Report from the Select Committee of the House of Commons on the Affairs of the East India Company, 1832. In *Irish University Press Series of British Parliamentary Papers. Colonies: East India*, 5:253–58. Shannon: Irish University Press, 1970.

Letter from the Right Hon. George Canning to the Chairman and Deputy Chairman of the East India Company, respecting Permissions to Proceed to India, 22 August 1818. In general appendix no. 5 to Report from the Select Committee of the House of Commons on the Affairs of the East India Company, 1832. In *Irish University Press Series of British Parliamentary Papers. Colonies: East India*, 5:266–67. Shannon: Irish University Press, 1970.

Life in India 1, Six Sketches Illustrative of Life in India. London, n.p., 1826.

Lyotard, Jean-François. *The Differend: Phrases in Dispute*. Translated by Georges Van Den Abbeele. Minneapolis: University of Minnesota Press, 1988.

Macaulay, Thomas Babington. "Warren Hastings." In *Critical and Historical Essays,* ed. Hugh Trevor-Roper, 400–512. New York: McGraw Hill, 1965.

MacFarlane, Iris. *The Black Hole; or, the Makings of a Legend.* London: George Allen and Unwin, 1975.

Macpherson, C. B. *The Political Theory of Possessive Individualism.* London: Oxford University Press, 1962.

Mani, Lata. *Contentious Traditions: The Debate on Sati in Colonial India.* Berkeley: University of California Press, 1998.

Markley, Robert. "Sentimentality as Performance: Shaftesbury, Sterne, and the Theatrics of Value." In *The New Eighteenth Century: Theory, Politics, English Literature,* ed. Felicity Nussbaum and Laura Brown. New York: Methuen, 1987.

Marsh, Charles. "Society in India." *New Monthly Magazine* 22–23, nos. 1–5 (1828).

Marshall, P. J. *The Impeachment of Warren Hastings.* Oxford: Oxford University Press, 1965.

Marx, Karl. "The British Rule in India." In *The Marx-Engels Reader,* ed. Robert Tucker, 653–58. New York: Norton, 1978.

———. *Capital,* vol. 1. Translated by Ben Fowkes. New York, Vintage Books, 1977.

McClintock, Anne. *Imperial Leather: Race, Gender, and Sexuality in the Colonial Contest.* New York: Routledge, 1995.

McLane, John R. *Land and Local Kingship in Eighteenth-Century Bengal.* Cambridge: Cambridge University Press, 1993.

Mehta, Uday Singh. *Liberalism and Empire.* Chicago: University of Chicago Press, 1999.

Mill, J. S. "The Subjection of Women." In *On Liberty,* ed. Stephan Collini. Cambridge: Cambridge University Press, 1989.

Millar, John. *Observations concerning the Distinction of Ranks in Society.* Dublin: T. Ewing, 1771.

Miller, Christopher. *Blank Darkness.* Chicago: University of Chicago Press, 1985.

"Minute of the Governor-General," 30 May 1829, in the general appendix to the Report from the Select Committee of the House of Commons on the Affairs of the East India Company, 16 August 1832. In *Irish University Press Series of British Parliamentary Papers. Colonies: East India,* 5:274–80. Shannon: Irish University Press, 1970.

"Minutes of Evidence Taken before the Whole House and the Select Committee on the Affairs of the East India Company (Public)," 1813. In *Irish University Press Series of British Parliamentary Papers. Colonies: East India,* vol. 4. Shannon: Irish University Press, 1968.

Mitter, Dwarka Nath. *The Position of Women in Hindu Law.* 1913. Reprint, New Delhi: Inter-India Publications, 1984.

Moir, Martin. *A General Guide to the India Office Records.* London: British Library, 1988.

Monkland, Mrs. *Life in India; or, the English at Calcutta.* 3 vols. London: Henry Colburn, 1828.

Montagu, Mary Wortley. *Turkish Embassy Letters.* Athens: University of Georgia Press, 1993.

Montesquieu, Charles de Secondat, baron de. *The Spirit of the Laws.* Translated by Thomas Nugent. New York: Hafner Publishing Company, 1959.

Morgan, Lady (Sydney Owenson). *The Missionary.* 3 vols. Delmar, N.Y.: Scholar's Facsimiles & Reprints, 1981.

Mudimbe, V. Y. *The Invention of Africa.* Bloomington: Indiana University Press, 1994.
Mullan, John. *Sentiment and Sociability: The Language of Feeling in the Eighteenth Century.* Oxford: Clarendon Press, 1988.
Musselwhite, David. "The Trial of Warren Hastings." In *Literature, Politics, and Theory: Papers from the Essex Conference,* ed. Francis Barker et al., 77–103. London: Methuen, 1986.
Niranjana, Tejaswini. *Siting Translation: History, Post-Structuralism, and the Colonial Context.* Berkeley: University of California Press, 1992.
Novak, Maximillian. Introduction to *The Manufacturer,* by Daniel Defoe. Delmar, N.Y.: Scholars Facsimiles and Reprints, 1978.
Nussbaum, Felicity. *Torrid Zones: Maternity, Sexuality, and Empire in Eighteenth-Century English Narratives.* Baltimore: Johns Hopkins University Press, 1995.
O'Hanlon, Rosalind. "Issues of Widowhood: Gender and Resistance in Colonial Western India." In *Contesting Power: Resistance and Everyday Social Relations in South Asia,* ed. Douglas Haynes and Gyan Prakash. Berkeley: University of California Press, 1992.
Pateman, Carole. *The Sexual Contract.* Stanford: Stanford University Press, 1988.
Perry, Ruth. *Women, Letters, and the Novel.* New York: AMS Press, 1980.
Philips, C. H. *The East India Company, 1784–1834.* New York: Barnes and Noble, 1961.
Pocock, J. G. A. *Virtue, Commerce, and History: Essays in Political Thought and History, Chiefly in the Eighteenth Century.* Cambridge: Cambridge University Press, 1985.
Pope, Alexander. *Rape of the Lock.* Boston: Bedford, 1998.
Pratt, Mary Louise. *Imperial Eyes: Travel Writing and Transculturation.* London: Routledge, 1992.
Prinsep, Augustus. *The Baboo and Other Tales Descriptive of Society in India.* London: Smith, Elder and Co., 1834.
Randell, Philip. "A Tale of East and West." In *Bungalow Ballads: Echoes from the East.* London: Simpkin Marshall, 1910.
Ray, Sangeeta. *En-Gendering India: Woman and Nation in Colonial and Postcolonial Narratives.* Durham, N.C.: Duke University Press, 2000.
Raynal, Guillaume-Thomas. *Histoire philosophique et politique du commerce et des établissements des européens dans les deux Indes.* 10 vols. Paris: François Maspero, 1781.
Records of Fort St. George. Despatches from England, 1721–1724. Madras: Government Press, 1928.
Records of Fort St. George. Despatches to England, 1719–1727. Madras: Government Press, 1929.
Records of Fort St. George. Diary and Consultation Book of 1721. Madras: Government Press, 1930.
Remarks by Rammohun Roy, on Settlement in India by Europeans, 14 July 1832. In general appendix no. 5 to the Report from the Select Committee of the House of Commons on the Affairs of the East India Company, 1832. In *Irish University Press Series of British Parliamentary Papers. Colonies: East India,* 5:341–43. Shannon: Irish University Press, 1970.
Renan, Ernest. "What Is a Nation?" In *Nation and Narration,* ed. Homi K. Bhabha. London: Routledge, 1990.

Report from Committee on Petitions, 8 May 1781. In *Reports from Committees of the House of Commons, 1715–1801*. First series, vol. 5. London: House of Commons, 1803–1806.

Richards, Thomas. *The Imperial Archive: Knowledge and Fantasy of Empire*. London: Verso, 1993.

Richardson, Samuel. *Clarissa; or, The History of a Young Lady*. London: Penguin, 1985.

Roberts, Emma. *The East India Voyager or the Outward Bound*. London: J. Madden & Co., 1845.

———. *Hindostan: Its Landscapes, Palaces, Temples, Tombs; the Shores of the Red Sea and the Sublime and Romantic Scenery of the Himalaya Mountains*. London: Peter Jackson, 1850.

———. *Scenes and Characteristics of Hindostan with Sketches of Anglo-Indian Society*. London: W. H. Allen, 1835.

Rocher, Rosane. "British Orientalism in the Eighteenth Century." In *Orientalism and the Postcolonial Predicament*, ed. Carol A. Breckenridge and Peter van der Veer. Philadelphia: University of Pennsylvania Press, 1993.

Roy, Rammohun. "Address to Lord William Bentinck." In *The English Works of Raja Rammohun Roy*, ed. J. C. Ghose. Calcutta: Oriental Press, 1885.

———. *Translation of a Conference between an Advocate and an Opponent of the Practice of Burning Widows Alive*. Calcutta: Baptist Mission Press, 1818.

Ryan, Michael. *Marxism and Deconstruction: A Critical Articulation*. Baltimore: Johns Hopkins University Press, 1982.

———. "Self-Evidence." *Diacritics* 10, no. 2 (summer 1980): 2–16.

Said, Edward. *Culture and Imperialism*. New York: Alfred A. Knopf, 1993.

———. *Orientalism*. New York: Vintage, 1979.

Sangari, Kum Kum, and Sudesh Vaid. *Recasting Women: Essays in Colonial History*. New Delhi: Kali, 1989.

Scott, Helenus. *Adventures of an East-India Rupee: Wherein Are Interspersed, Various Anecdotes Asiatic and European*. 1782. Reprint, Philadelphia: Robert Bell, 1783.

Scott, Joan Wallach. "Gender: A Useful Category of Historical Analysis." In *Feminism and History*, ed. Joan Wallach Scott. Oxford: Oxford University Press, 1996.

Scott, Sarah. *The History of Sir George Ellison*. Lexington: University of Kentucky Press, 1996.

Sharpe, Jenny. *Allegories of Empire: The Figure of Woman in the Colonial Text*. Minneapolis: University of Minnesota Press, 1993.

Skinner, Gillian. *Sensibility and Economics in the Novel, 1740–1800*. New York: St. Martin's, 1999.

Smollett, Tobias. *The Expedition of Humphry Clinker*. New York: Rinehart & Co., 1950.

Sorenson, Janet. " 'I Talk to Everybody in Their Own Way': Defoe's Economies of Identity." In *The New Economic Criticism*, ed. Martha Woodmansee and Mark Osteen. London: Routledge, 1999.

Spear, Percival. *The Nabobs: A Study of the Social Life of the English in Eighteenth-Century India*. 1967. Reprint, Calcutta: Rupa and Co., 1991.

The Spectator. 5 vols. Edited by Donald F. Bond. Oxford: Clarendon, 1987.

Spivak, Gayatri Chakravorty. *A Critique of Postcolonial Reason: Toward a History of the Vanishing Present*. Cambridge: Harvard University Press, 1999.

———. "Feminism and Imperialism." In *Contemporary Literary Criticism: Literary and Cultural Studies*, ed. Robert Con Davis and Ronald Schleifer. New York: Longman, 1991.

———. "Neocolonialism and the Secret Agent of Knowledge." Interview by Robert Young. *Oxford Literary Review*, nos. 13.1 and 13.2 (1991): 220–51.

———. " 'Other Things Are Never Equal': A Speech." *Rethinking Marxism* 12, no. 4 (2000): 37–45.

———. *Outside in the Teaching Machine*. New York: Routledge, 1993.

———. "The Rani of Sirmur: An Essay in Reading the Archives." *History and Theory* 24, no. 3 (1985): 247–72.

———. "Subaltern Studies: Deconstructing Historiography." In *In Other Worlds: Essays in Cultural Politics*, ed. Gayatri Chakravorty Spivak. London: Routledge, 1988.

———. "Theory in the Margin: Coetzee's Foe Reading Defoe's Crusoe/Roxana." In *Consequences of Theory*, ed. Jonathan Arac and Barbara Johnson, 154–81. No. 14 in Selected Papers from the English Institute, 1987–1988. Baltimore: Johns Hopkins University Press, 1991.

———. "Three Women's Texts and a Critique of Imperialism." In *"Race," Writing, and Difference*, ed. Henry Louis Gates Jr., 262–80. Chicago: University of Chicago Press, 1986.

———, ed. *In Other Worlds: Essays in Cultural Politics*. New York: Routledge, 1988.

Starke, Mariana. *The Sword of Peace; or, A Voyage of Love: A Comedy in Five Acts*. London: J. Debrett, 1789.

Stokes, Eric. *The English Utilitarians and India*. Oxford: Clarendon Press, 1959.

Stoler, Ann L. *Race and the Education of Desire*. Durham, N.C.: Duke University Press, 1995.

Stone, Lawrence. *The Family, Sex, and Marriage, 1500–1800*. New York: Harper Books, 1979.

Strobel, Margaret. *European Women and the Second British Empire*. Bloomington: Indiana University Press, 1991.

Suleri, Sara. *The Rhetoric of British India*. Chicago: University of Chicago Press, 1992.

Tharu, Susie, and Tejaswini Niranjana. "Problems for a Contemporary Theory of Gender." In *Gender and Politics in India*, ed. Nivedita Menon. New Delhi: Oxford University Press, 1999.

Thompson, Henry Fred. *The Intrigues of a Nabob; or, Bengal the Fittest Soil for the Growth of Lust, Injustice, and Dishonesty*. N.p., 1780.

Tinniswood, Adrian. *Life in the English Country Cottage*. London: Weidenfeld and Nicolson, 1995.

Tobin, Beth Fowkes. *Picturing Imperial Power*. Durham, N.C.: Duke University Press, 1999.

Todd, Janet. *Sensibility: An Introduction*. London: Methuen, 1986.

Tomaselli, Sylvana. "The Enlightenment Debate on Women." *History Workshop Journal* 20 (autumn 1985): 101–24.

Trumpener, Katie. "Rewriting Roxane: Orientalism and Intertextuality in Montesquieu's *Lettres Persanes* and Defoe's *The Fortunate Mistress*." *Stanford French Review* 11, no. 2 (1987): 177–91.

Varadharajan, Asha. *Exotic Parodies: Subjectivity in Adorno, Said, and Spivak*. Minneapolis: University of Minnesota Press, 1995.

Verelst, Harry. *A View of the Rise, Progress, and Present State of the English Government in Bengal.* London: J. Nourse, 1772.

Viswanathan, Gauri. *Masks of Conquest: Literary Study and British Rule in India.* New York: Columbia University Press, 1989.

———. *Outside the Fold.* Princeton, N.J.: Princeton University Press, 1988.

Wheeler, Roxann. *The Complexion of Race: Categories of Difference in Eighteenth-Century British Culture.* Philadelphia: University of Pennsylvania Press, 2000.

Wildenthal, Lora. *German Women for Empire, 1884–1945.* Durham, N.C.: Duke University Press, 2001.

Williams, Raymond. *Marxism and Literature.* Oxford: Oxford University Press, 1977.

Williamson, Thomas. *The East India Vade-Mecum; or, Complete Guide to Gentlemen Intended for the Civil, Military, or Naval Service of the Hon. East India Company.* 2 vols. London: Black, Parry, and Kingsbury, 1810.

Young, Robert. *White Mythologies: Writing History and the West.* London: Routledge, 1990.

INDEX